BEYOND
POSSIBLE

BEYOND
POSSIBLE

ONE MAN, 14 PEAKS,
AND THE MOUNTAINEERING
ACHIEVEMENT OF A LIFETIME

NIMS PURJA

NATIONAL
GEOGRAPHIC

WASHINGTON, D.C.

Published by National Geographic Partners, LLC
1145 17th Street NW, Washington, DC 20036

First published in Great Britain in 2020 by Hodder & Stoughton, a Hachette U.K. company

ISBN: 978-1-4262-2253-5

Printed in the United States of America

21/MP-PCML/1

To my mother, Purna Kumari Purja,
for working so hard to allow me to live my dreams,
and to the climbing community of Nepal,
home of the 8000ers

Your extremes are my normality.

CONTENTS

1 DEATH OR GLORY 11

2 HOPE IS GOD 17

3 BETTER TO DIE THAN TO BE A COWARD 33

4 THE UNRELENTING PURSUIT OF EXCELLENCE 45

5 INTO THE DEATH ZONE 55

6 SWIMMING TO THE MOON 79

7 THE MISSION 97

8 THE HIGHEST STAKES 111

9 RESPECT IS EARNED 123

10 THE NORMALITY OF THE EXTREME 137

11 RESCUE! 153

12 INTO THE DARK 167

13 IN TIMES OF CHAOS 179

14 SUMMIT FEVER 193

15 THE POLITICS OF A MOUNTAIN 205

16 QUITTING'S NOT IN THE BLOOD .219

17 THROUGH THE STORM 233

18 THE SAVAGE MOUNTAIN 247

19 A MOUNTAIN MIND 257

20 THE PEOPLE'S PROJECT 273

21 EPIC 283

Afterword 297

Appendix One: Lessons From the Death Zone 305

Appendix Two: Fourteen Mountains: The Schedule 313

Appendix Three: The World Records 315

Acknowledgments 317

1

DEATH OR GLORY

Dateline: July 3, 2019

The world slipped from beneath me as I careened headlong down the side of Nanga Parbat's slushy, snowy face. Thirty, 65, 100 feet rushed by in a blur.

Was this the end?

Only seconds earlier I'd felt secure, leaning hard into the mountain's plunging slope and battering winds with solid footing. Then my grip suddenly sheared, the teeth of my crampons unable to bite into the white as I plummeted, slowly at first, then faster, much faster, building speed every second, calculating the moments until I'd sail away from the mountain forever, my body across jagged rocks below or smashed into a deep crevasse.

Brother, you don't have long to un-fuck this.

If I died, there would be no one else to blame for such a bloody end. *I'd* decided to climb the world's ninth highest mountain in

11

brutal, whiteout conditions. *I'd* embarked on a wild effort to shatter old speed records, aiming to reach the pinnacles of all 14 "death zone" mountains in only seven months—each summit above 8,000 meters, an altitude where the air is so lacking in oxygen that human bodies and brains wither and fail. And *I'd* chosen to let go of a fixed rope during my descent, in a friendly gesture to allow another climber to pass as he nervously made his way down the mountain. But after I took one, two, three steps forward—one human without anchor on a mountainside in the sky—the snow jolted awkwardly, sloughing away, collapsing in on itself and sucking me down with it.

I was out of control now, and the two rules I'd set for myself on expeditions were being pressure tested. One: Hope is God. Two: The little things count most on big mountains.

By stepping away from the rope, I'd already forgotten Rule Two. Now I had only Rule One to fall back on.

Was I scared of dying in those brief seconds? *No.* I could accept death, especially if it came while attempting to push myself to new levels of human achievement. Testing physical limits was exactly my hope in 2018, when I announced a plan to challenge the previous best time for climbing Earth's 14 death zone peaks. The benchmark had been set in 2013 by Korean mountaineer Kim Chang-ho, in a record time of seven years, 10 months, and six days. Polish climber Jerzy Kukuczka had achieved the same feat in 1987 in a similar time frame of seven years, 11 months, and 14 days.

Although both men had established the record before I came along, the idea of a speed record for such a dangerous feat wasn't something other climbers had really attempted. It was a wild idea, and aiming to shave away so much time seemed absurd—perhaps beyond what was humanly possible.

But I wanted to try. And to do so, I quit the British military, where I served as a Gurkha soldier for several years before joining the Special Boat Service (SBS)—a wing of the special forces and an elite group of soldiers operating in some of the most lethal battlefields on Earth. Walking out on my career felt risky, but I was prepared to gamble everything for my ambition.

Fueled by my belief in myself, I treated the challenge like a military mission. During the planning phase, I'd even named my attempt "Project Possible." The title later came to feel like a one-fingered salute toward the people who wouldn't, or couldn't, believe in my dream. There were plenty of them—doubters appeared everywhere, and even the more supportive voices sounded skeptical at times. In 2019, an article on the Red Bull website said my goal as an unknown climber was as likely as a "swim to the moon." Still, I believed differently.

When judged against the expertise of a lot of high-altitude mountaineers, I probably seemed fairly green. I had only started operating above 8,000 meters a few years previously, but I quickly adapted to high altitudes. Much of that, I believed, had to do with my unusual physiology. Once I started climbing into the death zone, I found it relatively easy to move rapidly at great heights, taking 70 steps before pausing for breath where other mountaineers were only able to make four or five.

My powers of recovery were also surprising. I often descended from high peaks at speed, partying through the night in base camps, and moving onto my next expedition the following morning, hangovers be damned. I felt nothing could hold me back, no matter the circumstances—apart from death or serious injury, that is.

Another 30 or 40 yards raced by on Nanga Parbat. I had to find focus—focus on my movement and increasing velocity; focus on the people fading into the clouds above as I slipped farther and farther away; and focus on the techniques of a lifesaving self-arrest.

Could I use my ice ax, digging it into the mountain to slow my fall? Muscling my ax underneath me, I held onto the head firmly, jamming the pick into the snow. But the snow was too soft and I couldn't gain purchase. I pushed again. Nothing. *No hold.*

Any confidence I'd briefly felt in my ability to solve the problem was fading fast. My plunge grew still faster. I'd lost all control, when . . . *there!* Through the spray of snow I spotted the fixed rope we were using to descend moments earlier. If I could reach for it with enough force, I might have a chance to hang on. It was my last hope. I twisted, thrust out my arm, and made a grab for the cord . . . *Contact!* Gripping with all my strength, my palm burning as if aflame, I gradually slowed my plummeting body to a stop.

For a moment I was still. Then, the world seemed to suck in a deep, settling breath. *Was I OK?* By the looks of it, yes I was, though my legs shook with adrenaline and my heart banged against my chest.

Taking a second or two to gather myself, I rose to my feet and adopted a new rhythm, a more cautious stride.

To climbers on the line above, I may have appeared unflappable, as if I'd instantly returned to a regular operational setting and nothing out of the ordinary had happened. But the fall had rattled me; my confidence had taken a dent. I gripped the rope tightly, and double-checked each and every footfall; a different mind-set was in play now. As I planted my boots in the shifting snow, I told myself that death was going to come for me at some point—maybe on a mountain during Project Possible, maybe in old age decades down the line—but not on Nanga Parbat, and not within the next heartbeat.

Not today.

Not today.

But when?

And would I finish what I'd started?

2

HOPE
IS GOD

'd been inspired to attempt climbing all 14 of the world's biggest peaks at an unheard-of speed. My goals were to top the Nepali peaks of Annapurna, Dhaulagiri, Kanchenjunga, Everest, Lhotse, Makalu, and Manaslu; to race up Nanga Parbat, Gasherbrum I and II, K2, and Broad Peak in Pakistan; and finally, to summit Tibet's intimidating 8,000ers—Cho Oyu (which was also accessed from Nepal) and Shishapangma.

But why? These were some of the most inhospitable places on the planet; a challenge of that magnitude, with a deadline of only half a year or so, might have sounded like madness to most people. But for me, it was an opportunity to prove to the world that everything, *anything*, was possible if you dedicated your heart and mind to a plan.

The adventure started with Mount Everest, the world's tallest peak and an epic Himalayan monument within my homeland. To people outside the small, landlocked country of Nepal, Everest carries a near-mythical quality. But as a kid, it felt like a distant entity. My family was poor; the trek from where we lived to Everest and back was expensive, even for locals, and the journey took around 12 days. It also required a traveler to stay overnight in a series of teahouses—small hotels in the villages that lined the route—so I never experienced the adventure.

After I moved to England in 2003, as a Gurkha soldier serving with the British Armed Forces, people always asked the same question: "What's Everest like?" Friends unfamiliar with Nepal's geography imagined that the mountain loomed majestically outside my back garden. They looked unimpressed when I admitted I'd not even seen base camp, let alone climbed above it. It even caused some peers to question my strength.

"It's on your doorstep, mate, and you haven't bothered? And we thought Gurkhas were tough . . ."

After 10 years, the joking and sniping finally got to me. OK, I thought, I'll start climbing.

I took my first steps toward the highest point on Earth in December 2012, when I finally made the trek to the foot of Everest's intimidating massif at the age of 29. By that point, I had progressed from the Gurkha regiment and into the military elite; through a friend, I'd been connected with the famous Nepali mountaineer Dorje Khatri, who offered to guide me to base camp on a trek set to last several days. Dorje had scaled Everest several times and was a champion for the Sherpa* guides: He defended their rights and

---

* Sherpa means two things: It's an Indigenous group from Nepal, but it's also a slang catchall for the Nepali Himalayan mountain guide, as used by foreign explorers.

campaigned for better pay, but he was also a climate change activist and tried to alter the way the world viewed the Himalaya's fragile ecosystem.

I couldn't think of a better person with whom to make the journey. But staring up at Everest's peak as it loomed 8,848 meters above, I decided that trekking wasn't enough; it was time to go higher, and I didn't care about the risks.

After a fair amount of persuasion, I convinced Dorje to teach me some of the skills I'd need to climb an 8,000er. At first, I begged him to let me attempt Ama Dablam, a nearby peak that towered 6,812 meters above sea level, but Dorje laughed off my idea.

"Nims, that is a very technical mountain," he said. "People who have climbed Everest even struggle to get to the top." Instead, we traveled to the nearby peak Lobuche East, picking up some rental equipment in a nearby village before trekking to the summit. The work was slow, but steady, and under Dorje's tutelage, I pulled on a pair of crampons for the very first time, walking across a grass slope and feeling the bite of their steel points in the turf. The sensation was odd, but it gave me an idea of what I might experience during a proper mountain ascent. As we slowly worked our way to the top, into the cutting cold and powerful winds, I felt the buzz of an expedition for the first time.

Each step caused me to pause and overthink. At times I'd experience a surge of fear; at others, falling to my death seemed like a real possibility. But after wasting so much energy on stress, I eventually located the confidence to stride forward purposefully and my anxiety faded.

On the summit, I was blown away by the view around me: The jagged Himalayan vista was shrouded by a blanket of cloud, but here and there a peak penetrated the gray mist. My adrenaline soared as Dorje pointed to Everest, Lhotse, and Makalu. A sense of pride washed over me, mixed with a feeling of anticipation. I'd already decided to climb those three peaks in the distance, even though I could be considered something of a late bloomer in high-altitude mountaineering terms.

I wanted more. Around that time, I'd caught wind of some exciting news: In 2015, the Brigade of Gurkhas—the collective term for Nepal's Gurkha fighting forces—was marking two centuries of service with the British military in a celebration called the G200. A series of prestigious events were being arranged—among them, a memorial service at the Gurkha statue in London, a reception at the Houses of Parliament, and a Field of Remembrance at the Royal Albert Hall. But buried within the packed cultural program was mention of an expedition to Everest.

The Gurkhas had previously built a reputation as being sturdy climbers, but because of the high turnover of war and the regiment's recent deployments in Afghanistan and Iraq, no serving Gurkha soldier had ever made it to the top. (It was also extremely expensive for Nepali people to climb Everest, even with some of the discounts afforded to local residents.) That was all set to change when an ambitious plan was announced in 2015 to take a dozen or so Gurkhas to Everest's peak via the South Col route, as part of the bicentennial celebrations.

The mission, called the G200 Expedition (G200E), was set to be both challenging and history-making. Even better, as a serving Gurkha in the United Kingdom Special Forces, I was eligible to climb. I was proud of the regiment, I'd do anything to further their standing, and this felt like an honorable cause.

As I sharpened my skills, my ambition grew. An advantage of being in the British military was the access to a variety of highly specialized courses. I joined one on the art of extreme cold-weather warfare and soon became a member of that unique cadre of mountain warfare specialists. Next, in 2012 I climbed Denali, the highest peak in the United States and one of the Seven Summits, the highest mountain on each continent, which comprise Denali (North America), Everest (Asia), Elbrus (Europe), Kilimanjaro (Africa), Vinson (Antarctica), Aconcagua (South America), and Carstensz Pyramid (Oceania).

A 6,190-meter climb, Denali was a serious undertaking. Isolated and brutally cold, the temperatures there sometimes dropped to minus 60°F, which was a serious problem for a novice climber like me. But it was also a perfect training ground. I learned rope skills and put my special forces–forged endurance to good use, dragging my sled through thick snow for hours on end, taking care not to fall into one of the many crevasses on the mountain.

Then in 2014, I climbed my first peak in the death zone. Dhaulagiri was nicknamed the White Mountain because of the deep powder coating its steep and intimidating slopes. It was also considered one of the most dangerous climbs in the world, thanks to a terrifying death toll. At the time, more than 80 climbers had perished there, and its South Face was yet to be scaled, even though the likes of Reinhold Messner, the first mountaineer to climb Everest solo, had attempted what was an apparently impenetrable route.

Dhaulagiri's biggest danger was the risk of avalanches, which erupted out of the blue, sucking everybody and everything away in their path. In 1969, five Americans and two Sherpas were swiped from the mountain. Six years later, six members of a Japanese expedition were killed when a wall of snow buried them alive. Dhaulagiri wasn't an adventure to be taken lightly, especially for a climber with only 18 months' experience and limited knowledge of the perilous conditions found on extreme peaks. But eager to improve my climbing skills whenever I was granted leave from fighting in Afghanistan, I decided to attempt it.

A brother from the Special Air Service (SAS), a wing of the British Special Forces—we'll call him James—accompanied me on the trip. Neither of us looked the part, arriving at base camp in flip-flops, shorts, and Ray-Bans. And our timing was bad. We were joining a larger expedition that had been acclimatizing to the thin air for a month. An avalanche in the Khumbu Icefall had curtailed their trip to Everest, so they'd moved across to Dhaulagiri to climb there instead.

The pair of us were behind schedule because of our limited leave with the military. Therefore, there was no way for us to enjoy the usual procedures afforded to mountaineers hoping to function at high altitude, such as full acclimatization rotations.* Meanwhile, our climbing buddies looked to be the real deal, and when we all set off for the trek to base camp, James and I soon fell behind. James was really struggling with the altitude. It took us three days longer than the others to complete the preliminary journey.

---

* Mountaineers usually spend a couple of months on 8,000-meter peaks. Over a space of weeks, climbers move from base camp to Camp 1 to get used to the debilitating effects of high altitude. They then move between Camps 1, 2, and 3, climbing high in the day and sleeping low, until the symptoms of acute mountain sickness (AMS), such as nausea, breathlessness, and banging head-aches, have subsided. These climbs are called "acclimatization rotations." Once settled at high altitude, they wait patiently, sometimes for weeks on end, until a suitable summit window opens up, when the weather is considered good enough to climb. Then they'll push on to the peak.

"What do you guys do?" asked one of our expedition partners later. He'd noted our appearance when we'd first arrived. I knew what he was thinking—were we loose cannons to be avoided at all costs during a dangerous summit push?

I shrugged. Neither of us was about to reveal our full military roles, as we were bound to certain levels of secrecy. Also, we preferred to be judged on the mountaineering skills we might have possessed, rather than our combat expertise.

"Oh, we're in the military," I said eventually, hoping for an end to the questions.

The climber raised an eyebrow. Our travelling kit looked fairly piecemeal, although the climbing equipment James and I brought was of high quality. Still, some expedition mates seemed to write us off as clueless tourists. I suppose the assumption was half-right, but I wasn't going to let anyone pick holes in my weaknesses. So at base camp, we prepared enthusiastically for our first acclimatization rotations. Over the coming week, we planned to climb daily up to Camps 1 and 2, the first of four tent camps along the route to the peak. We'd then hike back to base camp and sleep lower on the mountain until we felt ready for our summit push.

As soon as we geared up and began our first acclimatization ascent, it was clear that James didn't possess the same physiology as me. It had first become apparent on our base camp trek, but once we started the serious business of climbing on our first rotation to Camp 1, he was unable to maintain the pace as I pushed ahead. Once we stopped to rest at Camp 1, I realized he was suffering from altitude sickness.

As I climbed from base camp the following day on another acclimatization effort, James fell behind again. But before too long, I also blew myself out. In an effort to show off my speed, I pushed too far ahead, and as I rested at Camp 1 for a couple of hours, brewing a cup of hot tea, my small party yet to arrive, a horrible thought struck me.

Was James still alive?

As well as regularly trembling with avalanches, Dhaulagiri was known for its deep crevasses. With no one else in sight, James and his Sherpa might have tumbled into one, in which case it was unlikely they'd be discovered for days, if at all. In a slight panic, I packed up my pot and cup and headed down toward base camp to find them. (I'd learned early on not to leave my kit anywhere on the mountain; it was best to keep everything with me at all times, just in case.)

It didn't take long. Two people moved slowly below me. It was my climbing party, but James was in a worse state than before.

"This is a big mountain, brother," I said. "You're struggling with acclimatization, let me take that backpack for you."

I reached out to lighten his load, but James hesitated.

"Listen, forget your ego," I said. "If you want to summit, let me help you."

James relented, and slowly but steadily we worked our way back up to Camp 1. Now I, too, was hurting. The day's effort had taken a toll. I'd overreached and the mountains were delivering their first major lesson: Never burn yourself out unnecessarily. From then on, I vowed never to waste vital energy; I would work hard only when I needed to. When the time arrived to make my first ever 8,000-meter summit push a few days later, I made sure to hang at the back of the leading group as we snaked our way from base camp to the peak of Dhaulagiri—partly out of respect for the several

Sherpas leading us to the top, but also because I'd never climbed such a huge mountain before and I didn't want to experience another energy slump.

That's when I noticed the ever changing work of the guides within an expedition party. Every so often, the leading Sherpa would take a break from bodily plowing a path through the waist-high drifts, allowing one of his teammates to take over for a while. He would then fall to the back of the line until it was his turn to head the charge once more while the rest of us matched his prints in the snow, making for fairly easy work. This was a technique known as trailblazing, and with his selfless exertion, the lead Sherpa was helping the expedition party to follow a much smoother route upward. I respected the effort that every guide was making.

When it came to trailblazing, there were two techniques to learn.* The first was applicable in shin- to knee-deep snow, where climbers made footfalls by lifting their knees toward their chest with every step, then firmly planting their feet. The second was for extreme conditions with thigh- or waist-high powder. In those cases, leading climbers had to muscle forward with their hips, creating a pocket of space before lifting their leg out, working it forward through the snow, and making the next step.

---

* I also learned about the different styles of climbing. On Dhaulagiri, we worked with a fixing team who set ropes to the mountain with anchors. The climbers used those lines to assist their efforts on steep inclines and sheer faces. Alpine-style climbing involved a team moving quickly over the terrain while roped together for safety. If one of the group slipped or fell, the others braced hard to stop them from tumbling too far. Finally, solo climbing—as I saw it—required a mountaineer to work toward a peak alone, while trailblazing and climbing on his own path.

Suddenly, a climber in front of me stepped out of the line and started his way to the front of the pack to help.

I shouted up at him. "Hey, bro! What are you doing? The Sherpas aren't going to get upset, are they?"

He waved me away. "No, man, I'm doing my bit, helping the Sherpa brothers . . ."

I assumed that leading the group in such a way was disrespectful to the expedition guides; it looked as if someone else was trying to play the hero, which I'd previously believed was a dangerous step on such a risky mountain. It turned out I was wrong, and a Sherpa soon put my mind at rest.

"Nims, the snow is so deep. If you have the energy and can help out up front too, please do . . ."

Encouraged, I soon took the lead and drove forward. My legs felt like pistons as I pumped my feet in and out of the powder. The effort was huge, but by regarding every forward step as significant progress and part of a greater team effort, I was able to move steadily. My thighs and calves ached with the strain, but my lungs were light. The fatigue that hindered other climbers at altitude didn't seem to be striking me down. I was strong—*Boom! Boom! Boom!*—and every step arrived with power. When I turned to see how far I'd come, I was shocked to see the rest of my climbing party. They were little black dots below.

Wow, this is *my* shit, I thought, admiring the deep footfalls I'd left for the expedition. I'd been working without much thought, operating in the flow state that athletes often describe when they set world records or win championships. I was in the zone.

Careful not to overextend myself like before, I worked my way slowly to the next ridgeline, waiting an hour until the remainder of the group caught up. When they gathered around me, the lead Sherpa guide shouted excitedly and slapped me on the back. Others in the expedition, climbers who'd looked down on me a few days earlier and written off my chances of summiting, were now shaking my hand.

Everyone seemed relieved at my legwork, and my effort totally changed the attitude of the team. I was no tourist anymore. My mind-set had shifted, too. By the time I reached the peak, having broken trail for more than 70 percent of the route, I was not only surprised at what I'd achieved, but emboldened.

"Brother," I thought. "You're a badass at high altitude."

THIS CAME AS A SURPRISE. I hadn't been primed genetically for any success in the death zone, and climbing certainly wasn't part of my family life. As a kid, I wanted to be one of two things. My first option: to serve as a Gurkha soldier, like my dad. Renowned for their fearlessness, the regiment had been historically spread between the Nepali, British, and Indian armies, as well as the Singapore police. Everyone within their ranks came from Nepal, and all were known as bighearted and loyal, with an unswerving belief in queen and country.

Enough history books have been written about the Gurkhas' inception, should you want to go there, but here's the briefest of backstories. During the Anglo-Nepalese War (1814–16) between Nepal (then known as the Gorkha Kingdom) and the British East India Company (or EIC, a private army, which was double the size of the regular British Army), the skills of the Nepali fighters were so admired that any defectors turning to the EIC for work following a treaty agreement were employed as "irregular forces."

The Gurkhas later became a highly respected regiment in their own right, and were deployed in the Second World War, as well as Iraq and Afghanistan during the War on Terror. Two of my older brothers, Ganga and Kamal, had followed the same path as Dad, and whenever they returned to Nepal on leave, people looked at them as if they were rock stars. Gurkha soldiers were legendary—and their motto, "Better to die than to be a coward," conjured images of heroism.

My second career ambition was to be a government official. But I wanted to be Nepal's version of Robin Hood, stealing from the rich and giving to the poor. The country I grew up in was very small, and the common people had been disenfranchised for too long; even as a child, I understood the people around me had very little, and poverty rates were incredibly high. Many Nepali citizens were Hindus, and despite their lack of wealth, they would often give their money to the temple whenever they visited.

Not me. If I ever had money, I was happier emptying my wallet to people in the street who were homeless, blind, or disabled outside the temple. I'd do the same on a bus, where buskers would often play, unable to work because a terrible injury or debilitating illness had left them incapacitated. Every donation arrived with a contract: *This is for you, brother, but don't spend it on alcohol. Make sure your family gets the food it needs.*

I've always been this way. Money never attracted me, but as a kid, I dreamed of taking a job of authority, one with a uniform. Not because I wanted power or status, but because I liked the idea of draining money from Nepal's superrich—especially those who were corrupt—and handing the spoils to the people with nothing.

I was poor from the beginning, born July 24, 1983, in a village called Dana, in western Nepal's Myagdi district. It's a small village only a mile above sea level, so it wasn't like I was raised with crampons on my feet and a physiological connection to high altitude. Dhaulagiri was the biggest mountain in the region, but it was still a long way from my front door.

There was a gap of around 18 years between me and my older brothers, Ganga, Jit, and Kamal, and three years between me and my younger sister, Anita. We didn't have any money, and the thought of owning a car was unimaginable. But we were a loving family, and I was a happy kid. It didn't take a lot to keep me amused.

By all accounts, Mum and Dad—from different castes, or classes—faced many challenges long before I was born. Their problems began after they married. Marriage between castes wasn't done in Nepal, and their families were resentful. They were cut adrift from their parents and siblings, which meant they had to start their new lives together with next to nothing.

Dad was serving with the Indian Gurkha regiment at the time, but his salary alone wasn't enough to support the family. So when Ganga, Jit, and Kamal were born, Mum started working on the village farm for money. Most of the time, at least one of the kids was strapped to her back in a cloth. The workload of caring for a young family while bringing money home through hard labor must have been exhausting. A lot of my work ethic came from my mother; she was a huge influence on me, as she was for many who met her.

Mum had not been educated, which must have annoyed her, because she had a vision for helping other women in the area. Eventually, she became an activist in Nepal, working to change outdated attitudes toward gender and education. Mum fought for what she believed in, and though she barely earned enough to put food on the table, the family survived. Once my brothers were old enough, they were put to work too, waking at 5 a.m. and walking for two hours to find and cut grass for the family's three buffalo, before traveling to school for a full day of classes.

I had it a little easier. Our garden held several orange trees, and once the fruit ripened in autumn, I'd climb into the branches and shake the limbs until they were empty. The ground was soon covered in fruit and I'd eat until I was full. The next day, I'd scoop up more and repeat the feast.

But when I was four years old, my family moved to the jungle village of Ramnagar, in Chitwan, 227 miles away from Dana in the hottest and flattest part of the country. My parents worried about landslides threatening Dana, where several fast-flowing rivers were prone to flood and wreak havoc.

Not that I was bothered by the relocation. With the jungle on our doorstep, Mum could easily go into the undergrowth and gather wood for the fire. Meanwhile, adventure was easy for me to find—on the streets, in the woods, by the water—and the potential for exploration was huge.

From an early age, I'd learned it was fairly easy for me to thrive emotionally on the bare minimum. This might explain how I was later able to live so much of my life in the chaos of combat, or in a tent pinned to the side of a mountain. My mum was strict, but on weekends, when I wasn't at school, she was happy for me to explore Ramnagar alone.

I was happiest in nature. Most of the time I headed for the nearby river, hanging out on the banks all day and hunting for crabs and prawns (though Mum often turned her nose up whenever I proudly brought her back my catch). "Why have you brought me insects?" she'd say.

Life soon improved. When my brothers left to join the Gurkhas, they said they hoped to help me have a better life. Every month, they sent some of their wages home to fund my education at Small Heaven Higher Secondary, an English-language boarding school in Chitwan; I had been sent there when I was around five years old. This was a luxury, and far from guaranteed. Mum often mentioned the temporary nature of my brothers' generosity.

"One day they are going to be married," she said. "They'll have families of their own to look after and they won't be able to support your education anymore."

But even as a young kid, I already had a plan in mind to support the family. "It's fine," I told Mum, trying to shrug off any pressure. "I'll pass my exams when I'm older and then I'll become a teacher at the school, or even a nursery. Then I'll be able to look after *you*."

But the truth was that I really wanted to be a Gurkha. I seemed to have the makeup to cut it in the military. Though I was young when I started boarding school, the rhythm of a life away from home suited me. Everyone slept in a hostel, where the older kids held the power and teachers beat the children if they stepped out of line. It was my first challenge: learning how to survive in a tough environment.

As I grew older, negotiating daily battles in the playground grew trickier. I was tough for my age, but had plenty of older kids to deal with; when Mum visited with food or supplies, one of the senior school bullies often came knocking when she left. Sometimes my food was snatched away, and I could do nothing about it.

My initial survival instinct was to run off, sprinting into the trees before anyone could rob me. I was fast, with plenty of stamina, and I enjoyed track-and-field events in physical education. But my second survival instinct against school bullies was to fight back. As my strength grew and I reached my teens, I took up kickboxing, learning to defend myself and breaking down competitors until I became the regional champion.

By the time I reached year nine at school, I'd suffered only one defeat: to Nepal's national champion, who was several years older. Now, when a bully came for my food, I stood up to him and unleashed my new skills. Not many kids challenged me after that. Kickboxing was my first step to becoming a man.

My next was to apply for the Gurkhas.

3

BETTER TO DIE THAN TO BE A COWARD

"If a man says he is not afraid of dying,
he is either lying or he is a Gurkha."
—*Indian Army Chief of Staff Sam Manekshaw*

From an early age, I believed in the power of positive thinking and willed my way through illnesses and chronic ail-
ments. Around the age of 10, I contracted tuberculosis,
which was a serious and worryingly common disease in
Nepal, but I emerged unscathed. Later, I was diagnosed with
asthma. When the doctor explained some of the long-term impacts
it might cause, I listened, but knew that nothing would stop me
from living my life. Eventually, I was running through the woods

and over long distances in school races for fun. Sometimes, I felt like a human antibiotic because I'd taught myself to think that way: I trusted myself to heal. *I believed.* The same attitude powered me into the British military, where I showed great resilience under pressure. It surrounded me like a force field and I soon learned that with relentless self-belief, anything was possible. I'd need every ounce of it once accepted into the Gurkhas.

The selection process to join the regiment was notoriously brutal and unforgiving from the start, and I'd heard all the stories from my brothers. Before being allowed into Gurkha training, every applicant between the ages of 17 and 21 was subjected to a thorough physical and mental assessment. For example, anyone with more than four fillings was given the boot. False teeth, or even overly large gaps in the mouth, were grounds for rejection. Brains were as important as physical ability.

I needed to pass my Nepali School Leaving Certificate, an exam that grants the equivalent of a high school diploma in the United States; I managed this thanks to the schooling provided for me. When my time came to try out for the regiment in 2001, a retired British Gurkha—assessors were then known as Galla Wallahs— inspected me in the village. My entire body was checked; any scars could have gotten me rejected, though fortunately I'd avoided picking up any nasty kickboxing injuries. But in the end, I failed. Why exactly, I'm not sure, as I had passed all the physical and education assessments. But my hunch is that the assessor had taken a bit of a disliking to me.

Although I was one of only 18 applicants to have passed the physical tests, the Galla Wallah ranked me in 26th place on the final candidate list. Only 25 individuals were accepted into the next phase of Gurkha Selection that year, and the rejection was demoralizing. Infuriated, I railed against the unfairness of it all and for a little while considered giving up on my dream of joining the regiment.

In the end, I overcame my disappointment (though I was still grumpy about it) and was successful on my second attempt a year later. I moved on to the next stage, regional selection, where I grunted my way through a series of push-ups, sit-ups, and pull-ups before taking an English and math test. I was then ushered into the third and final phase, central selection, where the work would get much harder.

One of the better-known tests in the Gurkha's central selection phase was the "doko race," in which applicants were ordered to carry *doko* (bamboo baskets) on their heads, each filled with 65 pounds of sand. Potential Gurkha had to complete an uphill circuit of three miles in less than 48 minutes.

The running part didn't worry me; in the intervening years my enthusiasm for track and field had grown into something more serious. As a year-seven student, I'd helped organize a series of trials for kids who hoped to represent the boarding school in regional championships. The athletes were older than me by two or three years, and my job was to outline the track with a white marker. But when the 400-meter race started, I joined in for fun. At the first turn I was near the front of the pack, but on the second I felt unstoppable and burst ahead of the front-runners, crossing the line in first place.

My teacher grabbed me by the arm. He imagined that somehow I'd joined in mid-race as a prank.

"Purja, where did you come from? Is this a joke?"

"No, sir," I said, nervously. "I started with the others . . . Ask them!"

When it was confirmed that I'd raced the other kids fair and square, the school was left with little choice. They had to thrust a year-seven pupil into a regional competition typically dominated by boys from year ten.

"Despite your age, we're putting you up," said my teacher.

I was completely naive as to what was expected of me, or how to prepare. Even so, when it came to the inter-boarding-school championships, in which I was running the 4x400-meter relay, 800-meter, 2,400-meter, and 5,000-meter races, I felt ready. I decided to race barefoot, because I believed that running shoes or spikes might weigh me down. My only tactical thought was to "hang back for the first half of the race . . . then go!"

With that simple strategy, I won both the 800-meter and 2,400-meter events; I led my school to victory in the 4x400 meter relay, too. What must have felt like a major gamble on my school's part had paid off.

With my running background, that part of the doko race wasn't a concern. I'd previously taken an unorthodox approach to race preparation at school and would often sneak away at 4 a.m. to run through the nearby streets, increasing the physical effort by slipping some metal rods I'd found lying around into an elastic support bandage, which I then strapped to my legs. When the sun came up, I crept back to bed before anyone noticed. I hoped that hard work would pay off now.

Bamboo baskets loaded with sand were a new challenge, however—though at least I'd experienced some background training. It helped that both my brothers had endured the same grueling exam and knew what to expect. Kamal was on leave shortly before my assessment, which was taking place again in Pokhara; Ganga, who had retired from the military in 2002, was also there. They joined me for a couple days, and together we formulated a plan.

"OK, Nims, we're going to have to intensify your preparation," said Kamal one afternoon, handing me a bamboo basket. He then dropped a heavy rock into it. My arms buckled a little under the load. "Now, get used to that weight for a bit and let's run."

We moved over the rough terrain of Pokhara, along the river and down steep paths, the basket on my head feeling like a 10-ton weight. The pain bit into my neck, back, and calves. When we finally came to a stop, Kamal looked down at his watch. A frown creased his brow.

"An hour, Nims. You're not going to pass with a performance like that. We'll go again tomorrow."

The following day, I was faster, bringing my time down to 55 minutes. A day later, I sped along the course, completing three miles in just under the required time of 48 minutes. I thought I was going to be fine.

But when I eventually joined a doko race that included a large group of teens hoping to pass the same central selection as I was, I looked across the line and felt worry creep in. Some had paid a local athletics company to prepare their bodies with an intense training program; others even had new shoes and military-style haircuts, as if they'd already qualified.

My concern proved unfounded. When I finished the race in the leading pack, I knew I had it within me to join the Gurkhas.

FROM THERE, the assessments were a blur of push-ups, pull-ups, sit-ups, sprints, cross-country runs, and beep tests. I passed everything, including tests in English and math; I even finished first in a mile-and-a-half race. Finally, I was accepted as part of the British Army. After years of training, education, rejection, and unrelenting effort, my dream was finally coming true.

Within two weeks of passing central selection, I flew to England to join the Gurkha Training Company at the Infantry Training Centre in Catterick, Yorkshire. I'd never been outside Nepal, let alone as far away as England. But I assumed integrating into a different culture would be a relatively straightforward challenge.

No bother, I thought, I've been to boarding school. My English is excellent. I'll be fine.

My plane landed at Heathrow in January 2003. On leaving the airport, I was immediately shocked. It was cold, and the wind and rain were so strong they seemed to be blowing horizontally. I assumed our coach would drive us through central London on a mini-sightseeing tour, where I might glimpse Big Ben, St. Paul's Cathedral, and Buckingham Palace. Instead, we hit the motorway and sped to the north of England through a landscape of sheep, hills, and the occasional service station. My confidence at settling into the local culture was dissipating fast.

I had also been wrong about my English skills. Conversations with locals were indecipherable. My written English had been pretty good at school, but I was absolutely lost when it came to accents. Geordies, Mancunians, Cockneys—every dialect sounded alien. The very first person I met in England was from Liverpool, and when I shook his hand to say hello, he responded in a thick accent that startled me. *I had no idea what he was saying.*

Nobody in my English education in Nepal had warned me about regional dialects. Now, in real-life situations in Britain, I was at a loss. Those first weeks I often drifted through conversations thinking, What the hell?

I did learn some unexpected skills at Catterick, like how to dress well. One of the many rules we were forced to follow was to be "suited and booted" in our uniforms at all times. On our first trip to the beach, my platoon strolled across the sand in bare feet, our pants rolled up and our suit jackets slung over our shoulders. We must have looked ridiculous to passersby.

Then there was the business of fighting: the reason I was here. I was ready, maybe even eager to get started—but it would take four years to get there. In a 36-week course, I learned the core principles of the Gurkha regiment, including modules on cultural training and infantry battlefield training.

After passing recruit training, I joined the Gurkha Engineers— schooled in trade skills due to the nature of their work on the ground—and made a selection from a list that included carpentry and plumbing. I opted to work in building and structural finishing, and for nine months lived in Chatham, Kent, where I was taught how to plaster walls, as well as the intricacies of painting and decorating. It may have been dull, but I knew it was worthwhile. If life didn't work out for me in the military, at least I had a handy profession to fall back on.

The time was drawing near to take my skills into the real world of armed conflict. I completed my education as a combat engineer in a series of field exercises and the 13-week All Arms Commando Course at the Commando Training Centre Royal Marines in Lympstone, Devon. In 2007, I was deployed to Afghanistan as part of

Operation Herrick, a 12-year strategy to maintain a military presence in the country. We were also tasked with watching for any terrorist activities the Taliban might be orchestrating, as well as helping locals build a new government.

At times, my role was to sweep vast areas of land for improvised explosive devices (IEDs). On operations, the Royal Marines Commandos would often go in first; if a suspected trigger device was confirmed, my team was tasked with clearing the area, pinpointing exactly where the bomb was positioned before dismantling it. Our unit was then able to move forward safely as a whole. The work was always intense, because one misstep might blow us to pieces, and we were always in a hurry. We had no time to dawdle in exposed land; the enemy might strike at any moment.

For the most part I was assigned to work with 40 Commando, the Royal Marines' battalion-size "formation." One of our joint operational tasks was to move from door to door on patrols, checking for ammo, weapons, or Taliban drug stashes. I was a loyal soldier, proud of the Gurkhas' reputation within the British military, and I'd do anything to defend it. I was also respectful of the queen and the crown; they meant everything to me, and I wasn't afraid to speak my mind.

During one operation, I was charged with sweeping an enemy compound for booby traps; because my unit wasn't vulnerably standing out in the open at the time, it seemed wise to take extra care, and I didn't want to miss a spot. But over my shoulder, I sensed a commander watching me, his impatience building.

"Purja, hurry up," he barked. "What's the problem?"

"Yeah, I *could* hurry up," I said. "Maybe, I could just skip this and say, 'Job done!' But the reason I'm doing this properly is because I don't want the Gurkhas to be blamed for missing any IEDs. It's not only about me."

I was irked by my commander's suggestion that something was wrong. Was he insinuating that I was too scared to work quickly? Having walked around the room aware a bomb might go off at any second, the truth was that, yeah, I was a little edgy. I was sane, after all. But even in Afghanistan, fear didn't play a role in my world.

"You think I'm fucking frightened of this?" I continued, dropping the Vallon detector we used to locate bombs and mines, and striding around the potentially explosive floor of the unscanned room, my voice rising. "My life doesn't mean anything here. But reputation does. That's why I'm doing this job properly."

"Oh . . ." said my commander. He seemed too taken aback to punish me for insubordination.

The more time I spent in Afghanistan, the more I grew to respect the Royal Marine Commandos. I loved their ethos. They were super-soldiers, but they were humble. Although I had plenty of confidence, I wasn't a fan of overpowering egos. And whenever the two groups were caught in gun battles together, there was a mutual respect.

Often in those situations, the Gurkhas' job was to provide close combat support; sometimes, we were called in to attach L9 bar mines to the doors of enemy compounds. Originally designed as an antitank land mine, these explosive devices were also useful for removing obstacles; they could blow through the thick walls so common in Afghanistan. My job was to creep up to a door, fix the mine, run away, and . . . *BOOM!* The unit then pushed into the smoking hole to clear any enemy fighters engaging us from the other side.

On other occasions, I was deployed with a light machine gun (LMG). I'd rise at 4 a.m., patrolling through open valleys in the desert to make our presence known to anyone watching nearby. My unit then wandered through towns and villages in the baking heat, checking in with the friendly locals, while taking potshots from the not so friendly. The work was stressful but rewarding. When weapons fired, adrenaline surged through me.

My day-to-day life was about the battle, and the risks were clearly defined. Somebody had to die, which was unfortunate, and at some point that person might be me. But I was ready. And when it came to my combat duties, I was ready for more.

I'D HEARD STORIES about other operations: hostage rescues, hard arrests on serious Taliban players, and door-kicking raids, all performed by the Special Air Service (SAS) or Special Boat Service (SBS). These shadowy regiments made up the U.K. Special Forces, and as far as I was concerned, their work represented a step up, even on the Gurkhas. When I'd first learned about them at Catterick, I was impressed.

Wow. I want to be one of those guys.

Of course, I loved being a soldier, but I also liked the idea of being top of the league even more—and the special forces were the elite. Toward the end of 2008, I sized up my options, learning that the SBS was aligned with the Royal Marines, and the SAS with the British Army. I initially registered my interest in joining the SAS and looked into the squadron's modus operandi and application requirements. I was impressed; they operated across land, sea, and air. Then a friend gave me a little more intel on the SBS.

"These guys do parachute jumps, they fight on land, and on the water," he said. "It's everything the SAS does, but they dive and swim in combat, too."

That was what I was looking for: joining the pinnacle of combat forces. Having worked with the Royal Marines in Afghanistan, I knew I'd blend in well (mentally, at least). Shortly after returning to England from Afghanistan, I attended an SBS briefing course. My application to join U.K. Special Forces Selection—the intense, six-month-long trial that separated those with the guts to join the group from those without—was accepted in 2008. After six proud years with the Gurkhas, I was moving on. My moment to join the military elite had arrived.

THE UNRELENTING PURSUIT OF EXCELLENCE

Nobody believed me when I said my mission was to join the Special Boat Service—probably because no Gurkha had made it before, though several Gurkha brothers had progressed into the SAS. But the SBS was a bit harder to crack, because everyone in the squadron had to be capable of diving and swimming during combat. Gurkhas come from a landlocked country, so the odds were stacked against me from the start—and everybody around me knew it.

Even if I managed to make it through the selection program, I had to pass a series of specialist courses to make it into the SBS.

Operating in the water was completely foreign to me, but I was eager for the challenge. Still, doubting voices arose from within the Gurkha regiment; people thought I was joking or saying that I was applying for show. I ignored them and focused on researching my ambition.

I understood that to become a special forces operator, it was important to adapt—not only to an increased workload and intense style of fighting behind enemy lines in dangerous war zones, but also to the people around me. I was, after all, from Nepal.

Nobody else in the squadron would look like me. To prepare for the culture shock, I decided to learn a portfolio of British jokes: dad jokes, dirty jokes, jokes from old sitcoms and stand-up shows. The Nepali sense of humor is a world apart from the kind found in the SBS, so I memorized gags and funny stories.

Why did the blonde stare at the orange juice bottle? Because the label read: "Juice: concentrate."

I was that eager to fit in.

And I had another reason to familiarize myself with British culture. When assessing who was cut out for the special forces, the assessors, or directing staff (DS), sought recruits who could fit into a squadron of highly focused soldiers. When fighting in some of the world's most dangerous combat environments, team morale is a vital factor. If a potential SBS operator isn't able to crack jokes or get the typical gallows humor, it could be used against them.

It was imperative that I slipped comfortably into their world; I couldn't just say, "Oh, I've come from the Gurkhas, so I don't get it." Or "I wasn't schooled in England. That one went right over my head." I needed to be fit for the purpose on every level.

To prepare myself physically, I pushed myself hard. While based at the Gurkha barracks in Maidstone, Kent, I'd work through my military commitments during the day. But when 5 p.m. arrived, I rushed back to the house to shovel down a small dinner before heading to the gym for a 70-mile bike session.

Combat swimming was a major part of SBS training. But because I wasn't exactly adept in the water, after cycling I dove in the pool and swam as many kilometers as my body could handle. I swam freestyle length after freestyle length, blowing out after 2,500 meters. I rarely made it to bed before midnight, when I'd collapse, sometimes getting up again at 2 a.m. to carry a 75-pound load 10 miles from Maidstone barracks to Chatham.

On weekends, my daily routine involved running for hours at a time. I'd rise at 8 a.m. to haul my ass around the streets with two or three Gurkha buddies; we operated in a relay system, where I was the only soldier prevented from taking a break. One guy would accompany me for six miles, leading me along at a strong pace. Once he completed his distance, another running partner took over, and together we'd go six more miles. This went on for hours, and left me physically and psychologically pummeled.

Getting out of bed in the middle of the night with rain hammering outside was demoralizing, but I pushed through. When snow arrived, I resisted temptation to hit snooze. Emotional control was only one of the many traits I'd need to possess to become an elite soldier.

There was no rest. I understood that if I were fighting with the special forces, we'd have no time for such luxuries, so training as hard as I could seemed like my best hope. Sometimes I worked alone, muscling along under a backpack loaded with 75 pounds of weight for hours on end. The self-inflicted program was the toughest challenge of my life to that point. Every step of the way I fought against the doubt of others: My teammates and senior officers in the Gurkhas assumed elite military service was beyond me, but none of them grasped how dedicated I'd become, or how my mind-set would fuel incredible feats in the years ahead. I had hope. *And hope was God.*

I wasn't, however, a religious person. Although my parents were Hindus, I didn't follow a single higher power. Instead, I liked to celebrate a bit of everything. Sometimes I went to church; other times I visited a Buddhist monastery. But I always wanted to learn new ideas. I was open and human, and I respected every religion in the world.

But more than anything, I had faith in myself. When I was a kid, becoming a Gurkha was my hope. It was my god. Joining the military elite six years later was my next hope. That became my god, too. And I needed to believe in it. Without belief, a challenge the magnitude of passing selection was doomed to fail, so I needed a far higher level of commitment than mere satisfaction or bragging rights. Becoming an SBS operator was more like a cause, and I gave everything to it.

When I finally made it to selection in 2009, every day of the six months was a test of physical and emotional will. It began with the Hills Phase and included a series of timed runs over the Brecon Beacons mountains in South Wales. Determined not to let the pressure get to me, I didn't let myself worry about the succession of tests lined up over the following weeks; I focused only on the 24 hours ahead.

Today I will give 100 percent and survive, I thought at the beginning of each day. *I'll worry about tomorrow when tomorrow comes.*

I held back nothing, kept nothing in reserve because I knew that anything less than my full effort would result in failure. I broke myself on the hills every day, regrouping at night, where I'd summon the will to put in the same effort again over the next 24 hours.

From the start, I seemed to be operating on the back foot. A key attribute of anyone operating within the British Special Forces is their ability to become the "gray man." In a military or surveillance capacity, the gray man blends into the surroundings to avoid detection or unwanted scrutiny.

Sometimes, it helped to adopt gray man tactics during selection, too. Potential operators that continually found themselves at the front of the pack could expect mental pressure from the DS. Those unable to keep up with the physical workload were often verbally thrashed before being kicked off the course and sent back to their regiments.

Because of my skin color, I found it impossible to blend in or to hide in the middle of the group. Everyone made mistakes from time to time, but the DS usually spotted my mistakes immediately, and often from a distance. The yelling and jeering started shortly after, but I maintained my focus—for the most part. During one test march, I failed the course's time requirement by just over a minute. The pressure was immediate and intense. I knew each day was increasingly harder. My dreams were now on the line.

The following morning was set to be brutal, too: The penultimate day of the Hills Phase was a speed march over almost 18 miles. This was followed by the infamous final march—a test of endurance over more than 37 miles while shouldering a loaded Bergen backpack, weapon, water, and supplies, with a weight of around 80 pounds.

After missing the march time, I was presented with a death-or-glory situation: Finish the time trial and final march within the required limit of 20 hours and I still had a shot at making the cut; fail, and I was heading home to the Gurkhas. Except there was no way I was returning to my old regiment. I'd decided that if selection was beyond me, it was time to quit the military for good.

Either do this, Nims, or go home, I thought, gathering my gear the following morning.

My mind was made up, but during a spot-check on all the recruits' equipment on the start line, my stress grew. I'd made a mistake.

"What's this, Purja?" asked the DS, as he rummaged through the Bergen still strapped to my back.

He was waving my water bottle around. My heart sank. *The protective cap was missing!* Even worse, some of the liquid had leaked out.

A key element of making it through selection was the maintenance of personal equipment; without high standards, an operator would likely fail in conflict. Leaving behind something as small as a water bottle cap might be the difference between a covert mission going well and being detected by the enemy. The fatigue of the Hills Phase had affected my attention to detail, but that was no excuse; I should have had enough in the tank to cope. And now I would face the consequences.

"Looks like you'll be carrying some extra weight today," the DS said smugly.

I felt my Bergen being opened. A rock was dropped inside, and the pack's straps strained under the new weight. But the effect it had on me was unexpected. Now, I was even more inspired to succeed.

I thought, Well, Nims, one way or another you're going to have to prove you're one of the strongest here, whether or not they can see you.

Settling into the familiar sensation of pain first instilled in me by those heavy training sessions for the doko race, I charged forward. I'd learned that the selection process wasn't about discovering soldiers made of iron. Instead, the DS were looking for people who were flexible and able to mold themselves into any situation.

Mentally and physically, I felt it within my grasp to adapt to the toughest challenges the Hills Phase had to offer. I felt strong as I yomped up steep hills. Flats and downhill stretches were taken at a running pace, mile after mile, hour after hour, until after nearly a full day of exertion, I crossed the finish line as the fastest recruit of the day.

In the face of my toughest challenge yet, I hadn't cracked. I'd bent and flexed. I was malleable.

MANY TIMES DURING TRAINING, my soldiering skills were pushed to the limit—none more so than when we were in the jungle. In military terms, the remote rainforest locations I worked in were horror shows. It was hot and sticky, the experience gloomy and wet. Everyone stunk. Operating in the jungle is a test of military skill; the vegetation is booby-trapped with bugs and snakes, and the tropical conditions are adversaries to be feared in their own right.

Yet whenever I was there, often for weeks at a time, I always smiled my way through the mud. I was in my element, productive and happy, while a few of the guys around me suffered. Some of them even thought something was wrong with me. One morning, while cheerfully climbing a hill on a navigation check, I noticed camouflaged faces in my unit staring back at me in disbelief.

"Fucking hell, Nims," whispered one of them. "I'm hanging out on these patrols, piss-wet through, and you're . . . *enjoying it?*"

I laughed, explaining that it was an environment I'd grown up in. The jungle was home ground. I still made many of the same mistakes as everybody else, as I had throughout my career so far. But I worked under the theory that the military elite would require me to be resolute and flexible when I got there, and nobody was going to do me any favors or encourage me to work harder. I had to motivate myself at all times. If I was in a bad situation, it was up to me to dig myself out. At times, it was hard not to snap under the emotional stress.

I also had to bite my lip in the face of criticism. One time, a guy in my patrol screwed up in a reconnaissance exercise, but because success in the jungle is based on teamwork, the whole group was punished afterward. When the patrol called us together, we were dressed down, and I was told I'd achieved the distinction of being the worst soldier in the world.

"What the fuck are you even doing here, Purja?" someone shouted.

When I tried to answer, I was cut off. "Speak English," he said, referring to my strong accent. I wanted to punch him in the face, but I held back, knowing it was all part of the test. I couldn't react to provocation. So I kept my mouth shut.

I'll just have to hang in here. These bastards might try to break me, but I'm going to last the course no matter what.

It was their job to crush my spirit; mine was to fight on to the very end.

I dealt with every test the military could throw at me, from live-firing drills to mock casualty evacuation (CASEVAC) operations. My resolve was unbreakable. Come and test me, I'd think. By the end of jungle training I felt ready for battle, and with each step I was closer to becoming a fully fledged member of the SBS, *my new god*.

After passing a series of additional specialist courses, it became official. I was a member of the Special Boat Service. On my badging day, I took my first ever drop of alcohol during an induction ceremony with the other guys. First, a glass of whisky. Then a liter and a half of lager, wine, and spirits, all mixed together. I had to down it all in one hit—not that I minded at that point. *I had met my god*. I was now a special forces operator and part of an elite club, having proved myself capable of fighting at the highest level. I was one of them. I felt like a rock star.

As soon as my first hangover ebbed, the pace of life became intense. One minute I was training in a boat, the next I was throwing myself and a parachute out of a Hercules plane over the sea. My new life was demanding, but it was never dull.

After joining the SBS, each operator assumes one of several roles to develop their skill in a particular discipline. I chose to become a trauma medic. My job was to patch up any wounds or injuries my teammates sustained during a gun battle; I learned how to deal with bullet-wound trauma and injuries from IED detonations.

Finally, I was thrust into real life-or-death action in July 2010, where I operated in a series of war zones and worked on hard-arrest raids. My role was to rush through houses and enemy compounds with a unit of men, facing off with enemy forces and IED booby traps.

Kicking in doors was exciting, but terrifying, and I soon became a seasoned operator. Something inside me switched on during a fight; I stayed calm under pressure, thanks to my training and experience but also because of the Gurkha spirit. We had a reputation to uphold: We were known as one of the toughest fighting forces on Earth, and I was determined to maintain that image.

I had a code: bravery above all else. There was no other way for me to live.

5

INTO THE
DEATH ZONE

Once I entered wars for prolonged periods, life became even tougher. There was no hiding place, and the hostile forces we battled against were adaptable and unwilling to surrender.

But I didn't crumble. I wasn't one to express my feelings openly, even to my wife, Suchi. And as a soldier, I soon learned to mask any grief I might have felt on the job. I believed hiding any emotional pain I might be experiencing while fighting was important.

During selection, I didn't want the DS to think I was unable to cope when operating at my limits; during war, I certainly didn't want the enemy to sense I'd become weak, tired, or scared. That would only give them a psychological lift. Disguising my pain and suffering was a skill I practiced at all times, and I did so by focusing intensely on the job at hand; it helped to shut out the chaos around me.

Even when I was shot during one mission, I didn't show fear or vulnerability. It happened during a gunfight at a border outpost, when I was asked to provide fire support for a raid. We were pinned down, and had sustained a handful of casualties. I was on the roof of a compound, firing my weapon while lying flat on my belly, when I was struck by something—I wasn't sure what at first, but it was powerful enough to knock me from the building.

I hit the deck with a thud, and having fallen 10 feet or more, my senses took a few seconds to flood back to me. *What the hell happened?* I tasted the warm, metallic tang of blood in my mouth. A puddle of red grew around me on the floor. For a split second I worried half my face had been shredded away, though I didn't feel any pain.

Was I in shock?

Was my jaw in one piece?

I pawed nervously at my chin. *Thank God. It was still there.* But clearly an enemy bullet had nearly ended me, leaving a nasty wound, slicing across my face, carving my jawline and lips to ribbons. Only when I checked my weapon did it become obvious how close to death I'd come. The round had struck my butt extender, the supporting arm that allowed me to rest my rifle into the crook of my shoulder as I fired.

A sniper had taken his shot. I reckon he was probably aiming for my neck, or head, but the aim was a fraction off. The bullet had ricocheted off the metal extension and smashed through the rifle's trigger housing mechanism, exiting at an angle across my face. The energy from that one round had carried enough power to force me off the roof from a prone position. My weapon was now useless; I tossed it aside and rolled into cover. The shooting wasn't over, so I resumed fire with a pistol, calling in to the unit that I'd been hit.

Once our operation was concluded and my wound patched up, I returned to base a few days later. But news of my injury had arrived in advance. Word spread that I'd been hurt in a gunfight and that the squadron's welfare officer had even called Suchi to explain that I'd suffered a bullet wound, though no details were passed on. Understandably freaked out, she called the base for an update. Not that I had any idea. As I rested, my sergeant major knocked on the door.

"Fucking hell, you Gurkhas!" he laughed. "Do you guys not bother telling your family you're OK?"

What do you mean?

"Your wife, she's called wanting to know you're still in one piece."

I hit the roof and called Suchi back angrily.

"What the fuck?" I said. "Why are you calling?"

Suchi explained how she'd feared the worst. The family was also worried that I might have been in trouble. Slowly, I realized my reaction had been excessive—I was a young man at the time and I hadn't put myself in her position. Calmly, I reassured Suchi that I was fine and that I'd decided not to tell anyone about what had happened until I made it safely home at the end of my military tour. The thought of upsetting my wife or parents while I was away seemed more stressful than any gunfight.

I explained to Suchi that the only time she truly had to worry was if two uniformed officers from the Royal Marines wearing black ties ever knocked on our front door; by then, it would be too late. Other than that, she was to carry on as if everything was fine. That might sound like a strange attitude to some people, but it was one of the many defense mechanisms I carried with me to manage a chaotic role.

Having survived a succession of gunfights over several years, I focused on the opportunities available within the military's highly specialized climbing courses, scaling challenging peaks and abseiling down sheer rock faces until my place on the forthcoming 2015 G200E Everest climb was all but assured.

I was then required to train a number of recruits from the Gurkha regiment: hopefuls looking to join the same expedition. Together, we scaled around 6,200 meters of Makalu's southeast ridge, chosen for its technical climbing. The expedition team-in-waiting learned how to jumar and belay effectively, while building confidence in their crampon work and climbing skills. They experienced severe exposure on sharp ridges at extreme altitude, and the work was rough.

After a celebratory drinking session at expedition's end, I decided to take on Ama Dablam, the mountain I'd fallen in love with during that trek with my friend and climbing mentor, Dorje, in 2012, scaling the near-vertical face of the Yellow Tower. Utilizing the unorthodox strategy of going directly from base camp to Camp 2 in one burst, rather than resting and acclimatizing at Camp 1, I soon reached the top of a technical Himalayan peak in around 23 hours.

But shortly afterward, I was struck by a double whammy of tragedies. The first was news that Dorje had been killed on Everest on April 18, 2014, when seracs* from the western spur collapsed,

---

* A serac is a pinnacle or block of ice found among crevasses on a glacier, usually on a steep slope. Commonly the size of a house or larger, they are dangerous to mountaineers, because they can topple without warning and can cause avalanches.

triggering a huge avalanche. A tsunami of snow, rock, and ice swept through the Khumbu Icefall, wiping out 16 Sherpas. It was one of the mountain's most deadly disasters, and Everest was closed for the rest of the season after guides refused to work as a mark of respect for the deceased.

The news, which I heard while on a military tour, hit me hard. But in a war zone there's little time to grieve; the enemy rarely affords moments of contemplation, and I had to get on with my work, acting as if nothing had happened.

Several months later, in what felt like another body blow, it was announced my squadron was being rotated into military action in May, right when the 2015 G200E trip was scheduled. I was off the team. It was demoralizing; I'd been working hard with my sights set on the expedition, and by scaling the likes of Dhaulagiri and Ama Dablam, my body and mind felt ready.

But I had to forget my disappointment; my job wasn't as a professional mountaineer. My role was to operate in war, and there was no space to grumble or sulk—though in hindsight, perhaps fate played its part.

As the Gurkha expedition prepared at Everest Base Camp in May, an earthquake measuring 8.1 on the Richter scale triggered a massive avalanche that barreled into base camp yet again, killing 22 people: the greatest single loss of life in Everest's history, though nobody from the expedition team was seriously injured. It made headlines around the world, and from my desert base I learned that the G200E was being abandoned, as was every expedition that year. When a new date was set for May 2017, I hoped to make it back on the team.

Not that my position was assured. Anything could happen in two years, and as I'd learned, my commitment to the military overshadowed any personal ambitions. I didn't let myself get overly excited, though I made sure to improve my climbing skills so that if 2017 went according to plan, I'd be ready for Everest.

And then, unexpectedly, an opportunity emerged in the spring of 2016, when my military deployment plans were altered at the last minute. Having spent the early part of the year training for one top secret combat environment, I was suddenly asked by high command to operate in another.

"We need your experience out there," said my sergeant major.

My disappointment was palpable. "I was only there six months ago . . ."

But my transfer was already set in place. And a happy twist was coming.

"Look, Nims, we'll give you four weeks' leave rather than the standard three," said my sergeant major. "How does that sound?"

This was both good news and bad. The good: I'd previously promised Suchi that we'd take a beach holiday after a grueling six-month tour I'd spent fighting the Taliban, and I was looking forward to a little rest and recuperation. The bad: There was no way I'd last four weeks sleeping on a beach lounger, reading, listening to music, staring out at sea, sunbathing. Boredom would overtake me within five minutes. Instead, I spied an opportunity.

Maybe I could climb Everest?

Logistically, it was a long shot and the expedition came loaded with risk. Because of the time constraints, I wouldn't have the luxury of a two-month acclimatization period, as most people take when climbing 8,000ers. But screw it, I'd done the same thing on Dhaulagiri—how would this be any different?

Financially, the odds were stacked against me, too. The costs of climbing Everest were extortionate, and the estimated bill came in at around U.S. $80,000. Suchi was a bit annoyed at first, though she eventually came around when I pointed out that my place on the G200E team wasn't guaranteed. Knowing the opportunity might not present itself again, I figured, *So what?* and went to the bank for a personal loan.

"Can I ask what you need the money for, Mr. Purja?" asked the banker.

"I need to buy a car," I lied.

A few minutes later I secured a U.S. $20,000 transfer. I then promptly booked a flight to Nepal's capital, Kathmandu.

This financial chicanery was only the first step of many, however. As I left England, I estimated most people climbing Everest were already moving toward one of the mountain's higher camps and were acclimatized in preparation for their summit push via the South Col route: the wind-raked ridge that linked Everest to Lhotse's nearby peak. With Sherpa support, I'd be able to make the trek to base camp from Lukla Airport, "The Gateway to Mount Everest," and then move to the higher camps with ease—but I didn't want Sherpa support.

I wanted to climb Everest solo.

It was a crazy idea and I knew it, especially as I'd only accumulated a couple years of experience on big mountains and was still honing my skills.

Any anxieties I might have felt about my relative inexperience in solo climbing were tempered with a little pep talk regarding my background. If I got into any trouble at high altitude, my medical skills might come in handy, but they alone wouldn't be enough to save me from the dangers of an 8,000er. Instead, my mortality would be decided by the ability to perform quickly at extreme altitude. Thank goodness, my now extensive military climbing training, and those expeditions to Dhaulagiri, Ama Dablam, and Makalu, had given me a fair idea of how to survive.

More important, I'd learned how to control my emotions during combat. Fear barely affected me, even when I was close to getting dropped by the enemy—an increasing occupational hazard in my line of work. Climbing a mountain with hundreds of deaths to its name seemed like a risk, but one I felt qualified to take.

I also realized that if I wanted to be considered an elite climber at some point, this was exactly the type of challenge I'd have to accept, regardless of the increased workload and lower odds of success. Sure, climbing with a 77-pound backpack, complete with climbing equipment, a tent, and supplies, would be a challenge. But I felt it was within my skill set. I also intended to use supplemental oxygen above 7,400 meters, which some elite climbers who operated at extreme altitudes considered controversial. The extra kit would add weight, but I figured it was vital because I was working alone.

The greatest risk, however, was psychological: I was taking a chance with my reputation—What would people in the military think if I screwed up? As I flew to Kathmandu and then Lukla Airport, I tried not to think about the potential for disaster.

My mission was in place. I was taking on the world's tallest peak.

"YOU'RE BLUFFING."

With a rapidly narrowing summit window at the end of May, the majority of people I encountered at Lukla didn't believe I could make it to the top of Everest in only three weeks. Nor did the American film crew on standby to film a documentary they were loosely calling *Everest Air*. They planned to trail a rescue team that was in place to conduct medical evacuations on the mountain. Given the perilous nature of 8,000ers, *Everest Air* was sure to have plenty of action to edit. While readying my gear, the film crew bombarded me with a series of friendly questions in the kind of conversation that always took place between adrenalized climbers on the brink of a risky expedition.

"Where are you from, Nims?"

England.

"Oh, right. Long way, dude. What do you do?"

I'm a medic. I work in London.

Following my trip to Dhaulagiri, I'd decided this was the perfect alibi, mainly because the story had a pinch of truth. If someone became nosy about my concocted medical career, I'd at least be able to throw them off the scent with a little talk about my experience in treating trauma injuries. Telling anyone I worked with the British Special Forces was out of the question.

The main guy in the film crew was sizing up my kit. "That's a lot of stuff. Are you here for the trekking? Because you're too late to climb Everest in time."

No, I'm here for the climb. And I'll make it in time—I have to.

There was a pause. "What? Where's the rest of your team then?"

I'm doing it solo.

There was a snort of disbelief; someone else laughed. "You're fucking kidding!"

I shook my head and shrugged it off. The glass-half-empty attitude went against everything I'd been taught in the military, where

63

grumbling or giving up wasn't an effective strategy. If problems or challenges came my way, I was supposed to find solutions, having been trained to adapt and survive. I picked up the last of my gear and tried my best to forget the snarky comments, knowing that gloomy thinking was both destructive and contagious.

No. No jokes, brother. I'm fucking doing this.

Besides, I didn't have the time for small talk. My plan for making it to the summit in such a limited window was to do everything more quickly than was recommended, without wasting too much energy.

I trekked to base camp at speed, making it to the bottom of Everest in only three days. Rather than taking a few acclimatization climbs through the Khumbu Icefall's notorious valley of toppling seracs to Camp 1, I headed straight for Camp 2 at 6,400 meters—a progression that usually took most people a month as they settled into the high altitudes. I was foregoing the luxury of time and rest, trying to adapt and survive—and quickly paid a heavy price for my impatience.

Having passed Camp 1, and stuck midway between the two camps, I noticed the first indicators of an oncoming physical failure. I was exhausted. My lack of acclimatization was taking its toll, the heavy backpack was pressing down on me, and every step in my crampons along the icy climb felt like a monumental effort. I'd also become seriously dehydrated. The sun had been high; at times it felt as if I were melting under its intensity. Sweat burned my eyes and I could barely see. But dangers were everywhere.

I was negotiating the Western Cwm, a route riddled with crevasses, and I was close to my breaking point from the physical and emotional effort. My eyes rimmed with tears; for the first time in years, self-doubt seeped into my thinking.

I'm not strong enough to make it to Camp 2. But I don't want to go back to Camp 1 either.

I knew I had to lose the negative internal chitchat, and fast. Whenever I'd been in life-or-death events in the past, I'd used visions of Suchi to restore my focus and determination. I thought of her during gun battles whenever my unit was pinned by enemy fighters; the emotions were fuel, and I was able to reset and concentrate on the job at hand. Now, I used the thought of her waiting for me to return home as inspiration to push toward shelter at Camp 2. I rummaged in my pockets and found my phone, recording a brief video message.

"Look, baby, I'm struggling massively, but as always I'm going to make this happen . . ."

I didn't send it; I only wanted to capture the moment. Then I worked on course correcting.

Let's do this.

After taking a few deep breaths, my heart felt full again. Before long, I located an extra reserve of strength, my internal pep talk jolting me from a doomy headspace. The walk along the Western Cwm was ordinarily mellow, the route fairly flat. And though one or two areas required a little technical mountaineering, I could spend most of the climb pulling myself along the fixed lines without too much stress, taking a couple diversions to avoid crevasses.* I gathered my gear and pressed on to Camp 2.

---

* Fixed lines are roped routes set at the start of the season by a designated team. They allow expeditions to move up steep inclines more easily throughout the same season.

Boom! Boom! Boom! My momentum returned, and every step felt like an achievement. *Boom! Boom! Boom!* Every footfall was a positive push to the Western Cwm's end.

As I'd discovered on Dhaulagiri, burning out at high altitudes was fairly easy, but I had yet to experience firsthand the full medical consequences of that kind of mistake, though that moment was soon to arrive. By the time I set up my tent at Camp 2, I was feeling good again, so I ate lunch and hung out with a couple Sherpa friends, before pushing up another 150 meters and back.

By acclimatizing a little higher, my hope was to avoid the pounding headaches that sometimes dogged me when sleeping at high altitude. But I overdid my effort, and by the time I lay in the tent to rest, my lungs were gurgling—a sure sign I was developing a high-altitude pulmonary edema (HAPE), an accumulation of fluid in the lungs and a nasty condition in which the chest wheezes and heaves, the skin turns blue, and the heart pounds like a kick drum. Without treatment, I had every chance of dying.

As I recovered in my sleeping bag, listening to the wheeze of my straining lungs, it was impossible not to feel the sting of frustration. I'd been stupid. Now every breath was a heavy effort.

Nims, you should have known . . . you're a mountaineer and a medic! You have all the knowledge in the world about altitude sickness. Why couldn't you have taken more care?

When it came to the high peaks, Dhaulagiri had taught me that a thin line separates success from failure, just as in battle. But I'd naively believed that my military training, plus the lessons learned elsewhere in the mountains, would guide me through knife-edge judgment calls on Everest. I'd also wanted to test my limits by pushing up the extra distance.

I was wrong. The critical divide between good and bad decisions during war becomes even narrower in mountaineering, because the physical extremes are so dramatic on 8,000-meter peaks. After only 24 hours on Everest, I was learning that to cross the line led to disaster. Embarrassed, I returned to base camp for a medical check and a period of recuperation to regroup for my summit push.

"You can't go back up," said the first doctor I checked in with as he listened to my rattling chest through a stethoscope. "By the sounds of it, that's a very big pulmonary edema."

Remembering my childhood success as the human antibiotic, I decided to get a second opinion.

What does he know? I'll find another medic who understands.

But the next mountain doctor was just as pessimistic. "I'd advise you not to climb any higher," he said. "The first assessment was right. In your condition you might get into some serious trouble up there."

Again, I shrugged off the diagnosis. *These guys are erring on the side of caution. That's fine in a civilian hospital, but I'm at Everest Base Camp. Everyone's taking a risk here, one way or another.*

My mind was made up.

These doctors are wrong.

A doctor friend of mine was also operating somewhere on base camp, so I tracked him down, hoping for a more casual diagnosis, one that would allow me to return to climbing in 24 hours. Instead, I was given the third and final warning of the day.

"Nims, man, you've got to get off the mountain. That's a pulmonary edema. You can't mess around."

Shit. I finally understood that I was going to have to take my recuperation seriously after all. The *Everest Air* team, impressed by my effort, offered me a ride back to Lukla by helicopter for x-rays and some downtime for a few days, where I learned that my diagnosis could have serious implications in the future. According to every medical journal I skimmed through online, HAPE was a potentially returning condition, and the smartest move was to go home and recover. Without care, my lungs could fail again. So if I was going to make another attempt I would have to ascend Everest cautiously—which didn't bode well given my rapidly diminishing leave from the military and the climbing season's closing window.

Still, I was determined to not allow a medical concern to derail my plans. As I recovered, I filled my head with positive thoughts. I told myself I'd make it to the top, no problem. By focusing only on success, I forced myself to believe.

And I had another sobering realization to deal with. Any hope I had to summit Everest solo was gone. I now needed a Sherpa to help me, but no way would I take an easy ride to the top. When it came to selecting assistance, I wanted to employ the least experienced guy I could find. First, because I still hoped for a serious challenge. Second, the Nepali Sherpa was an unappreciated and underpaid worker. Although climbers scaling Everest usually travel light, their Sherpas and porters generally lug 65 or 90 pounds of rope, kit, and provisions, while receiving little pay and next to no credit. However, once a Sherpa summits Everest, his service fees soar, and I wanted to give somebody that money-making opportunity.

There was another self-imposed restriction. Although I had the knowledge and expertise required to climb Everest, I also felt it important to be self-sufficient: If I struggled with HAPE again, I wouldn't need to call in a rescue party, because a Sherpa could help me down the mountain. So later, when I met Pasang Sherpa, a young porter from Makalu who'd never reached Everest's peak, at Everest Base Camp, I knew he was the perfect candidate. Pasang was so unprepared that he only owned an old summit suit and a beat-up pair of boots.

"This is great, Nims," he said, pulling on the thermal layers, gloves, and other bits of kit I'd given to him. "If I can get you to the top, I'll be able to charge three times as much for my services."

Knowing the trip could change both our lives forever, we started our climb, hoping for the best, silencing any talk of the worst.

WE MOVED STEADILY through the Khumbu Icefall and across the Western Cwm again. The wind strengthened, but our two-man team pressed ahead through harsh alpine conditions from Camp 2 to 3, pitching a tent and sleeping as the winds built and battered our shelter's thin nylon walls. My lungs felt good. I was holding up physically, and my brush with HAPE felt like a distant memory. We set out for the summit that night, pushing ourselves through the Himalayan dark. I was determined to not take unnecessary chances on my first Everest summit push, and closely watched the line of headlamps from the expedition ahead of us. I'd already had one brush with death and didn't fancy experiencing another.

With the peak in sight, I pulled myself along the fixed line that tethered me to the mountain. By 4 a.m., I had made it past the infamous Hillary Step, the technically challenging 40-foot-tall boulder jumble that every climber on the southeast route has to negotiate to reach the world's highest point. (In the 2015 earthquake, the Hillary Step was altered when its largest boulder fell away, but people still refer to it as a landmark.) A rush of excitement pulsed through me. *I'm going to do it!*

Our timing was perfect; the sun was about to appear over the Himalaya. And then, in a grand moment I will never forget, we stepped onto the summit of Mount Everest at 8,848 meters above sea level. Yet, as I finally basked in a reflective moment, Pasang seemed edgy. The strong winds had intensified, and we were both becoming a little unsteady on our feet.

"Nims, we have to go back," he said.

"But we just got here!"

"Yeah, but this is a dangerous time. People die on the way down because they wait too long and get caught out by the weather."

Despite Pasang's lack of experience on Everest, I knew he was right. There were too many horror stories of people wasting precious time taking selfies, or unveiling flags in the belief that their mission was complete, when in reality their job was only 50 percent done. The most important part of any climb was getting back down quickly and safely—to say nothing of the summit winds that have been known to reach 100 miles an hour.

I checked my oxygen levels, and according to my watch I had plenty of time for a safe descent. I told myself that Pasang was probably panicking because he was new to the mountain. Turning around for base camp was his priority now.

"Listen, brother, I risked everything to be here, but I'm feeling strong," I said, "so I'm not going down until I see the sun rising."

"No, Nims. *No, no, no!*"

"I can make it down, no problem," I told Pasang firmly, giving him the permission to leave.

He shrugged his shoulders and turned away sadly, but I was happy to wait alone. As he trudged down the mountain, I watched the sun climb above the Himalaya, washing orange and pink over the snowcapped peaks, burning through the wispy clouds below. Himalayan prayer flags whipped in the wind behind me. At that moment, I was the highest person on the planet; it felt like a life-defining event, and I took off my goggles to feel the cold air against my eyes. The view was every bit as wild as I'd imagined, and waiting had been the right decision. But I wasn't going to stick around for long.

At that altitude, situational awareness—an important facet of military life—was a tool every bit as valuable as my down-filled summit suit or insulated climbing boots. I took one last look at the epic views around me and began trudging down, picturing a celebratory beer at base camp. Days earlier, HAPE had knocked me down, and yet I'd still been able to climb the world's tallest mountain. My self-belief was soaring.

When I saw the stricken climber on the terrain below, abandoned to die by his teammates on an expedition gone wrong, I knew I'd have to draw on every last ounce of it.

THE MOUNTAINEER was incapacitated, or dead; I couldn't tell at first. Leaning in, I checked for vital signs. The woman was seemingly pinned to the spot, unable to move. Her goggles were gone, and when I looked around in the snow, I saw no sign of them anywhere. Perhaps her mind was overcome by altitude sickness and she'd thrown them in a panic or dropped them in confusion.

Physically, she was a mess, semiconscious and barely able to speak. I struggled to find her faintly beating pulse. She wasn't going to make it unless somebody moved her down quickly.

Fortunately, I was still feeling fairly strong; I had it in me to drag her to Camp 4, where I hoped she'd receive the assistance she badly needed. But time wasn't on our side. (I was also aware of my brush with HAPE, and the fact I hadn't committed to as many acclimatization rotations as most climbers on Everest.) If I couldn't find her a pair of goggles before the sun rose higher in the sky, the woman could suffer snow blindness, a painful burn to the retinas caused by the powerful UV rays at high altitude that can feel like having sand rubbed in your eyes. I cranked up the oxygen in her tank and tried to rouse her.

"Hey, you're going to be OK," I shouted, shaking her gently. "What's your name?"

I heard a mumble. She was talking. I leaned in closer.

"Seema . . ."

Seema! That was something to work with. If I could keep her chatting, I had a fighting chance to save her life.

"Where are you from?"

"India . . ." she whispered.

"OK, Seema, I'm going to get you home."

She seemed to nod. I heard her mumbling again, but I couldn't tell if she was showing signs of delirium, or if she was trying to tell me something. I switched into an operational setting and radioed down to Camp 4, where I knew the rescue team working with the

Everest Air crew rested, having made a high-altitude mission several hours previously.

"Guys, it's Nims," I said. "There's a woman, Seema, stuck here. Can you help her?"

A voice responded straight away. "Look, Nims, last night we rescued this climber all the way from the South Summit, and now we're spent. Can you bring her down to Camp 4 yourself? We can help her from here. If we come up again, one or two of us might die."

"Sure, no problem," I said.

Under the circumstances, those guys had made the correct call.

Here's a controversial reality: On 8,000-meter peaks, the attitude *every person for themself* sometimes rings tragically true. People climb, people struggle, and people die; badly injured individuals usually go through a moment when the inevitability of their death becomes clear to everyone around them. They might succumb to exhaustion or high-altitude cerebral edema (HACE), a severe and potentially fatal medical condition in which the brain swells with fluid, causing confusion, clumsiness, and stumbling. If either takes hold, people can become unable to think straight. In a confused panic, they unzip their summit suit in the false belief they're overheating. When intense cold sinks its teeth into flesh, a painful ending becomes unavoidable.

I've also heard of people wandering away from their group in the belief that they're nearly home; then they take a nasty tumble off the mountain's edge. At times, high-altitude expeditions can resemble a war zone. Many climbers want to stay with struggling friends as they die. Though they might exhaust themselves or run low on oxygen, remaining close, delivering comfort, and reassurance are very human reactions.

But that's actually the worst choice. With every minute wasted on the mountain, the chances of survival shrink for a tired group; before they know it, one death has become two, three, or even more.

If the healthy members cannot physically rescue the injured, the best response is for the group to leave and move down the mountain and radio for help in hopes that a stronger climber might be descending behind them or that a rescue team with enough oxygen can climb from a lower camp. I guessed that's what happened on Everest that day.

Camp 4 was a descent of almost 1,500 feet in altitude and from there, where the air was a bit thicker, Seema's condition could be assessed more effectively. The *Everest Air* team would have oxygen, too. If she was able to walk at that point, or even stagger, I had a good chance of being able to guide her all the way to base camp. The alternative was to hand her over to the rescue crew in Camp 4, while I descended to base camp before my oxygen ran out.

Either way, moving her down was going to be a challenge. What I'd planned on doing wasn't going to be the most comfortable evacuation for her, or for me. But it would certainly be the quickest and most effective.

Gathering a length of old, unused rope dangling from one of the fixed lines on the mountain, I wound it around Seema's waist, securing it tight. I then heaved, dragging her slowly down toward Camp 4. With every pull, Seema moaned in pain.

"I know, I know," I shouted out over my shoulder. "It feels so bad right now. But take my word, please: This is the best way to get you back safely, and if we don't act now, it's not going to happen."

The effort took around an hour, and having been dragged for 656 feet, Seema seemed capable of standing. I pulled her up, encouraging her to attempt a few steps, then a few more, until gradually we started making progress. But the effort was painful.

Finally, with around 25 meters to go until Camp 4, I realized that Seema didn't have it in her to move any farther. She was too weak. I was in a bad way myself, barely able to stand and on the verge of collapsing from the effort. My climb through the night had finally caught up with me, and the adrenaline of scaling Everest had worn off. I fell to my knees and radioed for help. A team of Sherpas rushed from a nearby tent and dragged us both to safety. Once sheltered from the freezing winds, I summoned the strength to call base camp.

"Guys, this is Nims. I'm at Camp 4 with Seema. She's in a bad way, but the rescue team is looking after her now . . ."

I heard a crackle on the other end of the line. One of Seema's expedition buddies was shouting excitedly. In the background, I heard other voices as people gathered around the radio.

"Nims, that's amazing! Thank you."

There was a pause. "Are *you* OK?"

I found myself at the tipping point. My oxygen was close to running out and if I hung around for too long, there was a chance I might die. Knowing that Seema had enough in her own tank, and that rescuers were with her, I realized my work was done.

"Guys, if I stay here any longer, you may have to rescue me as well. I'm going down now."

Hours later, I staggered into base camp and collapsed, instantly falling asleep in my tent. When I woke the next day, it was to good news: Seema had been successfully extracted and was alive, and as word passed around the tents, people wanted to know more about the unknown climber who had rescued her. Well-wishers, thankful expedition leaders, and even one or two family members were trying to figure out who I was.

At one point a media request came through. A journalist had been tipped off and wanted to interview me for a story, but it was critical that I maintain my low profile as an elite operator; I hadn't told anyone back at the SBS HQ about what I planned to do on my holidays. My only chance of escaping unwanted attention outside of the Himalaya was to apply a little emotional pressure.

"I'm a member of U.K. Special Forces, and I'll lose my job if this story comes out," I said. "Please don't say anything."

My request was passed down the line.

In the aftermath of Seema's solo rescue, I'd learned a serious lesson: By using oxygen during my expedition, I had been able to save her. Without it, the chances of summoning the energy for a rescue would have been slim. For that reason, from now on I was climbing above the higher camps on 8,000ers with bottled air, even though some mountaineers didn't consider it the purest form of high-altitude climbing. *Who cared?* Nobody could dictate to me why or how I climbed the mountains, just as I didn't have the right to dictate to others.

I hadn't climbed Everest for fame or reputation. If anything, I needed to keep my achievements quiet, because as a former Gurkha I'd jumped the gun: I was now, as far as I knew, the first serving member of the regiment to scale the world's tallest mountain. Were that publicized in the media, G200E might be scrapped. I needed anonymity, and upon returning home, my family and close friends were sworn to secrecy.

Every morning for a week, I scanned the newspapers for any news of my rescue efforts on Everest. From what I could see, nothing had been written—at least, nothing that mentioned me by name. The mission had been achieved by strength and guile. Shortly after returning from Kathmandu, I flew home to Suchi, happy for the rest and grateful that my secret and job were safe. A few days later, I was back scrapping with the military, where I kicked in doors and took down bad dudes, counting the days until it was time to climb another mountain.

6

SWIMMING TO THE MOON

May 2017 arrived all too quickly, but my deployment schedule had been kind. I'd been confirmed as a member of the G200E, where I would work as a team instructor. A second attempt at the world's tallest peak was back on, but this time I wouldn't have to secure a hefty bank loan to finance the trip. I was a member of the British Armed Forces, my expenses would be paid, and I intended to squeeze the experience for every last drop of adventure.

I'd been harboring the idea of climbing Everest and the neighboring peak of Lhotse before taking on nearby Makalu in a two-week period. Though all three mountains were 8,000ers, I reckoned I had it in me to climb them in around a week or so. But the schedule would require me to move quickly after summiting with the G200E: no mistakes, no holdups. Our celebratory expedition was made up of around 20 climbers and included Gurkhas, a couple faces from the military elite, and a handful of officers, one of whom was the expedition leader.

If I eventually summited, I'd have to break away and descend at speed to South Col.* From there I hoped to move quickly, climbing Lhotse and heading down to base camp. If everything worked as planned, I'd then party in Kathmandu for a bit with my Gurkha brothers before taking on Makalu.

I felt ready for the challenge. The way I'd made it to the summits of Everest and Dhaulagiri affirmed my hunch that I was a strong high-altitude mountain climber. But it wasn't simply about physical strength; my mind-set felt different, too. I seemed to have unusual drive compared to many climbers.

During operations I constantly reminded myself of my commitment to the Gurkhas, the British Special Forces, and the United Kingdom. I needed to do them proud. The last thing I wanted was to dent their image by failing on a mission, and I felt the same way on expeditions. I knew if I could climb Everest, Lhotse, and Makalu, the reputations of institutions I believed in

---

* Everest and Lhotse share camps from base camp up to Camp 3 on the South Col route. After Camp 3, a climber hoping to top out at the world's tallest mountain travels to the left across the South Col to Everest's Camp 4. Those hoping to climb Lhotse move straight up. Makalu was a helicopter ride away from the shared base camp.

would be enhanced, which could boost my brothers within them. I also wanted to test my limits. The mountains were there to be climbed. Did I have the minerals—British military slang for "guts"—to take them on?

Prior to the G200E, I even mentioned my ambition to my officer in command. "I want to climb Everest, Lhotse, and Makalu while I'm there," I said. "I won't need to take any time off. I'll do the climbs while the other lads are resting in Kathmandu after the expedition and I'll be on the same flight home."

"That can't be done, Nims," he said dismissively. "It sounds impossible."

Untroubled by his pessimism, I readied myself for the challenge anyway. I had to give it my best shot.

We traveled to Nepal in April, and once we arrived at Everest the G200E party was divided into two teams. My first job was to guide one team through the acclimatization rotations required to reach the summit. The process, which happened gradually, took the expedition into Camp 1 and then over the Western Cwm to Camps 2 and 3. From there, we'd return to base camp, by which point everyone should be physically primed for a summit push.

When compared to my first attempt at the world's tallest peak, this felt like a tactically wiser operation, and I thrived. My confidence had grown so much, and it also helped that some of the group I was leading were both strong and resolute, operating comfortably at high altitudes. However, others weren't so well equipped and were slow to acclimatize; a handful of climbers, including senior leaders, looked exhausted by the time we reached Camp 1 for the first time. I wondered how they could lead if they weren't up to speed on what was considered a fairly straightforward acclimatization rotation.*

Because it was clear which climbers had juice and which ones were fading, I decided to take the strongest on to Camp 2 and then 3, while the slower team members rested at Camp 1 for an extra day of acclimatization. After completing their respective climbs, the two teams took a couple days to rest in the nearby town of Namche Bazaar, before briefing day in base camp—the moment when the groups would be organized into two expedition units.

Team A was set to lead the climb. Team B would start their ascent once the first group had summited. But when the two parties for our historic expedition were revealed, it had been decided that the slower, struggling leaders should go first, which conveniently included the officers in the group. (I found that a bit weird—most officers I'd served with in the military elite typically put the interests of their men before their own.) Meanwhile, most of the stronger climbers—myself included, as well as two Gurkha Special Forces instructors—were set to follow in Team B. For some reason, we'd been relegated to the back of the line. I was pissed. *Hadn't we earned the right?*

---

* In the past, climbers using bottled oxygen organized their acclimatization rotations very differently. Expeditions would climb to Camp 1, sleep there, and then descend to base camp. On the following climb, the group would move to Camps 1 and 2, sleep, and then climb all the way down again. Finally, for their third rotation, it was considered best to go all the way to Camp 2, rest, and then climb up to Camp 3 before returning to base camp. For the past few years, it's been considered more effective if a climber summits after completing only one acclimatization rotation, moving quickly through the camps and sleeping at Camps 1 and 2, and moving up to Camp 3. This tactic also reduces the threat to climbers' lives, because they don't have to move through the very dangerous Khumbu Icefall, over and over.

"Why are the fastest climbers not in the lead party?" I asked as the meeting drew to a close. "Your mission, the mission of the British government, is to put the first serving Gurkha on the summit. But the strongest have been put to the back."

The room fell silent; there wasn't a lot for anyone to say. Their decision had been political and it was painfully transparent. Team A was made up of slower leaders with a handful of Gurkhas chucked in. One of Team A's members tried to end the dispute by claiming that everybody was now fully acclimatized and equally strong, but I wasn't convinced.

"I saw you all at Camp 1 during the acclimatization rotations," I said. "You were knackered and struggling to keep up. How can you lead the strongest members when you are slower than they are? What happens if a rescue situation kicks off?"

I was exasperated. Finally I said, "OK, if you want to play politics, play politics. It's not my fight. Good luck."

Tensions had been running high for days, probably because the mission was looking increasingly precarious. The weather conditions on Everest had been horrific. High winds ravaged everything above Camp 2, and a series of storms were expected the following week. Then, 24 hours before setting off for the summit push, it was announced that some of the fixed lines still weren't in place. The team charged with setting the last of the rope* had given up around the Balcony, a crest on the southeastern ridge, 8,400 meters above sea level.

---

* A line-fixing rotation, like acclimatization, requires a series of climbs to set the ropes for an expedition, sometimes all the way to the top. The team designated for the job usually features the best climbers on the mountain at that point, but the work is hard going and can take weeks to complete, depending on the terrain, weather conditions, and mountaineers involved.

Apparently, the weather was too bad to climb any higher, and with the work incomplete, the G200E suddenly seemed in jeopardy. The mood turned bleak, especially as this was our second attempt, taking into account the tragedy of 2015. If the decision was made to abandon our climb, we knew we might not get another chance. As a Gurkha, I couldn't live with the knowledge that we'd failed to scale Everest, even though it was in our home country.

When I looked through the climbing order again, which included all the parties on the mountain hoping to summit, I realized I might be the only one who could fix the lines. A number of more experienced mountaineers who'd planned to climb were packing up and going home. I believed I was the strongest climber left. I had the experience and capability to function in extreme temperatures, and as an elite operator, I possessed the resilience needed to complete the mission. Plus, I knew I could break trail with the best.

As the worrying intel about the fixing team spread through the group, I made an announcement: "I'll go up and set the ropes."

Most of the lads around me assumed the mission was effectively over and seemed pleasantly taken aback at my offer, even though everybody on the G200E team had learned about my mountaineering skills. The fact that I'd scaled two 8,000ers already, one of which was Everest, was now common knowledge too, as was my rescue of Seema.

My role on military operations was to get the job done, no questions asked; personal agendas or politics were always put to the side. I adopted the same attitude with the G200E team. Negativity was ignored.

"Trust me, I can do it," I said.

Eventually, the G200E leaders agreed with my plan and decided that I would lead a fixing team, which included two special forces operators, both of whom were Gurkhas, and eight Sherpa guides. The expedition schedule was also changed. If our against-the-odds, line-fixing mission was successful, the majority of climbers would switch to Team A. While they climbed, Team B would wait at base camp, only moving up once the first group had summited.

The pressure was high, but I was confident, climbing steadily by using the trailblazing techniques I'd first learned on Dhaulagiri. We worked comfortably to Camp 2, sleeping overnight before heading to Camp 4. Having rested briefly, we then made our summit push and, keen to lead by example, I climbed alone for 500 yards, from Camp 4 to the Balcony. It felt important that my teammates realized I was happy to put in the hard yards, rather than asking a Sherpa guide to do it instead. In situations like that, respect and credibility were earned.

The sun was up, burning so near through the thin atmosphere, and as we worked across the South Summit and, later, the Hillary Step, it was impossible not to be awed by the view of Nepal and Tibet on all sides.

But I had no time for gawking. As the leader of a line-fixing team, I knew that if we couldn't set these last few ropes, the expedition would collapse. According to comms, Team A was rapidly closing on Camp 4 behind us. If we were turned around now, everybody would need to leave for base camp, because the expedition's supplies of food and oxygen were about to be used up. The entire mission would need to be resupplied, and that would take time and serious effort. Given that the season for climbing Everest was about to close with no other weather window in sight, G200E hinged on our progress.

Thank goodness, my stamina was holding up. Around 10 yards from the peak, as some of the lads in the line-fixing crew caught up, I held back from making the final push alone. "Brothers," I thought, "We're doing Everest as a team."

Once everybody joined, we put our arms around one another's shoulders, making the last steps together.

This was history. We had set the fixed lines, and 13 soldiers from the regiment eventually made it to the top during the G200E. (Our ropes also provided a route for other climbers on Everest at the end of that season.)

For some of those lads, the climb was a clearly defined end-game. *Where else would they go next?* But when I looked across the mountain ranges below me, I knew the next phase of my adventure was waiting. A new beginning had been set in motion.

TO IMMEDIATELY CLIMB Lhotse and then Everest once more— where I was due to help the second G200E team to the top as the one designated instructor with the stamina to climb the peaks back-to-back—I'd need support. A Sherpa guide had been called in for each of my summit attempts, and several oxygen cylinders* had been distributed across the mountains for me.

---

* I had placed oxygen in high camps across the mountain during the acclimatization rotations and load carry climbs, where we dropped off equipment, such as oxygen, for use later in the mission. Big expedition teams rarely carry all their equipment with them on summit pushes.

But despite my preparation, things soon came crashing down. As I prepared to leave the South Col for my second peak of the day, word filtered through that the lines on Lhotse were also incomplete. Having experienced the same difficult conditions as the team on Everest, the fixing crew had temporarily halted their work shortly after Camp 4.

Even worse, the Sherpa I was slated to climb Lhotse with had fallen sick and was already descending to base camp. I moved from tent to tent trying to convince one of the other guides to join me, but no one seemed willing to make another summit attempt in such a short space of time.

My heart sank. Climbing Lhotse solo for the first time was probably beyond me, and one mistake would impact the hopes of Team B waiting at Everest Base Camp. They needed me to lead them to the summit. I didn't want to let them down; they'd worked so hard to achieve their dreams of summiting Everest. I packed up and headed down, fuming.

By the time I reached Camp 2 and rested overnight, it was announced that Team A had reached the top, around 18 hours after me. I felt triumphant; our efforts had been worth it.

But in a heartbeat, the good news was overshadowed when it was decided that the expedition was effectively over. Because a number of serving Gurkhas had already summited, the mission had been completed and it was decided the climbing should stop. The lads at base camp still waiting for their shot—blokes who had sacrificed their time and, in some cases, money to fulfill their dream—were going home. It felt like a selfish move. When I later met up with Team B, the scene was heartbreaking. A few of the lads were in tears.

What had been the point in cutting them down? Some people might argue that, yeah, the job had been completed, so was there any point in risking more lives on such a dangerous mountain? But those Gurkhas understood and accepted the risks associated with high-altitude climbing. And, although not the quickest in the group, they were certainly stronger than many climbers who would still go on to summit Everest that season.

In the fallout, I realized that, had everything gone to plan—if the official fixing team had done their job and the original Team A had made it to Everest's peak—my role in Team B would have been redundant, too. I'd have been stuck at base camp with the others.

I partied with my Gurkha brothers in Kathmandu a couple days later, but the buzz of success was soured by bitterness within the blokes who were held back. They were upset, and I couldn't blame them. As I knocked back beer after beer, the same question came back to me, over and over. *Yeah, but can you do even more, brother?*

My first attempt at Lhotse had been written off, but I was now hearing that the fixed lines had been set all the way to the top. That meant my aim of climbing Everest and then Lhotse and Makalu in the two-week window I'd previously set for myself was back in play, though the timing was tight. (And I'd have to climb Everest once again, but I figured, What the hell?)

I mission-planned my routes along the three peaks, estimating I'd need some luck with the weather to nail the schedule. I'd first work my way up to Everest's Camp 3, climbing across to the summit of Lhotse. I'd then backtrack across to the South Col before scaling Everest. Once that was done, I could then travel over to Makalu's base camp via helicopter.

This was a huge test of endurance, but logistically, I had zero concerns: My oxygen was already in place and I could scoop up the cylinders as I worked my way across the mountains. Plus, the Sherpas I'd booked for the initial attempt were still happy to climb. Yes, I was a little behind schedule. But I'd topped a couple 8,000ers before and never required anything in the way of recovery time afterward, so it was within reach for me to move quickly. All I needed was self-belief.

That's when disaster struck. An entire book could be devoted to what happened next.

Having arrived at the foot of Everest a day or so later, I noticed a cluster of oxygen cylinders on the ground alongside a pile of other discarded equipment from the G200E. When I looked closely, I realized the bottled air was mine. A Sherpa, having wrongly assumed that I'd decided to pack up and head home, had brought some of my air down from one of the camps. I hit the roof. And then, at the worst possible moment, my smartphone vibrated. My brother Kamal was calling. When I answered, he was shouting angrily.

"What the fuck are you still doing up there?" he yelled. "You've climbed Everest twice already. Last year you saved someone's life. This year, you saved a whole expedition from being a failure. Your name's already flying around. People know you . . . what are you hoping to prove?"

At first, I tried to explain. I wanted to tell Kamal about what I hoped to do. But we had no time and my brother wasn't in the mood to listen. Already emotional due to my dumped oxygen, avoiding any further flash points or setbacks seemed important. So I hung up. Kamal and his lecture could wait.

I needed time to think. Close to being overloaded with equipment and oxygen bottles for my next climb, I didn't have the space for the extra air I needed, but consoled myself with the fact that I had air waiting for me at another two camps across the mountain. Still, as I ascended to Everest Camp 2 and then Camp 4 at Lhotse, it became clear that nearly all of it was gone. Angrily, I searched the tents and scrabbled around in the freshly dumped snow, as the harsh reality of mountain life dawned upon me.

Someone had stolen it.

I was furious. Climbing without air would go against the principles I'd set for myself following the rescue of Seema. Yes, I believed I had the strength to scale Lhotse, Everest, and Makalu anyway, but if I started breaking the promises I'd made, it could become habitual and I'd never hit my targets. This was an ethos I'd long applied to life: If I ever got up in the morning and told myself that I was going to do 300 push-ups that day, I made sure to do them, wholeheartedly. To skip the effort would be to break a commitment, and breaking commitments led to failure.

Yet I also understood that getting angry about the situation wasn't going to help. Military training taught me that remaining emotionally strong was imperative: Flipping a negative event into positive momentum was the only way to remain focused on my primary objective.

Get it together, Nims. Stay tough. You'll find a solution to this problem.

Drawing in some settling breaths, I reframed the developing disaster. I visualized my oxygen going to a better place. I forced myself to believe the cylinders had been swiped to save the life of another climber. *Someone has survived because of your oxygen, Nims.*

Having emotionally reset, I adapted to the situation, tweaking my schedule and moving across to the South Col again. My plan was now to top Everest first, in what was shaping up to be a stormy event. I'd then climb Lhotse—where I'd arranged for a friend to drop some bottled air for me at Camp 4—and finally Makalu.

The wind howled around me, and for a brief moment, I was feeling self-doubt. What I was about to attempt was huge. *But could I make it?*

I steadied myself.

Yeah. You can.

I scaled Everest when the mountain was at its most vicious. Hurricane winds swirled at the peak, and shards of ice struck me like bullets in conditions so severe that a number of other climbers died that day. But leaning into the blasts, and knowing that my speed would help me, I worked as quickly as I could with my Sherpa. The pair of us feared for our fingers and toes in the cold as we waited 45 minutes at the Hillary Step for a traffic jam of climbers moving up and down its face to the peak. After reaching the top, I descended quickly and crossed to Lhotse with a new Sherpa, pushing on to Camp 4. Soon, I was on my second Himalayan summit of the day. I looked at my watch—I'd been climbing for 10 hours and 15 minutes. Now, only Makalu remained.

I had no idea at that moment that I'd broken the record for climbing Everest and Lhotse in such quick succession. It wasn't my aim; I was focused on topping three peaks. But when I was told at base camp that the previous best time had been 20 hours, I was shocked. I'd unintentionally cut nearly 10 hours from the fastest registered time.

Now another record was in reach. If I could climb Makalu in the next few days, I'd break the world record for the fastest time to top Everest, Lhotse, and Makalu. Even though I'd never climbed Makalu, the fifth highest mountain in the world, I figured my chances were good. With a helicopter set to take me to the next base camp, piloted by my friend Nishal, one of the best high-altitude pilots around, I buzzed with excitement at the potential of what was within reach.

"Brother, you've just smashed a world record," said Nishal, hugging me at the landing zone.

"Yeah, and I can get another one at Makalu."

I wanted to rush my next steps, but Nishal was keen to put my achievements into perspective. "Mate, you said you'd do all three mountains in 14 days," he said. "You've got a few days to crack Makalu and still catch your flight home with the G200E guys. Why don't you enjoy the moment? Party for a bit!"

He then pointed out that May 29 was coming up, an event in the Himalaya also known as Everest Day. The celebration marked the first ever summit of the mountain in 1953 by Tenzing Norgay Sherpa and Sir Edmund Hillary.

"Bro, there's going to be drinking and parades," said Nishal. "Everyone's going to be having a lot of fun. You should think about it."

Realizing I could celebrate Everest Day and still have time for the world record, I agreed. I was on holiday, after all. Nishal's helicopter swooped into Namche Bazaar and I partied hard, drinking and dancing with some business friends. All the while, though, I remained fixed on Makalu. And Nishal reckoned he had a scheme that would save me even more time.

"Nims, you don't seem tired at all," he said. "Why don't you stay here for a bit longer and I'll drop you off at Camp 2 on Makalu rather than base camp? No extra charge."

By my estimate, a chopper ride to Camp 2 usually arrived with an eye-watering price tag of several thousand pounds. What Nishal had proposed was an incredibly generous offer (and he'd stayed sober for my ride the next morning). But I couldn't accept it. To his surprise, I shook my head. By climbing Makalu the following day, from bottom to top, I'd break a world record and learn a lot about the limits of my physical and mental strength. There was no way I wanted to be accused of cutting corners. I needed everything to be legit.

"Thanks, but no way, man," I said. "I'm doing this properly."

Nishal scowled. His friends looked a little annoyed too, and I sensed my decision had been mistaken for rudeness, or a lack of gratitude. As the hours passed and the drinking became sloppier, they couldn't believe I'd passed up such a generous offer. The debate heated to the point where a fight seemed possible. Then Nishal made his final attempt at twisting my arm.

"But no one will know!" he shouted.

"I will! Sure, I *could* lie to the whole world. I *could* make out I've climbed all three mountains from bottom to top. But I won't lie to myself, brother. No way. I'm doing this properly."

Through the haze of beer, the guys around us gradually came to understand my motives. I explained to everyone that I'd appreciated the gesture, but that Makalu was now so much more for me than just scaling another peak, or one more achievement on a bucket list of mountains. It was about conquering the last in a hat trick of Himalayan peaks—but in the right way, with integrity. This was important, as the effort was a moment of self-discovery about what I could truly achieve if I threw all my physical and psychological resources at a bold expedition idea.

And it worked like a charm.

I left Makalu's base camp 24 hours later, brutally hungover, and charged to the peak: all 8,485 meters of it in one hit. I led from the front with my small team, trailblazing through heavy snow, high wind, and disorientating cloud cover until I reached the top. This in itself was an achievement; nobody had yet climbed Makalu that season (although a number of teams had tried, only to be pushed back by poor conditions).

Once I'd made it back to base camp in one piece and discovered our helicopter ride back to Namche Bazaar had been canceled due to poor weather, I promptly took on one of the hardest treks in Nepal on foot with my Sherpa team. We ran at speed all the way to Kathmandu, completing a six-day journey in 18 hours, stopping only to drink beer and whisky. Only Halung Dorchi Sherpa kept the pace with me, and I felt strong, drawing on my combat training to push through the pain.

I'd broken two world records—by climbing Everest and Lhotse in 10 hours, 15 minutes and then topping Everest, Lhotse, and Makalu in five days. I was also the first person to climb Everest twice, then Lhotse and Makalu in the same season. And I didn't feel done.

After making it back to England in one piece, joining my G200E brothers on the flight home, I eventually visited Kamal to see how he was doing. His voice cracked as we spoke. I could tell he was trying not to cry.

"You are my brother," he said, explaining his anger. "I was worried about you."

Any frustration I'd felt with him had faded. "Listen, it's all good. But when you called me, I was in a moment where I was doubting myself. And then when someone like you, who I respect, tries to put negative energy into my head, it can be hard work to turn it around. I needed positivity. That's why I had to hang up the phone."

"Why didn't you explain?"

"I had no time! There had been a mix-up with my oxygen. There was too much going on. And I had to focus on that rather than justifying myself to you."

By the time we'd finished chatting, Kamal understood the why of what I'd done. It was then my job to figure out the how.

7

THE MISSION

There were so many questions.

What did I have that many other climbers didn't?

How was it that I'd been able to climb three challenging peaks in record time without physical recovery in between?

For some reason I'd felt compelled to run to Kathmandu, when there was time to stroll back at a gentle pace, partying all the way. What was I trying to prove?

I was constantly trying to push myself, but that wasn't exactly a unique quality in the mountaineering community. I knew plenty of special forces soldiers who'd climbed Everest, and all of them were wiped out afterward. None possessed the engine to immediately attempt another peak. But for some reason, I had the physiology to climb and descend, *climb and descend*, fixing lines and leading expeditions over and over and over, with very little rest. My reserves felt limitless.

Not only was I climbing aggressively, trailblazing through waist-deep snow and leaving experienced Sherpas behind, but I was also adept at making highly pressurized decisions quickly, thanks to my military training. Assessing risk and reacting accordingly had become second nature. I understood the fine line between bravery and stupidity; negative situations didn't upend me, and I attacked everything with positive thinking. Those traits had the potential to turn me into a high-altitude machine.

Of course, there were technically better climbers than me out there, and at sea level I might have found myself at a disadvantage when my relative strengths and weaknesses were placed against other climbers. But not all of them were able to plan and imagine in the same way as I was. Above 8,000 meters, I could locate the self-belief required to take me to the peak of any mountain in the world—whatever the conditions.

I'd also been notified that an honor from the queen, an MBE (Member of the Most Excellent Order of the British Empire), was being arranged as a reward for my outstanding work in high-altitude mountaineering. This included my salvaging the G200E, rescuing Seema on Everest, and breaking records on Everest, Lhotse, and Makalu. Not everyone appreciated my achievements, though. When my records were announced, a number of highly regarded mountaineers pointed out that I'd used oxygen. I ignored them: There are many ways to climb mountains, and my ambitions mainly hinged on pace. I had no time for critics—I led from the front, fixing my own lines. That's *Nims style.*

However, it wasn't only about doing everything quicker than everyone else. Nims style required me to plan and to lead, yet I needed to be self-sufficient on the mountains at all times. Through hard lessons, I'd come to understand my strengths and limitations, and how to work with them to avoid trouble, for the most part. Sure, I'd rescued someone at high altitude, but I hated the thought of people having to abandon their own mission to help me. I'd have rather died.

As far as I was concerned, there were no set rules when climbing in the death zone. Everyone worked differently, and I hadn't complained that some of those same critics had stepped into my footfalls or used the lines I'd set on their own summit push, hours after my drive to the top.

But the snobbery was still annoying, so I worked to make it inspiring. I used it as fuel, and in the post-expedition buzz of my climbs through the Himalaya, I decided to up my game. If I could take three of the world's largest mountains in five days, maybe I had it in me to climb the five tallest peaks—Everest, K2, Kanchenjunga, Lhotse, and Makalu—in an equally impressive time—say, 80 days? The idea gnawed at me for weeks until I decided to act upon it.

There would be hurdles—I knew that. I realized my chances of securing the leave needed for such an ambitious project were slim, but I was going to take a shot anyway. When I made the request, I tried to be convincing. I reminded the senior officer of my outstanding record, in and out of combat, and my growing climbing expertise. I used my work with the G200E as leverage. *And don't forget I advanced the SBS's name even further with those world records.*

My senior officer glanced skeptically at the expedition plan. A negative response was coming, I could tell.

"Climbing K2, Nims? Many people who climb that mountain die there. It's the same on Kanchenjunga," he said. "This is such a huge project. And it's not as if you're climbing one mountain here. You're running up mountain after mountain in 11 or 12 weeks. Is this even possible?"

I tried to appeal to his sense of adventure. "When I was a Gurkha, I really wanted to join the special forces," I said. "Not for money, or for the name, but because I wanted to operate among the very best. I fixed lines on the G200E when everybody else gave up. Then I held the flag of the SBS high afterward. Now I want to attempt this."

The officer shook his head. There was no way he would authorize so much leave, he explained. It was too risky. Also, if it became known that a special forces operator was climbing K2, which was located on the border of Pakistan and China, it could lead to trouble.

"It's just not doable, Nims," he said.

I felt deflated, but I wouldn't abandon my dream; the back-and-forth over my expedition hopes went on for months. On some days, I felt that high command might relent. On others, they became increasingly resistant, until eventually, I decided to take matters into my own hands.

Well, that's it then, I thought, I'm going to quit.

I felt liberated. I was 35 years old at the time and knew that by resigning from my military commitments, I'd give myself the opportunity to think bigger and more boldly in a challenge of my own making. So rather than climbing the five tallest mountains in

80 days, what was stopping me from topping all 14 death zone mountains in the quickest time imaginable? I struggled to think of too many pitfalls. *Only politics or money. Or maybe an avalanche, or a crevasse, if I'm really unlucky.*

It was in my Gurkha blood to be fearless at all times, so although an avalanche might sweep me away on Annapurna as it had for dozens of others, I wasn't going to worry about it. Meanwhile, the dangers involved in climbing all 14 death zone peaks were manageable: I'd learned how to work in poor weather and deep snow; I could operate effectively, without fear. Better to die than be a coward, after all.

Also, I was comfortable with the idea of saying goodbye in my 30s. Hanging on until the age of 80-something, when I might be unable to look after myself, held little appeal. I preferred to leave while going full tilt.

The political and monetary aspects of the expedition were an entirely different story, though. There would be paperwork and permit requests, particularly from the Chinese and Tibetan authorities, who had closed Shishapangma for the entire 2019 climbing season. Then there were the bills. At least a million U.S. dollars— maybe more—was required to climb the full portfolio of death zone mountains, so I'd have to approach a series of sponsors, all while exploring alternative funding options. But for now, the primary mission—in theory—was exciting enough for me to contemplate my departure from the military. If I believed my goal of climbing all 14 8,000-meter peaks in quick succession was achievable, then it was achievable.

Every facet of my training and combat experience had told me so. While serving with the Gurkhas, I'd been frequently forced from my comfort zones into extreme pain and had learned that mental strength was more important than physical power. Likewise, the British Special Forces taught me how to push beyond any psychological limits I'd previously set for myself. The logistics of planning a series of high-altitude expeditions were intimidating, but I'd built connections in the climbing community through my work in the mountains. I possessed the skills and contacts to make it work.

I flipped open my laptop at home one afternoon, hoping to understand how long an expedition of this kind might take. A brief scan online told me that around 40 other mountaineers had climbed all 14 8,000ers. The fastest anyone had done so was Korean climber Kim Chang-ho in 2013, who took seven years, 10 months, and six days. Jerzy Kukuczka of Poland wasn't far behind him, with a time of seven years, 11 months, and 14 days, in 1987, though he was only the second mountaineer to have scaled all the 8,000ers after legendary Italian Reinhold Messner broke through the glass ceiling of what was considered possible in 1986.

So, the field was small and, on average, several years seemed to represent the likeliest time frame. No one really knew for sure, as neither of the two fastest climbers was trying to set a speed record; they had simply set out to summit each mountain in their own style, often ascending alone up unclimbed routes without bottled oxygen. Nims style was different—speed was the name of my game—and I was now pondering a question few had pondered before me: How fast could these giants be climbed?

Given the way I'd worked through Everest, Lhotse, and Makalu in five days—not to mention Dhaulagiri in two weeks—it was clearly within my reach to go quicker. The only question was by how much.

I worked on a pragmatic estimate. *OK, so there's no funding. It might take some time to get the money together, but if I can stay on home turf in Nepal for the first expeditions, I'll be fine. Plus, I have a ton of contacts there.*

I listed off the mountains I needed to climb: Annapurna, Dhaulagiri, Kanchenjunga, Everest, Lhotse, Makalu, and Manaslu . . .

Pakistan would be a different ball game altogether. The treks between mountain base camps are long, and the weather is unpredictable.

Nanga Parbat, Gasherbrum I and II, K2, Broad Peak . . .

But in Tibet, it might take you longer with the paperwork and permits.

Cho Oyu and Shishapangma . . .

I've only climbed four of these mountains before . . . so how about seven months? That should be enough time to climb all 14, give or take a few weeks.

The goal of shaving off an entire seven years from the world record was wildly ambitious, but I quickly embraced the idea. The bottom line was to climb as quickly as possible, whatever the weather, *Nims style.*

I had other incentives, too. Although I sought to push past physical and emotional limits I might have previously placed on myself, I also knew all too well how climate change was hammering my home country of Nepal. Alerting the world to the region's floods and disappearing glaciers was my priority too, as was spotlighting the plight of the people living and working in the affected mountain communities.

Most of all, though, I loved the thought of ripping up the rule book. If I could show kids and adults alike what was humanly achievable, then my far-fetched ambitions might inspire others to think big and push themselves in ways they previously considered unimaginable. I also liked that I might give the world a crazy story to remember.

I gave my grand mission a name—Project Possible. Then I prepared a battle plan, steadying myself for the inevitable doubters.

ONE TROUBLING FACTOR when quitting the SBS was psychological security. That might seem ironic, given that I'd put my life on the line over and over on patrol or in door-kicking operations. But for 16 years the British military had been everything to me. They'd told me where to be and when, and they'd provided me with a house and a daily routine. Yes, the job was dangerous with high stress, but it had comforting familiarities, even in war. In the military, I had structure, focus, and loyalty. Some days, as I planned my exit, I worried if I'd done enough for queen and crown in return.

My other big concern about resigning from the special forces was my pension. It was a life-changing chunk of money, and to claim it, I had only to serve a few more years. Quitting now meant giving up the lot, which was a worry and a financial stress I'd have to manage down the line.

Putting aside my doubts, on March 19, 2018, having logged on to the Ministry of Defense website, I submitted my resignation request. My notice period was one year, and at first some mates in the squadron tried to change my mind. High command also promoted me to the position of cold-weather warfare instructor, as a subject matter expert (SME), where my role became to teach other operators how to climb mountains, survive in harsh conditions at altitude, and ski across challenging terrain. It was a prestigious responsibility. It meant I was considered the best climber within the squadron.

Promotional persuasion wasn't enough, however. My superiors then asked me to consider the logistical pitfalls of my move, and they argued that by resigning, I'd lose out on financial security that would excite most people in the real world.

Except, I wasn't most people and I had a different take on the real world. I was raised a poor kid in Nepal. If I had to, living out of a tent for the rest of my life would have been no problem at all. The biggest surprise, though, arrived when the SAS learned about my plans to quit and invited me to a meeting at their base. An officer then asked if I'd ever consider switching regiments.

"Congratulations on the G200E and MBE, Nims," he said, looking over my records. "And we know what your strengths are on the mountains. If you were to join the SAS, we'll make sure you'll be looked after, of course. We'll give you better opportunities, which will help you and your family."

He then threw out some serious bait. I was promised a place on a prestigious, one-year climbing program in which I'd be able to focus purely on operating at high altitude. Most important, I'd be provided with a budget for equipment and travel.

It was a dream gig, but as far as I was concerned, jumping between the two wings of the special forces felt disloyal, like leaving one football team for a local rival. There was no way I wanted to let the SBS guys down in that way.

"I'm really humbled that you guys have seen something in me," I said, eventually. "And it's kind of you to offer me those opportunities. But I never joined the special forces to be a general, or for money. Going back to financial basics is cool with me. And besides, I couldn't switch teams."

Their response was short and sharp. "You're loyal, which is to be commended," said the SAS commander. "But you're fucking crazy."

I shrugged my shoulders and thanked him for the meeting, but I was torn. As I drove away from the barracks, it was hard not to wonder if I'd made the wrong decision. *If I did take up this offer, I'd be the first operator to serve in both the SAS and the SBS. There would be some serious kudos.* As I second-guessed myself over the next few days, Suchi even took to searching online for any job opportunities that might suit her in Hereford. But in the end, I stuck with my original plan: I wanted to climb the big mountains.

My friends and family seemed equally confused. As far as they were concerned, this was the latest in a long line of what they considered to be baffling career developments. My brothers accused me of being ungrateful. They argued that without the money they'd sent to Chitwan for my education, I wouldn't have learned English. Without English, it's highly unlikely I'd have made it into the British military. All this was true; I owed them everything. Kamal called me in another mood. He couldn't get his head around my plans.

"Brother, *everybody* wants to get into the special forces," he said. "You're there, but you're turning your back on it. You were 10 years in the war and now you are in the driving seat as a cold-weather warfare instructor. You'll get a great pension without losing your fingers, toes, and eyes in battle. But after all that graft, you're going to leave everything behind? What the hell?"

"Kamal, this isn't just about me," I said. "It's not about you either, or the family. We're a small part of a bigger worldwide community and I don't have long to do this. I'm not getting any younger. If I can make a difference now and show the world what can be done at high altitude, it's worth it."

We didn't speak again for two months.

My family life also presented a serious financial commitment. In Nepal, some families insisted the youngest son care for his parents if ever they go broke or become too old to look after themselves. In Mum and Dad's case, they really needed the money, and Kamal and Ganga had supported them as best they could. But now they had their own families to care for. Since joining the Gurkhas, I'd sent my parents a chunk of wages every month because they were my world.

But Mum had recently become very ill. She was suffering from a heart condition and had surgery to insert a stent. Then came kidney failure. Mum often had to visit the hospital for treatment, until she was placed permanently in a Kathmandu facility. (Chitwan didn't have a suitable clinic.) My dad, half-paralyzed, was unable to visit her in the city; my ultimate goal was to bring them together again, in the same house. But with Project Possible under way, all that paused, for a little while at least.

When I announced the news, it upset them at first. Because we had lived so close to Dhaulagiri, it wasn't uncommon for us to talk to climbers trekking through our village on their way to and from base camp. Sometimes groups passing through on their way up were visibly reduced in numbers during the return journey. On one occasion Mum met two climbers in the local teahouse. They were crying; their friends had been killed on the mountain, they told her. She never forgot it.

Years later, after the tragic deaths of so many people on Everest during the avalanches of 2014 and 2015, the thought of her son mountaineering filled her with dread. Whenever I showed her an expedition video on my phone, she winced. The images of me climbing across a crevasse ladder in the Khumbu Icefall upset her. Mum wanted to know what my new plan entailed.

"So, you know the 14 biggest mountains in the world, Mum?"

She nodded. "Some of them."

Mum listed a few names. *Everest, Dhaulagiri. Oh, and Annapurna.* "But what's that got to do with you?"

She was fretting. *Was her youngest son losing the plot?*

"Oh, Nims," she said. "Is it because we're very ill and it's such a burden to look after us? I think you are doing this because you want to kill yourself."

"It's okay, Mum," I said. "I'm going to do this. I'm going to show the world what I am capable of. And I'm going to come back stronger. I'll be a different Nims."

She offered a bittersweet smile. "You don't listen to what we tell you anyway, so I know you're going to do it, whatever we say. Our blessings are with you."

My family's concerns weren't the only emotional hurdle, however. Friends laughed whenever I talked about Project Possible; fellow operators mocked me. That was fair enough; the goal was supposed to be tough, improbable even. But only because nobody had achieved anything quite like it before.

Of course, there was a chance I might fail, as during any daring endeavor. Certainly, the odds I'd be killed along the way were fairly short. In the aftermath of screwing up, people were sure to laugh, or say, "I warned him." But at least I wouldn't die wondering, *What if?*

And if I could pull it off . . . *What then?*

8

THE HIGHEST STAKES

From the minute my one year's notice was accepted by the Ministry of Defense, I set two plans in motion. The first was to organize my operational detail for Project Possible. I pulled together a team of Nepali climbers that I knew would be up to the task of supporting me over the 14 peaks for the best part of a year. I determined which mountains to climb and when, based upon weather reports from the past five climbing seasons.

Having assessed the topographic conditions of each mountain, I decided to split Project Possible into three phases: The first was to take place in Nepal; my plan was to crash through Annapurna, Dhaulagiri, Kanchenjunga, Everest, Lhotse, and Makalu in April and May. Then I would head for the Pakistani mountains of Nanga Parbat, Gasherbrum I and II, K2, and Broad Peak in July. Finally, I aimed to return to Nepal for Manaslu in the autumn, before heading to Tibet to top Cho Oyu and Shishapangma.

Every mountain required legal work to obtain necessary climbing permits, but China and Tibet were particularly tricky because Shishapangma was apparently closed through 2019. I decided to worry about that particular battle when it arrived.

Prepping for missions was my bag, having been a part of my military life for so long. But the second part of the planning process was new to me: fund-raising. It was a daunting task because high-altitude climbing is an expensive sport. The cost of climbing Everest alone in 2019 ranged between U.S. $40,000 and $150,000, and the early financial estimations for Project Possible were intimidating. There was no way I could drum up a reserve of that magnitude without help.

I learned that to fund projects of this nature, I'd have to rely on a series of sponsorship deals, in which companies financed my trip in return for exposure and branding opportunities whenever I topped one of the 14 peaks. Some extra cash could arrive from guiding tours,* and I aimed to take experienced mountaineers to the peaks of one mountain on each phase—Annapurna, Nanga Parbat and Manaslu.

The work was relentless. While I planned the 14 expeditions throughout 2018, a friend worked on securing the financing. Between my military commitments, I tired myself out with meetings, planning sessions, and train journeys, running on fumes for seven days a week. Psychologically, the logistic effort felt as grueling as my time on selection. But like those early mornings on the

---

* I liked the idea of fusing my career to my passion and so I set up Elite Himalayan Adventures in December 2017. In 2018, the group began leading clients —experienced climbers who paid to be guided by a team of skilled guides—to the top of 8,000-meter peaks.

Brecon Beacons, I approached every day with a positive thought: *I can do this. I will navigate every problem the mission can throw at me. I've already climbed the world's tallest peak. The only thing standing in my way right now is funding. Get out there and smash it.*

In the same way that joining the Gurkhas, passing selection, and climbing Everest had represented personal deities—ambitions to lift myself up for—so raising money became a new and powerful idol. I gave everything to that.

With a business partner—an anonymous accomplice—we reached out to a series of potential investors. I knew that to excite funders for Project Possible, I needed to make bold statements about the mission that would generate headlines and get people talking.

Emboldened by my early success breaking world records, I announced my intention to break more. The first one, obviously, was the speed at which I intended to climb the 14 8,000ers. I also figured I could better my time on Everest, Lhotse, and Makalu (and with it, the fastest time from the summit of Everest to the summit of Lhotse). But I also revealed that I intended to set the world's fastest time for climbing the Pakistan 8,000ers, as well as for the time taken to climb the five highest mountains in the world: Kanchenjunga, Everest, Lhotse, Makalu, and K2.

My ambitions didn't gather much attention; maybe people didn't take me seriously. After several months on a conveyor belt of meetings and phone calls, I was dealt a crushing blow.

"Nims, we've raised barely any money," said my associate, sadly. "And it's not looking good."

He was right; there was nothing in the bank and Phase One already felt like a nonstarter. I was in trouble—or so I thought. I promptly switched tactics and decided to front the fund-raising drive myself, making my daily routine even more intense. Most mornings I got up at 4 a.m., working on my social media outreach for a few hours before racing to the 7 a.m. train into London from the south coast. I'd take multiple meetings a day, becoming numb to the empty promises and flat-out rejections. On the rare occasions my work was done before midnight, I'd open my computer to write follow-up emails, before rounding off the day with another session on Instagram or Facebook.

I wasn't exactly tech savvy at that time. Simply preparing a couple of Project Possible–related posts, while adding the relevant links and hashtags, could take me two hours. The work was a grind, and sometimes I voiced my frustration online:

> Another day of battle in reference to the fund-raising campaign for Project Possible: 14/7. The journey of fund-raising has been extremely hard for me, and also it's not my expertise. Whoever I approach, they say, "Nims, why not next year? If we do it next year, we will have enough time to raise the funds." My answer has always been the same: By saying we will do it next year, we are going for the easier option.

Next to nothing in the way of cash arrived for a couple of months. By the turn of 2019, with my clock ticking, I couldn't convince any potential sponsors; meetings often ended with a thanks-but-no-thanks dismissal. What I intended to do, some argued, wasn't humanly possible, and a few people even laughed off my plans.

I was in a rough spot. I'd left the military and my income was slashed. But despite it all, Suchi remained supportive. Though all my efforts went into a project that wasn't bringing in any money, she never applied any emotional pressure. I was grateful for the room to breathe.

My new role raising money for Project Possible, or trying to, challenged me in ways I didn't expect. The work drained me, and it became hard to step away from a never-ending to-do list. Mentally I was frazzled, but rather than talk to Suchi about the strain I was under, it seemed easier to pretend everything was running smoothly. Passing on stress to her was the last thing I wanted, so I crept out of bed at one or two in the morning to work on another email or letter while she slept.

I harbored so much desire for the mission that I found it impossible to slow down. I banished the thought of quitting, as I didn't want to transfer any pessimist vibes subconsciously to potential investors or sponsors.

To instill faith in others, it was critical that I maintained faith in myself. But at times it was bloody hard work.

I WAS FAST APPROACHING a crossroads when hope arrived. Through an SBS friend, I was introduced to an interested business partner. He understood my passion and immediately promised to bring roughly U.S. $28,000 to the planning kitty; I later spoke at a corporate event and earned another $10,000. It was barely a drop in the ocean, considering I needed to pull together around three-quarters of a million. But the money wasn't just money. It was progress.

From there, Elite Himalayan Adventures invited private clients to join me on Project Possible's Annapurna climb, and I created a

GoFundMe page, boosting my followers and donations with daily updates on Instagram and word-of-mouth buzz. Ant Middleton, another friend from the military, even pitched in a donation of $35,000. We'd served together in the same elite squadron, and he'd previously been a keen supporter of the Gurkha regiment.

But it still wasn't enough. In the end, after the entirety of my personal savings were put into the mission, there was only one way to ensure Phase One's launch: I needed to remortgage my house. It was a drastic sacrifice with an uncertain outcome. Although my retired friends from the military owned two or three homes, I'd invested everything into climbing.

I knew that if I could pull off Project Possible, the afterglow of success could bring a financial payoff and help to repay the loans I might take. I could expect to charge premium guiding fees, and there was a chance I might join the lucrative after-dinner speaker's circuit, like one or two of my buddies from the special forces. The consequences of failure, though, were massive. If I couldn't climb all 14 peaks in the time I'd promised, people could write me off as a loudmouth, and career boosts would be harder to come by.

Although I joked with friends that, if push came to shove, I could live in a tent for the rest of my life . . . I didn't really want to. A more sobering reality also struck me: If I didn't return from my mission in one piece, the financial burden of my failure would land on Suchi and the family. I needed her blessing to take this next step.

I had faith that she supported me. Suchi had always understood the physical and emotional sacrifice I'd made to protect my country at the highest military level. She also knew that Project Possible was a mission for the now because my recent engagement in combat meant I was physically fit and strong enough to finish the job. Waiting until the following year, or even five years down the line, reduced my chances of survival and success.

Psychologically, I was also in a very good place following my work in war. I'd seen some horrible things during service—acts of brutality and violence that I sometimes wished I could unsee. But I was mentally steady, and for the most part, the horror of conflict had seemingly bounced off me.

I suppose it helped that my retirement from the SBS had been a decision of my own making, and that I had a project to throw myself into. Many people were forced to leave through injury or because they weren't capable of doing a job that required razor-sharp focus anymore. Some operators left the squadron because they'd been emotionally broken. For those people, finding a new life—one with commitment, unity, and excitement—could be a challenge every bit as testing as war.

I was lucky. I quit the job because I had a new passion, and the idea of climbing 14 peaks gave me something to work for every day. In time, I built a similarly strong camaraderie with the people I'd chosen to join me for the ride.

I also understood the healing power of nature. It felt good to be outside, climbing at altitude across an environment that didn't care about race, religion, color, or gender. The mountains were impartial; only humans showed bias. There was no judgment. Whenever friends opened up to me about serious emotional problems they'd been having, I took them climbing. The mountains were the best therapy a person could experience. Life felt so much simpler when you were connected to nature by a climbing rope and a set of crampons.

So I sucked up my pride and asked Suchi.

"I've given everything to this dream," I said. "Without this project I won't be the same person. If worst comes to worst and I don't complete the 14 mountains, we can still make a living from the climbing company. We can survive anything. Even if we lose everything we've gained in life so far, and we have to start again, we'll be OK."

After everything I'd put her through—fighting in a dangerous job abroad for several years or retiring from work early and turning down a huge pension to climb mountains—was a bold ask. But I was out of options. Using our home as collateral on a massive loan was my only way forward.

She looked at me sternly. "OK, Nims," she said. "But you better be right."

It was reassuring to know that Suchi still believed in me, and that she had faith in Project Possible. She told me she had zero doubt in her mind that I'd succeed in the mission once it was up and running, but she was nervous about the financial hit we'd take to get there. I'd long known she had a power in her that few people carried—not only as a wife, but as a woman too—and I was grateful for all of it. She was prepared to risk everything we had for my dream.

In a strange way, the sacrifice wasn't so unsettling for me. I'd spent my military career living at my emotional limits, so the thought of losing our home was just another form of mental distress—one that I could manage effectively. My default setting was that if the worst happened, I'd find a way to make a living. I wasn't scared to struggle in uncertainty, but it was a very different scenario for Suchi, and she was prepared to gamble all the same.

FOR A MOMENT or two during the fund-raising drive, I nearly crumbled.

In February, only a month away from the beginning of Project Possible and following another chaotic week of endless, fruitless meetings, train journeys, and phone calls, I drove home along the M3 to Poole one afternoon. My mind was a blur of numbers, bills, and contracts. The $92,000 equity on the house was withdrawn, though I held back enough cash to pay the domestic bills while I climbed and guided throughout 2019. The rest of it was plowed into Project Possible. Slowly we made progress, booking flights, securing permits, and gathering together all the equipment and supplies I needed to start the mission.

But still I stressed. I was exhausted by the lack of support outside of my immediate bubble. Why would nobody back me? Meanwhile, the weight of Nepali tradition hung from me like a backpack loaded with bricks. What would happen to my parents if I couldn't finish? For a brief moment, as brake lights and indicators flickered on the road ahead, I became overwhelmed. My eyes brimmed with tears.

Fucking hell, Nims, why are you doing this to yourself? To everybody you love?

Pulling into a pullout to get myself together, I focused on what might happen if I *was* to achieve the unthinkable.

Project Possible wasn't just about me. That had always been my truth. Yes, the pressure was on my shoulders—and the ambition and hard work, not to mention any spoils at the end—would be undeniably mine. But I needed to remember my objectives. I was showing people what was achievable if an individual devoted mind

119

and body to reaching a seemingly insurmountable target—and that was a big deal. Reestablishing the Nepali climbing community as being the best in the world, as it had been during large chunks of the 20th century, was important, too. Then there were statements to be made about climate change. Finally, I was a bloody special forces soldier. Emphasizing the image of the SBS as an elite troop, in and out of combat, was another driving force.

I dried my eyes.

Let's get this thing done.

As I'd learned in war, every obstacle or enemy was another challenge to figure out and overcome. I needed to adapt and survive in my new environment, as I had while working through selection, fighting in war zones, and climbing the world's biggest mountain. I pressed ahead for the next few weeks, sucking up the rejections from a string of potential backers.

Why should we throw money at a plan that's set to fail?

Some people even wondered if they could push me toward a nasty end. *If we fund the impossible and Nims dies, will we be partially to blame?*

All the people who couldn't grasp the potential of my dream were demoralizing, but it made me more determined. Once the mission kicked off, I'd prove them all wrong with my actions.

Thank goodness, not everyone I spoke to was so pessimistic. The U.K.'s Nepali community and a group of retired Gurkhas organized a Project Possible fund-raising drive—pensioners and veterans were making donations of $5, $15, and $30, and the gesture was incredibly humbling. As the countdown to my first climb approached, I'd amassed around $163,000. It was barely enough to cover Phase One of the project, but I hoped to spur more interest with every climb that followed. As sponsors, media, and the mountaineering community watched my progress, I figured the skeptics would be shocked into action and their money was sure to roll in.

Relying on self-belief and momentum, I readied myself for the most ambitious operation of my life.

9

RESPECT IS EARNED

There were many reasons *not* to attempt Annapurna as the first expedition on the schedule. For starters, the world's 10th highest mountain had gathered a fearsome rep as the deadliest. By the start of 2019, around 60 climbers had died there in total, while only about 190 mountaineers had ever reached its summit and returned home safely. In other words, whatever your odds were for successfully making it to the top and back, you were about one-third as likely instead to die in the attempt. Much of the danger is a result of Annapurna's instability; a glacial war zone, it's prone to avalanches that spew snow, rock, and shattered ice walls onto anyone unfortunate enough to be in the wrong place at the wrong time. Unseen crevasses crisscross the mountain, and many people have fallen unknowingly to their deaths after a slip into a hidden crack beneath them.

Meanwhile, the weather in that part of the Himalaya is temperamental, changing in a heartbeat. And the conditions can be so extreme that around 43 people were killed in a snowstorm in 2014, including 21 trekkers. It's long been known that when the bad storms roll in at Annapurna, a fairly inaccessible peak suddenly becomes impenetrable.

Although we had every opportunity to start on one of the less intimidating climbs in the region, Annapurna presented me with the opportunity to assess my expedition team. To climb any 8,000er, an experienced mountaineer requires a support crew; because we'd have to fix a lot of lines ourselves throughout the 14 peaks, I wanted to work with the right number of climbing partners per mountain. For example, if I was leading the fixing team to the very top and we were the only expedition on the mountain, I'd need several guys. However, on some mountains where I was familiar with the terrain and the ropes had been fixed all the way to the top, I'd need only one climbing buddy, such as on Everest.

Discovering exactly how effective my crew could be was critical—and I had to find out quickly. Although everyone in the group I gathered throughout 2018 was a seasoned guide with a number of 8,000-meter peaks to their names, executing 14 climbs in quick succession was a challenge for the ages. My experience in war taught me that a person's true character always emerged when faced with a life-or-death event, and that reveal often took place in gun battle. A new Gurkha or Royal Marine Commando might breeze through training, but there was no way to assess their true battle-readiness until bullets and bombs were flying around for real.

In mountaineering terms, Annapurna was a gunfight. We would set the fixed lines, the work was bound to be heavy going, and potential death awaited us at every stage; it was the perfect test scenario for all of us. For the team setting the route, there was no easy path to the top. And for the person leading that fixing team, the pressure to execute was huge.

I needed to know which individuals I could trust to keep their heads in dangerous flash points. I also wanted to discover any weak links or flaws within the group, if any at all. Some guides that had joined me were already friends or associates from the mountain, such as Mingma David, Lakpa Dendi Sherpa, and Halung Dorchi Sherpa.

Mingma was Dorje Khatri's nephew, and I'd first met him in Kathmandu in 2014, shortly after the Khumbu Icefall tragedy of the same year. Through friends, I'd heard he was an impressive climber who had scaled Everest, Lhotse, Makalu, and K2. He was slight, around 120 pounds wet, but Mingma was built from taut muscle. Whenever I bumped into him during expeditions, he always struck me as one of the strongest guides I'd ever seen. And everybody had heard the stories of Mingma's high-altitude rescue missions. He had saved people on Dhaulagiri, Makalu, and Everest.

I knew that Mingma would want to join me after an encounter I'd had with him during my first successful ascent of Everest in 2016. I'd been working my way to the top with Pasang, while Mingma was supporting the *Everest Air* team I'd met at Lukla Airport. He spotted us as we worked our way steadily to Camp 4. High winds had blasted everybody on Everest that day, and as Pasang and I dug a temporary snow shelter for protection, I noticed Mingma and another Sherpa pitching a tent nearby. Waving, they called us over.

"We heard you were sick with HAPE," said Mingma. "What are you doing here, Nimsdai?"

In Nepali, the word *dai* translates to "brother."

"Yeah, I was in a bad way, but I've got my shit together," I said, laughing. "I just needed to take some time off. I'm going for it now."

I looked at the faces staring back at me in the fading light. Mingma seemed to be weighing up whether I was bold or simply had a death wish.

Eventually, he spoke up. "You know, Nims, our job is to help climbers to the top. We can follow anyone on any mountain."

He pointed to Pasang. "Your Sherpa is not experienced, so . . ."

So?

"I'll follow you, Nimsdai. I'll help you."

I felt torn. My scrape with HAPE meant I'd already blown the goal of making it to the top alone; I needed Pasang to summit Everest. But it was also important that I didn't become a burden to any other expeditions on the mountain. Also, I was so bothered by the thought of my lungs failing again that the stress of being rescued at high altitude made me feel a little uneasy. Still, Mingma's kind support was something to consider. Feeling humbled, I made myself comfy in their tent, waiting until the winds had died down enough for climbing to resume. Mingma was a reputable figure—the mountaineering equivalent to an elite operator. *And he wanted to team up with me?*

The gesture blew me away. Although I eventually declined their assistance and climbed Everest with Pasang, I knew Mingma was exactly the type of individual I would love to work with in the future. He was strong and fearless.

He was also well connected, and wanted to bring Gesman Tamang into the Project Possible family. Gesman was a strong, but relatively inexperienced climber—in terms of death zone peaks, at least. Like Mingma, he'd summited Everest, Lhotse, and Makalu, only not as frequently; he was also trained in avalanche and high-altitude mountain rescue.

"He's a good guy, a bull," promised Mingma, when he first mentioned Gesman. "He's done the right courses. You can trust him."

Although he hardly had a watertight résumé, Gesman came with Mingma's recommendation, and Mingma's word was as good as any. Physical strength wasn't the only asset Mingma and Gesman both possessed; they were positive spirits too, and I'd decided that everyone in the mission needed an optimistic mind-set. I wanted people who climbed for passion, not money or glory (though they'd be getting paid pretty well for the work). Just as important, they had to feel pride for the Nepali guiding community.

Project Possible was also my way of thrusting Sherpa culture into the limelight; for too long, the climbing industry had overlooked their heroic work. As far as I was concerned, they had been the driving force behind a lot of successful expeditions above 8,000 meters—and a support network of Sherpas that performed the heavy lifting propelled most against-all-odds expeditions. Who do you think sets the fixed ropes on Everest? And who carries the heavy equipment and supplies over huge distances while their paying clients move relatively freely?

They execute other, more specialized roles too. On Everest, for example, a unit of Sherpas called "ice doctors" place ladders and guide ropes over the hundreds of crevasses that scar the Khumbu Icefall. Typically, they were paid, but their small fees paled against the overall cost of an expedition. Without their work, most ascents would fail; relatively inexperienced climbers would die.

The Sherpa guide had been making the impossible possible for years, though for the most part their work was rarely celebrated.

The politics of the mountain annoyed the hell out of me. When I'd first started climbing 8,000ers, I watched, impressed, as excellent climbers scaled the death zone peaks and their achievements were glorified by climbing websites and magazines. Then I looked for the names of the guys supporting that particular climber—*the true heroes*. After all, they were carrying more weight, fixing more lines, and working so much harder than everybody else, but nobody ever mentioned them by name.

The disparity in respect pissed me off. Although a paid job, the work required of a Sherpa was incredibly dangerous. With Project Possible, I wanted to highlight the skills of Nepal's climbers—but for that to work, I needed my team to have the same philosophies as me. I didn't want sheep, or dedicated followers. I wanted a group of freethinkers.

There was a hierarchy, though. From the outset, I made it clear that my job would be to run the team, to make decisions under pressure, and to use all the skills I'd learned on the mountain, in the military, and while operating as a cold-weather warfare specialist. In the special forces, each team was made up of expert warriors; my aim was to build a climbing group with an identical dynamic. Sure, I was team leader, but the other guys would operate as specialist climbers. Each of them possessed expert skills and all were capable of looking after themselves in moments of high drama.

With a superior level of unity, I wanted us to break trail through the deepest snow and into the hardest weather toward the 14 summits. I wanted us to become elite—to be regarded as the special forces of high-altitude mountaineering. And from there, I wanted that respect to shine upon the entire Sherpa community.

In many ways, I was running a high-altitude equivalent of the U.K. Special Forces Selection on Annapurna. Project Possible's operators had to be strong, capable, and emotionally positive. The guys joining me had all proven they had potential to deliver, but our first climb would encompass all the most testing parts of selection rolled into one.

I was also looking for different things in different people, and intended to split the expedition into two groups. The core team would feature Mingma, Gesman, Geljen Sherpa, and Lakpa Dendi Sherpa; a secondary group comprising Sonam Sherpa, Halung Dorchi Sherpa, Ramesh Gurung, and Mingma's brother, Kasang Sherpa, would be on hand to provide backup if necessary. Another colleague, Dawa Sherpa, was in place to double-check all my expedition plans as we went along.

I was happy with the setup; the team was full of characters. Geljen Sherpa was initially tasked with fixing the lines as part of our team on Annapurna, but had offered to stay on for the duration of Project Possible. I liked the dude; his spirit brimmed with enthusiasm. Geljen danced; he smiled. Nothing seemed to dent or upset him, and as we readied ourselves at Annapurna's base camp and planned our infrastructure for Dhaulagiri, I noticed a shared mentality was building between us. The team worked hard and played hard; nobody moaned if the effort became too rough, as it so often did on the mountains.

Whenever I adjusted our plan for Annapurna, the others said, "Let's do this!" Every idea was tested and nothing was dismissed out of hand, as if everybody had forgotten how to say "no." Plenty of that had to do with our team spirit, but a number of the lads had heard about my previous efforts on Everest, Lhotse, and Makalu. I'd earned their respect, and they were in the process of earning mine. This was exactly the psychology we needed if Phase One was to succeed.

On the support team, Sonam Sherpa had been installed to look after the logistics of every summit push, as well as care for our clients during "paid-for" expeditions in which expert climbers were guided to the peak, as they would be on Annapurna, and also on Nanga Parbat in July and Manaslu in September. While on the mountain, Sonam would also help us fix lines and maintain eyes on the whole expedition from the rear, taking our radio calls from higher up while ensuring the expedition was running smoothly at base camp and beyond.

If an unexpected weather pattern was pushing in, Sonam acted as our early warning system. If a mission turned ugly, he'd be required to organize any necessary assistance, such as a helicopter rescue. Alongside him on the support team, Lakpa Dendi Sherpa was a climber who had previously helped me fix lines on the G200E in 2017. Together, we'd hauled 15 miles of rope to the top of Everest on summit day. By the looks of things, the dude could lift a mountain on his own.

Although the two units were both strong and experienced, managing their skills would be key. Though the guys in place had all climbed several 8,000ers, some mountains such as Gasherbrum I and II, K2, and Broad Peak were going to be new experiences for all of us; I had topped only four of the 8,000ers myself at that time. But by climbing them successfully, the individuals in the Project Possible crew would expand their experience and reputation; they would become more sought-after guides for any expedition parties looking to climb death zone peaks in the future.

Managing such a determined group would require all the leadership skills I'd gathered during my time with the military (though I'd also received an education in how *not* to lead, following my experiences with the G200E). There was no way I intended on letting people down at the very last minute. Keeping morale high was going to be key, especially when survival became a major issue.

The work would be a balancing act, but I intended on building our operational structure from the heart. When we were climbing unfamiliar mountains, such as Kanchenjunga, the likes of Mingma and Gesman would lack experience, as would I; this had the potential to unsettle everybody's confidence. But at the same time, our work ethic, desire, ambition, and camaraderie would drive Project Possible to the top and back. I also understood that to lead with passion, I had to climb more powerfully than the guys around me—though not by too much.

On previous expeditions, I'd worked with strength, trailblazing steadily until the other climbers in the group had been dots in my slipstream. That style of effort had two negative knock-on effects: (1) I often had to wait for an hour or two in the freezing cold while the others caught up with me, and (2) my spurts were demoralizing to everyone else. Imagine running a marathon with serious athletes; it's pretty discouraging to watch them sprint off into the distance. But if those same athletes stay in touch, pushing their colleagues to run a little more quickly than they'd previously been used to, their presence can be inspirational. It drags everybody along at a speed they previously hadn't considered possible.

I planned to adopt that same attitude. I would speed up when I thought it might benefit the team, but I would back off when assistance was needed. As a result, we'd hopefully always summit as a group.

If, by the end of 2019, everybody felt proud enough to say they were an integral part of a successful Project Possible mission, then my work would be done.

I EVENTUALLY ARRIVED at Annapurna's base camp on March 28, 2019, and as I readied myself at the small outpost at the foot of one of the world's most dangerous mountains, there seemed to be a dismissive attitude in almost everybody I spoke with. An expedition of hard-core climbers and seasoned guides had shown up; some of them knew about Project Possible and my plans to climb the 14 summits in less than seven months. Others heard the gossip and scanned my posts on social media. It wasn't hard to imagine what they were thinking. *OK, Mr. Big Climber. You've been up and down some pretty impressive mountains, but do you know what it really means to climb all the 8,000-meter peaks?*

I shut out the negative noise and told myself it was nothing more than a distraction.

The climbing community might have underestimated my determination to accomplish my goal, but at the same time I understood the skeptical mood. To a lot of climbers, Project Possible probably sounded like an unhinged flight of fantasy. A few people had accused me of overreaching; they wondered why I was shouting my plans from the rooftops when I could have approached the mission with stealth, without drawing so much attention.* Thank goodness, supporters were cheering me on too, and every now and then I'd read an encouraging message on Instagram, or chat with someone who was excited by the idea.

I'd need every scrap of their positivity.

A day or so before we began our first rope-fixing climb, the team performed a *puja*, a Nepali ceremony conducted with a lama, or spiritual leader, during which the group offered prayers to the mountain gods. Juniper was scorched, rice was thrown, and a mast of prayer flags was raised. The hope was that those same gods might grant us safe passage to the peak, sparing us from the wrath of an avalanche or crevasse fall.

Although I wasn't dedicated to one god, I believed in the power of prayer. I also liked to connect with nature alone and once the puja was completed, I took myself away from the group to stare up at Annapurna's summit. The sky was a bright blue; thick clouds drifted around the higher edges, but I was locked in a one-to-one conversation with the wall of rock and ice ahead. In a way, I wanted to ask the mountain for permission.

OK, can I? Or can I not?

Having watched and waited, I sensed hope.

Still, if anything was troubling me at that point, it was the lack of physical preparation I'd undertaken. Because of my departure from the military and the seemingly endless meetings and fund-raising efforts throughout the past year, I'd been unable to

---

* In many ways, executing the work in an off-the-radar style would have suited me nicely. The problem was, I was starting from scratch financially. To get money, I needed sponsorship. To acquire sponsorship, I'd have to put on a show, while working on and off the mountain.

expose my body to the types of pressure I'd once worked through in service. In and out of combat, I was always incentivized to exercise hard as an elite operator; I'd had plenty of opportunities to gain strength every day, either in battle or through training. But now that I was a civilian and my priorities had shifted to the logistical planning of Project Possible, as well as the occasional guiding expedition, I wasn't as sharp as I'd been during previous climbs.

I took any opportunity to ready myself for Project Possible. On the way to Annapurna's base camp, I lifted rocks in strength training sessions and took a 12-mile run. Although this—as well as the first session I'd had time to complete in nearly four months—was hardly ideal preparation, I knew that once we started the line-fixing process, I'd become stronger.

I needed to be. The route we were taking was a monster: a line over Annapurna's north face, an intimidating climb that the French climber Maurice Herzog first scaled in 1950. We decided to commit to the climb on April 2; shortly thereafter Mingma, Geljen, and I, plus a few Sherpa guides from other expeditions, headed out to set the ropes up to Camps 1 and 2.

The climbing route was unforgiving. Initially, the path led us through a snow-covered field of rocks that climbers could negotiate without too much bother. But beyond that, the route grew increasingly dangerous. The landscape was cracked by deep crevasses—some visible, others hidden below a carpet of thick snow. One wrong step could send a climber falling to their death, so it was critical that all of us were roped up. If somebody fell through the snow, the weight of the remaining mountaineers, bracing as a group, would hopefully arrest their fall.

Before long, we were high above base camp, but the weather conditions had worsened. As we anchored ropes and fixed lines, a heavy wind whipped around us in a fury. The snow packed into waist-deep drifts and the work became grueling. But as point man, my job was to lead the other team members along, lifting my legs high and planting my boots firmly, with focus, so that the others could fall in behind, all the while listening for telltale rumblings of an oncoming avalanche.

Not that I'd be able to correct course even with a warning. I reminded myself that I was strong, that I would reach the summit. But avalanches were an uncontrollable act of God that nobody could truly prepare for.

Feeling the crunch of snow under my boots and the icy burn of oxygen in my lungs, I climbed, slowly but steadily.

10

THE NORMALITY OF THE EXTREME

After hours of heavy work, having broken trail through mile after mile of knee-deep snow, the Project Possible team walked into Camp 2. We'd tackled steep ribs and buttresses, negotiating a series of crevasses along the way. Bloody hell, the effort had been grinding. But with the fixed lines in place, we were closer to being primed for our summit push.

We still had so much more to climb, but despite the fatigue, everyone was in high spirits, mainly because the strong winds had died down and the mountain felt calmer. The sun was low, the group danced and joked, and the smell of fried chicken and rice wafted over camp.

Then I heard a crack like thunder from somewhere above.

Oh no . . .

The all-too-familiar rush of adrenaline kicked in, a sensory call to action I'd previously only associated with incoming gunfire or an exploding IED. But this time the adversary was bigger and potentially more destructive. *Avalanche!* And a big one.

A large chunk of Annapurna's north face had sheared away, and an eruption of white billowed down the mountain at an unstoppable speed. For a split second I was paralyzed; the magnitude of what was about to happen shorted my nervous system. Everything in the avalanche's path was in danger of being crushed. And we were very much in the avalanche's path. There was no way of escaping it.

Move!

As I looked around for a point of cover, I realized that Mingma and Sonam were rigid too, frozen by fear. The scene wasn't unlike one of those CCTV clips sometimes shown in the aftermath of a tsunami, when shocked passersby stare at an oncoming tidal wave on the horizon, seemingly incapable of running away. By the time their fight-or-flight mechanisms have kicked in, it's usually too late; they're unable to escape. Now an equally terrifying fate was powering toward us.

"Fuck, we're going to go!" I shouted. "Everybody into the shelters!"

I'd often been told that it was always best to seek some form of protection in the event of an avalanche; even something as flimsy as a tent would do. *Well, it was better than nothing.* Acting on instinct, I ran for the nearest one and dove inside. Sonam and Mingma rushed in behind me, zipping up the door. Readying ourselves for impact, we huddled together, shoulder to shoulder, the

138

avalanche's roar growing ever louder as the ground trembled beneath us. Escaping the chaos seemed unlikely. Anticipating that we might have to cut our way quickly out of the tent once we'd been smothered, I shouted instructions to the others.

"Mingma, get your knife. Sonam, back yourself against the tent poles and brace."

But Sonam looked broken. He was mumbling a prayer to the mountain gods. I felt another shiver of fear. *Fuck, this is bad.*

I had a moment of wishful thinking: *I hope that prayer works, Sonam.*

And then God knows how much snow smashed over us at full force, hammering and tearing at the tent. For several seconds the fabric and fiberglass seemed to buck and wrench without breaking. I expected to be swept down the mountain at any second, all of us tumbling over one another. Then, suddenly, unexpectedly, everything became still again. There was a silence; then I heard the sound of panicked breathing. We'd survived.

"Sonam, are you cool?" I asked, pulling him closer, shaking him gently.

He nodded, mumbling a thank-you to whichever one of the benevolent deities had spared our lives. Around us, the mountain felt eerily calm, and when I left the tent to survey the wreckage of Camp 2, checking on our kit and equipment, it was clear that we'd been lucky. We had caught only the tail end of the violent event; nobody was hurt, and nothing had been destroyed. But the mood was uneasy among the local Sherpas, in place to assist with our line-fixing efforts. As far as they were concerned, our puja from a few days back hadn't worked and their gods were in a foul mood.

With the last of daylight fading, they trudged back to base camp fearfully. Although our goal of fixing lines to Camps 3 and 4 was immediately more daunting than before, at least we were still alive. Analyzing our options in the darkness, I speculated that the usual route—the one Herzog first climbed—was now too dangerous.

People are going to blame me if something goes wrong during the summit push, or if it later turns out to be unsafe . . . There must be an alternative route.

I stared at Annapurna's peak and asked the question yet again. *OK, can I? Or can I not?*

Then I joined the others for dinner, hoping the mountain might behave more mercifully from then on.

I WOKE with the sunrise—and a plan.

As part of the expedition inventory, I'd packed a few pieces of camera equipment with the hope of filming a lot of Project Possible as we moved from mountain to mountain. My aim was to record as much as I could while climbing, directing others on my team for the camera, and sometimes having one of them film me. Even though I had little moviemaking experience, I thought I could capture exciting material. Eventually, I hoped to show my expeditions to the world by making a documentary, or maybe presenting a live theater talk or two.

Recording had the added benefit of silencing any doubters who were sure to pop up once the operation was complete. Whenever somebody pulled off something really big in the mountains, it was all too easy for trolls to pick apart the results—unless those results were backed up with an exhaustive collection of footage.

Even then, it was tricky. Some people still believed the 1969 moon landing was faked; because the internet was swamped with all sorts of conspiracy theories and "evidence," I certainly wasn't going to expose myself to accusations of falsifying my achievements. I intended to make it home with as much film as I could. To help, I brought along two guys—Sagar and Alit Gurung—to assist with the editing and social media output. They'd shown so much faith in Project Possible that they'd each resigned from their previous jobs in the U.K. to join us.

During my fund-raising drive, I'd even approached production companies about buying the rights to the content. I proposed a camera crew join us for the entire mission, but nobody was keen. The general consensus seemed to be that I didn't have the funding and wouldn't even finish the project, so why should they send a film crew? Many people I encountered in those stressful months prior to reaching Annapurna were reluctant to believe my goal was humanly possible.

So I figured, if they're not interested, I'll do it myself.

BEFORE STARTING OUR CLIMB from base camp on day one, I distributed head cams to everyone in the team. A handheld digital camera was on standby, too. But the most exciting tool in my filming inventory was a drone. After checking it out at home, I was struck by its tactical potential. Of course, it would be great for filming aerial shots as we climbed and for capturing the impressive scale of our surroundings; we'd look like ants against the vast expanses of rock and ice. But it was also a handy reconnaissance tool. And as we tried to determine the best route up Annapurna's avalanche-ravaged terrain, I had an idea.

In the same way the British military used drones to improve the tactical understanding of a battle space, I'd be able to fly one across Annapurna, working out the safest route toward Camp 3. With Mingma and Sonam, we hovered the drone over a series of icy ridges, studying the footage on a phone for a new route up. *And there it was!*

A long vertical ridge that ran for a few hundred yards directly above us came into view. Dusted in snow, it resembled the bridge of a sharp, angular nose from a distance. I recognized it as the notorious Dutch Rib, a knife edge of powder and ice so called because a team of climbers from Holland, plus nine Sherpas, had originally scaled it in 1977. Very few people had attempted it since, probably because the line appeared so daunting. But by the look of things, there was just enough width on the nose's bridge to climb it.

The work would be challenging, mainly because anyone scaling it was bound to be very exposed. And a climber who slipped on the compacted rock and ice would have nothing to break a long and painful ride to the bottom.

That wasn't the only risk, though. As I scanned the drone footage, I realized that to get across to the Dutch Rib, we'd need to break trail through a no-man's-land of snow—another avalanche landing zone. But once we were on the ridge, we'd be protected from the fallout of any seracs that might collapse higher up the mountain; my guess was that the Dutch Rib was so thin and angled that any rushing debris from above would fall away on either side before it reached us. Our only problem was that the climb looked to be brutally tough.

When I returned to base camp later that day and announced my plan to the waiting expeditions, I was told that the Dutch Rib was a no-go zone. One Sherpa, an Annapurna guide with years of experience, instantly knocked the idea. "Nobody's climbed that route for years," he said. "It's too hard."

The reaction unsettled me a bit.

Maybe this is too massive a risk, I thought. But what other option do I have?

My military training, where I had to find creative solutions to difficult problems without whining or making excuses, had instilled in me a sense of inner positivity. I assessed the Dutch Rib drone footage once more and decided to put that mind-set into practice. Besides, I wasn't telling anyone they had to follow my plan. As the leader of the line-fixing team, I was merely giving them an option; it was up to them whether or not they took it. Yet days later, having edged my way slowly up the ridge with Geljen—my legs buckling as we dug into ice while fixing lines—I wondered if my Sherpa friend hadn't been right after all.

After a full day of rough work on the Dutch Rib, with the light fading, I found myself caught between Camps 2 and 3. Climbing in the darkness on such a precarious slope seemed risky, but heading all the way down to Camp 2 felt like defeat; we'd only have to repeat the same process the following day without making any significant progress. To push higher, we had to stay put for the night, and so we fixed our tent to the nose's bridge with around 30 anchors, Geljen and me resting above a sheer drop that would have meant certain death had either one of us forgetfully stumbled out of the tent at night.

That wasn't our most pressing issue, though. When we'd decided to set out for Camp 3 that morning, I'd originally expected us to make it all the way there, and back to Camp 2, in one push. At the time, in an effort to travel light, we hadn't packed overnight equipment, such as sleeping bags or food, so our meals and stove were stuck at Camp 2. Worse, a supply run wasn't scheduled to reach us until the following day. Pitched on the Dutch Rib's exposed surface, we soon began to freeze. Both of us were hungry and rapidly dehydrating.

I realized that by not being able to make my way up to Camp 3, the mission was in jeopardy. Without progress, we could be stuck in a perpetual loop for days, where returning to Camp 2 and climbing to the Dutch Rib's midway point, over and over, would eventually force us to give up. I was also pinned to my position by pride—for both the Gurkhas and the British military elite—and I had no right to dent either reputation by turning back and losing face.

I radioed everybody on the mountain for assistance.

"Hey guys, we can't go any farther than this," I explained. "If we come back down to Camp 2 now, we cannot progress, and we won't be able to summit at all, so I'm going to stay here and commit. But . . . we don't have food. Can someone bring up a stove and some noodles?"

My calls went unanswered. But I still wasn't in the mood to retreat. Besides, I was used to periods of discomfort in war, where I'd had to function in conflict with nothing in the way of food and very little water.

"We'll hold tight here," I told Geljen, defiantly.

But as we settled into our uncomfortable surroundings, fearful that a strong blast of wind might rip us away from the ridgeline, the radio crackled. A voice then cut through the static.

"Nimsdai, if nobody brings food and water from Camp 2, I'll bring you some from base camp."

Who's this?

"It's Gesman."

Gesman?

Geljen smiled. Gesman had arrived on Mingma's recommendation as the least qualified mountaineer of the team. Despite having climbed only a few death zone peaks, he was now offering to scale the Dutch Rib with supplies, when other considerably more experienced Annapurna guides and climbers had ignored my calls for assistance. That was a huge response.

"No, brother," I said. "We're good, but thank you. We can hang on."

I felt happy. Gesman's offer was both reassuring and inspiring. I instantly understood that if the least qualified climber on Project Possible could be as fearless and as dedicated in the face of adversity as the most experienced, then I'd found my new special forces. We were already the extreme altitude elite.

As far as I was concerned, selection was done.

FOOD SUPPLIES ARRIVED the following morning, and with new-found energy we climbed the Dutch Rib, set the fixed lines to Camp 3, and returned to base, readying the expedition team and accompanying Sherpas for our summit push. A plan was set: I would lead the way with Mingma, climbing a full day ahead of our paying clients, who Sonam would steer through the camps as they followed our deep footfalls in the snow. The fixing team intended to push to Camp 2 and sleep overnight. A day later, we'd scale the Dutch Rib, resting at Camp 3 before setting lines to Camp 4, from where we could expect to spend a full day trailblazing through the deep snow while anchoring lines to the mountain.

If everything went according to plan, our expedition team, plus the other parties climbing Annapurna that day, could meet us at Camp 4 shortly after the last lines were set. Then we could climb to the top as a group.

It was the first summit push of the mission. I was ready for the effort, but fixing lines meant I had to travel with a lot of weight on my back. I generally carried around 40 or 60 pounds in my rucksack, though a lot of this weight was rope. I'd also be trailblazing through deep snow, so the exertion would be huge. But as we moved upward and fixed lines, the load became lighter until I was usually left with around 22 pounds. I also carried very little in the way of food or water.

I never took energy gels, supplements, or snacks; everything I ate on the mountain depended on my mood, and I often was powered by egg-fried rice and dried chicken. I didn't like dealing with prepackaged meals; they were too awkward. When it came to hydration, I didn't need a lot to get me through a summit push, and I often conserved my water for other climbers. As a soldier, my body became accustomed to working with very little, but on the mountain I always kept a one-liter Thermos with me. My trick was to pack a cup with snow, melting it down with a splash of hot water from my flask. That was usually enough to get me through a summit push.

All of this kit had the potential to slow me down, but not by much. After two days of solid work, we were able to rest at Camp 4 for a few hours as the other parties caught up to our position. I was tired, but had plenty of energy left in the tank. As I relaxed in my tent, I was struck by an idea: I wanted to climb without oxygen. To scale the 8,000ers without gas had long been considered the purest form of mountaineering.

When Reinhold Messner and his climbing partner, Peter Habeler, topped the world's highest peak in 1978 without oxygen, it was rightly hailed as an incredible achievement—so much so that a number of people made claims that it hadn't happened at all. In their opinion, there was no way a climber could have topped the world's highest peak without oxygen. To silence the doubters, Messner repeated the feat, this time climbing from the Tibetan side of Everest, alone. By all accounts, his ascent was agonizing. But he managed it, and it's now considered perhaps the most groundbreaking accomplishment in the history of modern mountaineering.

In 2016, I'd made a promise to myself: that I was going to climb the 8,000ers with oxygen. That first trip to Everest had shown me how essential a supplemental air supply was when helping a stricken individual on the mountain, and there was every chance I might encounter at least one other incapacitated mountaineer while working through Project Possible. I'd never be able to forgive myself if I couldn't administer assistance. And I had other responsibilities to consider—namely, the fact that I was about to help lead a team of clients to the top. If one of them fell seriously ill or was injured, my chances of getting them back to base camp alive would be much lower without oxygen.

And yet, despite all this, I felt tempted to take the personal risk. (I still had oxygen with me should anyone else require it.) In hindsight, I think the altitude was playing with my mind. I wasn't thinking straight, and the lack of oxygen in my blood was conspiring with my competitive spirit. The same drive that had once inspired me to take those middle-of-the-night training runs as a teenager in Chitwan, or those grueling load carries to Maidstone while I prepared for U.K. Special Forces Selection, was now goading me into taking a risk on Annapurna. And all because one other climber had challenged my reputation.

It had started a week or so earlier. As I rested between line-fixing efforts, Stephen—a European mountaineer from another expedition team—had made a comment or two about my use of air on the 8,000-meter peaks. He was a seriously fit guy, an ultramarathon runner, and proud of it. "With this body, I can climb the big mountains without oxygen," he announced when we were first introduced.

"That's cool, brother," I said. "We all have our own reasons for climbing the way we do."

I soon forgot the comment, but in time it became apparent that Stephen wasn't a team player. He hadn't offered to help with the line-fixing work like the Sherpa guides from his expedition. Resting, drinking tea, and chatting was more his vibe. A few days later, as I partied with Mingma, Sonam, Geljen, and Gesman, Stephen walked by once more. Trying to unify the different groups on the mountain, I shouted out to him, offering him a bottle of beer. But Stephen turned it down.

"Nah, man, I'm climbing a mountain," he said, stiffly.

"Yeah, we're all climbing the mountain."

"But you're using oxygen."

There it was—*the challenge*. Some in the mountain-climbing community were making a big deal about the Project Possible team's use of air at high altitude, and it was starting to annoy me.

"Yeah, but not until after Camp 4," I said. "And you haven't had to break trail up to Camp 3 like us, so calm your ego down."

Nothing more was said about it. But once the summit push began, my competitive streak took over. During a brief catch-up period, all the mountaineers had congregated at Camp 3. My team was about to spend the day fixing lines to Camp 4. Everybody else was resting and by the looks of it, a lot of them were in dire need of it—especially Stephen. Hours earlier, I'd watched as his expedition team, small dots on the landscape below, fought hard to scale the Dutch Rib. When they eventually staggered toward our shelters, Stephen had vomited blood. His body was blowing out; I felt sorry for him.

Had he been a client of mine, one of us would have been forced to take him down for medical treatment. We'd likely have used oxygen to maximize Stephen's chances of a swift recovery. But the dude wasn't quitting—he announced he was still fit enough to climb.

Twenty-four hours later, at Camp 4, I was struck with an idea. One climb, no oxygen: *the critics silenced*.

The odds were certainly in my favor. This was our first expedition on schedule. I was feeling strong, and because Annapurna's promontory was just barely in the death zone at 8,091 meters, the thought of climbing without air was appealing. But when I mentioned my plan to Mingma in our tent, he shook his head. He worried the mission might lose its momentum if I wasn't able to power forward at my usual speed.

"We need your aggression, Nimsdai," he said.

I tried using reason. "I've been leading from the front the whole expedition. I know I can climb any mountain without oxygen."

The chances of him backing down, I knew, were slim, but I pressed ahead anyway. "Mate, just for the sake of these people and their opinions, let me climb without air."

He laughed. "No, Nimsdai!"

Mingma's opinion was important to me. His uncle, Dorje, was regarded as a totemic figure in Nepali climbing, and had shared his knowledge with the mountaineers in his family. Mingma had since become a hugely knowledgeable guide in his own right and a Sherpa of the Year in the making—the highest accolade anyone could expect to receive in that noble profession.

I knew Mingma was right, too, and his strong opinion forced me to recall an ideal I'd once held as a kid hoping to make it into the Gurkhas: *You don't have to prove anything to anyone.* Then there was the promise I'd made to myself about always carrying gas on the 8,000ers. Breaking it might lead to bad habits. Bad habits might result in failure.

And so I backed down.

I didn't have time to lose focus. To function effectively during combat, it was important to shut out any pain such as heat, discomfort, hunger, dehydration, and emotional upset, and I applied the same attitude to Annapurna. I understood the final push to the top would be brutally hard, even with air. I had around 3,200 feet to go, and some of the route required me to break trail through another blanket of waist-high snow (though the slope was gentle enough for us not to need fixed lines). I'd also have to scale a steep climb through an ice cliff before negotiating a final section of tricky, slippery rock shortly before the peak.

Once the team departed from Camp 4 at 9 p.m., I realized that most of the Project Possible route-fixing team were now guiding private clients, one-on-one, and that the work to come would be hard going and intense. By the looks of things with our clients, only Mingma and I were available to power through the snow. Realizing that we didn't have enough manpower, I pulled my guides in close.

"Guys, from now on everyone does 10 minutes of trailblazing," I said. "Twenty minutes if you can. Whatever you have in the tank, use it. When the person leading the team gets too tired, he should stop and move to the side, waiting to join the end of the line. The second guy then becomes point man for his 10 minutes or so. This will keep our momentum going."

With a clear operational brief in place, we set the rope and broke trail for most of the route, each of us taking turns to lead the way, one by one, until Annapurna's peak was finally in sight. We understood other expeditions were following, and they were relying on us to break trail to the top.

Since Dhaulagiri, I'd come to realize that my comfort zone generally opened up at around 8,000 meters—the point where most people break down. I owned that ground and rarely asked, "Can I really do this?" If ever a sliver of doubt seeped into my self-belief, I remembered my new god: proving to the world that imagination was the greatest power of all.

During previous expeditions, the buzz of achievement usually kicked in a few yards before the peak, in those minutes when every climber sensed that the hardest yards were done and the final steps were within reach. But at the top of Annapurna, weirdly, I felt no rush, no feeling of overwhelming emotion. Well, apart from the realization I was fortunate to be alive—our close call with that powerful avalanche had been a little *too* close. But any mountaineer taking on a climb as high risk as Annapurna needed a heavy slice of luck to match the other attributes required above 8,000 meters: strength, resilience, a sense of team, and an optimistic mind-set. The environment had been uncontrollable and savage, but at 3:30 p.m., we were perched atop it.

I took some time to soak in the view below, the jagged teeth of the Himalaya swaddled in cloud, laid out around of us. From my position, Dhaulagiri was clearly visible. My home village of Dana was somewhere in its shadow; I'd succeeded on home ground.

Maybe the massive challenges scattered around me on the landscape dampened the charge of euphoria I'd experienced on previous expeditions. I knew my work was just getting started.

And how the hell was I going to get all that money?

But the first peak on the list was done, and I remained undaunted. I recorded a quick thank-you message to my sponsors at home and made another appeal for funding. There was no harm in asking—and I was bloody desperate.

The date was April 23, 2019. The clock was ticking, and the world was watching. My race was on.

11

RESCUE!

Nims! *Nimsdai!*

I woke in Camp 4 on Annapurna to the sound of shouting. Shrinking into my sleeping bag, I let the events of the day rush back to me. For the past few weeks I'd barely slept, and having summited Annapurna, my strength was dwindling. I was in agony; my legs and back ached, and shortly after topping out, Mingma, Gesman, and I had trudged to Camp 4 and collapsed into our tents. But around us a new drama had unraveled. A panicked Sherpa was moving from group to group in the camp.

"Nims, I've left my client," he said, frantically. "He's still up there. His oxygen ran out and mine was low, so I gave him my cylinder to keep him going until I managed to get him some help, but I don't know if it's too late. I don't even know where he is—"

I remembered the man he was talking about—a 48-year-old Malaysian doctor named Chin Wui Kin, who was a fairly experienced climber. When my team had performed our puja, Dr. Chin had joined us for a while. We'd shared a drink and I remember him watching us and smiling as we conducted the ceremony. We'd even danced and taken selfies. I'd also seen them both on the summit; they seemed to be a little tired, but in fairly good shape, though I had warned them to leave quickly.

"Guys, let's get down as soon as we can," I'd said as they hung around to take photographs. "Then we can celebrate." Had we known that they were running low on air, I'd have handed over a cylinder, no problem. Maybe the guide hadn't anticipated that Dr. Chin might struggle at the peak. Perhaps he'd overestimated his client's abilities.

"I think he might be dead," said the Sherpa. "He's very tired. Nims, can you help?"

I nodded wearily. The idea of leaving Dr. Chin behind was too upsetting to consider. I had experience with rescues after my first climb of Everest, and I was probably the strongest and most qualified on the mountain to conduct a search and rescue operation at that point. Saving Dr. Chin was a risk, but I was up for it on one condition: I needed extra oxygen. My team was running low, and it would require all three of us to find and then extract the casualty from his position, wherever that might be.

"I'm happy to go up there and conduct a search and rescue mission," I said. "But we're going to need the insurance company to pay for some oxygen cylinders to be flown up here so we can get to him."

The Sherpa looked at me blankly.

"Listen," I said. "One: I don't know if the man is alive. Two: I'm not going to wander up the mountain searching for Dr. Chin without air. It puts my whole team at risk, which is a chance I'm not prepared to take, especially as he might be dead already."

A call was made to base camp, but by 6 a.m. our requests for a drop had gone unanswered. I knew any rescue attempts at were now out of the question, because we simply didn't have the oxygen to conduct a search, but I wasn't going to give up on Dr. Chin just yet. Maybe there was an alternative way to find him? I reached for the drone, and after warming it up in the morning sun, attempted to lift it into the air, hoping we might catch sight of the casualty by flying it across the terrain above—that is, if Dr. Chin hadn't already stumbled off a cliff edge. But the motor wouldn't start. I tried again—no luck.

After making one last call to confirm the insurance company hadn't changed its position, I descended to base camp, believing Annapurna had claimed another victim and eager to escape in one piece myself. It was around 10 p.m. by the time we made it to the bottom. I was exhausted, physically and mentally, though not so fatigued that I couldn't drink whisky until three in the morning. I was trying to shake away the heavy emotions I was feeling: I hated the thought that a guy had been left behind. The impact on his family would be devastating. But it was also a reminder that I might end up in the same position one day.

I eventually fell asleep to the sound of other returning climbers, while a man was probably dead, or dying alone, above us on the mountain. But several hours later, as I slowly woke up, the drama was starting again. Mingma was calling my name.

What the fuck?

"Nimsdai! Dr. Chin, they've seen him . . . he's alive!"

I heard the *whomp-whomp-whomp* of helicopter rotary blades.

A chopper had been called in to conduct a search and rescue operation.

"Are you sure?"

Mingma nodded. *Yes, brother.*

"Right, let's get eyes on him. We'll take that helicopter to his position and I'll ready a rescue team."

I quickly pulled on my clothes and started planning for the mission. I even sent out a call for help on social media, outlining the situation to anyone following our expedition that might be able to come to our aid:

Chin Wui Kin is still alive on Annapurna (HELP)
Action required: His insurance company to authorize the rescue.
Request: Can someone with media power help us, please?
Current situation: My team is waiting at the base camp for heli support (to bring six oxygen cylinders), but this can only be achieved if the rescue company authorizes the rescue.
Let's save a life.

I gathered my kit together and clambered into the chopper, later circling above Dr. Chin's last known location. *There!* A man, stranded on the ice in a bright red summit suit, his body buffeted by winds, was waving up to us.

"Yeah, that's Chin!" I shouted to the pilot. "We have to get down there."

I had no other choice but to help. If I had been in his position, the emotional turbulence would have been too intense. I imagined his thoughts and feelings as we approached from above. *I'm seeing a helicopter—I think. I'm waving at them and they're waving back . . . I'm saved!* Then to be forced into a feeling of false hope, waiting for a rescue that might never come, seemed like a cruel end.

Even though I'd been physically thrashed by the summit push on Annapurna and my second team was waiting for me in Dhaulagiri, having set the lines to Camp 2 already, I had no other option. Project Possible now hung in the balance. Our weather window on Dhaulagiri was closing rapidly; a storm was rolling in, and if I couldn't make it to the top within a couple days or so, the schedule could be thrown into disarray. With only one mountain checked off the list, my chance of completing Phase One in the required time would be severely reduced.

When we circled back to camp to brief Gesman, Mingma, and Geljen, I outlined our mission plan. Dr. Chin's wife, we were told, had self-financed a rescue mission, and oxygen was en route. (The Project Possible team did not charge anything for our manpower.)

"We can't leave him there," I said. "This is a tough mountain, but I think, together, we have the strength to save him. I've never left anyone behind in war. I'm not going to do it on the mountain, either."

Descending directly onto Dr. Chin's position was too risky due to the high altitude. Instead, we strapped into harnesses and individually attached ourselves to the helicopter with a length of rope called a "long line." It required rescuers to steady their nerves as they were lifted off the ground, feeling the tension in the rope. The wind blasted my face, and even though I wore goggles and a face mask, the cold seared my flesh as I was sucked into the sky by the chopper. My peripheral vision became blurred as the helicopter's speed and whirring rotary blades above distorted the view of the mountains around me.

I couldn't let fear knock me off course; it was important to enjoy the ride. For five minutes I dangled precariously, suspended several hundred feet above an uncaring expanse of snow and rock, as the pilot sought a suitable drop zone.

In the military I was often called to "fast rope" (or zip down a line from a helicopter) into boats moving at speed or enemy compounds. The process became routine during combat—but dropping onto a Himalayan peak was a totally new experience (though at least no one was shooting at me this time). Once we'd all arrived on the ground, one by one, we moved quickly along the arduous route to Dr. Chin's position.

A few days earlier, as we'd broken trail and fixed lines between camps, it had taken us around 18 hours to get from our drop zone to where Dr. Chin was lying stricken. But charged with adrenaline, we now moved at far higher speeds: a team of mountain-climbing Usain Bolts. Our lungs fought for air until the form of Dr. Chin, lying prostrate on white snow, came into view.

We had covered the distance in four hours, but I feared our efforts might be for nothing; Dr. Chin was in a bad way. As we gathered around him, he didn't react, although he seemed to be alive. His eyes were moving, so I gave his shoulders a shake. I needed to communicate with him if we were to extract him to safety.

"Hey, Dr. Chin!" I shouted. "You're going to be OK."

I checked him over. He looked close to death. The man had been stranded for around 36 hours. One hand was completely frostbitten and his face was ravaged by the cold. Even if we could get him to a hospital, the injuries would be life changing. Still, something about his movements told me he hadn't given up. Dr. Chin was trying to talk, and seemed to be fighting hard for his life as I tested his levels of consciousness.

"Hey, Dr. Chin, how many people are here?" I shouted, pressing my ear to his mouth so I could hear any mumbled responses.

"Four."

Four! Dr. Chin was hanging on.

"You're doing great, brother. Can you drink?"

"Water . . ."

I pressed a canteen to his lips as the others carefully packed him into a rescue sleigh.

We had no time to lose. The sun was dipping behind the mountains, and because the rescue helicopter was unable to lift us away in the dark, it was critical that we moved Dr. Chin as quickly as possible into a suitable shelter, where we could attempt to keep him alive until the chopper arrived the following morning.

We pushed on down the mountain, clambering into a tent another climbing party had left at Camp 4, where we worked to keep the doctor conscious for as long as possible. We rubbed his body in an attempt to increase his circulation. At one point, I even tried to remove one of his boots to assess the damage to his feet and to warm his toes; the intense cold had caused the fabric to freeze to Dr. Chin's flesh, and removing his footwear was impossible, even with a knife. His body would have to thaw first.

At times I was confident of saving him. Every now and then, if I felt Dr. Chin was drifting into unconsciousness, I'd try to rouse him. "You've got to stay strong now, man. You can stay alive." He'd respond with a groan.

I questioned our decision to conduct the rescue. "Have we done the right thing coming here?" I asked Mingma. "He might die, and we'll have risked our lives for nothing."

I could tell Dr. Chin was in pain. His lungs rattled with every breath, and his resilience seemed to be fading; I recognized this signal from my experience patching up wounded soldiers. An individual, having clung on to life alone for so long, was often offered a window of psychological rest when the CASEVAC team showed up. Rather than thinking solely of self-preservation, casualties were able to put their lives into the rescuer's hands. The responsibility had shifted; survival became dependent on the efforts of others.

In this case, our arrival and shelter had presented Dr. Chin with some respite, but it was a dangerous time. For the briefest of moments, he relaxed, which was all it took to kill a climber in such a precarious position.

But we were exhausted, too. All of us had paid the price for climbing Annapurna's summit 24 hours earlier. Still, we'd raced toward Dr. Chin's location the following day and, in the early hours of the morning, while working to keep Dr. Chin warm, I nodded off to sleep, until . . .

WHACK! I felt the sharp sting of an open hand. Mingma had given me a slap on the legs.

"Wake up, Nimsdai!" he shouted. "Wake up!"

I jolted. Aware that fatigue would smother me again, I energized myself even more by giving myself a smack on the jaw, and then another. Gesman and Geljen did the same. It was all we could do to stay awake, until someone had the idea that we should shout and scream at one another instead. It might have looked like mad-

ABOVE: At home with my younger sister, Anita, in Chitwan. As a small boy, I'd turn over rocks for hours in the nearby stream looking for crabs.

LEFT: The Purja family. Two of my older brothers, Ganga and Kamal, went on to become Gurkhas. It was only natural that I would follow in their footsteps.

TOP: Joining the Gurkhas in 2003. I put everything into making their ranks. ABOVE: On patrol in Afghanistan with the Queen's Gurkha Engineers

TOP: Scaling the Dutch Rib on Annapurna, a treacherous blade of powder and ice ABOVE: A moment of calm on Annapurna. The mountain very nearly killed the Project Possible team during an avalanche.

Before a climb, the expedition team will perform a *puja*—a Nepali ceremony in which prayer is offered to the mountain gods for a safe passage to the peak.

Even though I'd been physically thrashed during the climb, I couldn't leave an injured climber stranded, and did all I could to help Biplab on Kanchenjunga.

TOP: Climbing through the Khumbu Icefall on Everest ABOVE: A rare moment of peace at Everest Base Camp OPPOSITE: With one photo I captured the chaos that sometimes kicks off on Everest.

Lhotse *(above)* and the view from Makalu *(below)*: I would break the world record by climbing to the summit of Lhotse from Everest, and then scaling Makalu in 48 hours and 30 minutes.

TOP: Our tents at Camp 3 on Nanga Parbat. The weather was so much more unpredictable in Pakistan. ABOVE: A successful climb on Nanga Parbat was celebrated with cake. *Why not?*

OPPOSITE: Gasherbrum I, though not a headline-maker like K2, was a tough adversary. More than 30 climbers had died there since 1977. TOP: While looking to the peaks of Gasherbrum I and II, I told myself, *This is yours, Nims*. ABOVE: Atop Gasherbrum II

TOP: Broad Peak was smothered in snow as we looked at it from K2's base camp. The fixed lines had been buried. ABOVE: Establishing comms with the other Beyond Possible team members on K2

Heading toward Broad Peak with Mingma David and Halung Dorchi Sherpa

TOP: With Gesman and three Sherpa guides from another expedition at the summit of Cho Oyu ABOVE: At base camp on Cho Oyu, the pressure was building: The mountain was closing earlier than usual and we had to move fast!

TOP: Having scaled Manaslu in four days, only Shishapangma stood between me and the world record for climbing all 14 8,000-meter peaks. ABOVE: The tattoo across my back celebrates all 14 8,000-meter peaks. The ink is made of DNA from my wife, parents, and siblings.

With my mum. Everything I'd achieved was inspired by her.

All photographs courtesy of Nims Purja

ness, all of us packed into a tent, yelling loudly, crowded around a stricken man in the hope that our body heat might keep him alive. But we were in desperate times, and we resorted to desperate measures. Falling asleep could be the end for Dr. Chin.

We had other factors to consider, too: The helicopter was picking us up from Camp 3 at 6 a.m., and it was critical that we left on time to meet it. If we arrived too early, Dr. Chin would have to hang around, his body exposed to the wind and cold. Get there too late and our ride to the hospital would probably be delayed, which might prove costly in a situation where every minute counts.

Glancing at my watch, I realized we had only another couple hours to wait until the sun rose. When the time came, we labored down the mountain, dragging Dr. Chin with us. A helicopter soon hovered above us. We clipped Dr. Chin and his sled to the rope and just like that, he was lifted away to Kathmandu for treatment.

In Nepal, CASEVACs of that kind take place all the time. But sometimes, there was a game to play. Because of finances, search and rescue teams were usually left to make their own way down, because lifting climbers, one by one on a long line during a series of trips up and down the mountain, is costly. Turning the chopper around for rescuers in what would be four flights could add tens of thousands to the bill. But on this occasion, I was offered the next ride back down the mountain.

"Not yet," I said. "Please take all of my team first. Then come for me. I'll be the last man."

I understood the cruel reality that if I was winched away by the helicopter, they were unlikely to return for the others; the rides were too costly. But if I remained on the mountain, having led the rescue, there was no way they could abandon me—not after the hard work I'd put in to saving Dr. Chin. My reputation and connections in Nepal also lent me a certain level of power. So, to make sure they wouldn't be able to play games with my expedition team, Mingma, Geljen, and Gesman were transported to base camp shortly after the casualty.

By the time I was eventually flown into the helipad at the hospital in Kathmandu, where Dr. Chin was being treated, word of his rescue had spread. His wife had arrived to see him, as had a mob of cameramen and journalists who surrounded me once I'd left the chopper. When I met Mrs. Chin at the intensive care unit, she was relieved, but emotional.

"Thank you so much. I don't know what to say," she said. "The doctors aren't sure if he'll survive."

"He wants to live so much," I said. "He's been fighting up there for the past 36 hours. We did everything we could to help."

I was pleased to have brought them back together, but the rescue forced me to face the truths of high-altitude climbing and mortality. It was yet another reminder that life above 8,000 meters could be both savage and unpredictable (although whenever somebody signed up for an expedition like the one Dr. Chin had undertaken, they generally understood the dangers of mountain adventure). Succumbing to altitude sickness or suffering a serious injury rarely came as a shock when it happened—and it happened all too often on Annapurna.

But presented with the choice between dying slowly and uncomfortably through age, or passing away during an expedition or mission, my feelings were clear: I would take the latter. I wasn't afraid to die on the mountain; I'd rather burn out in style than drift away quietly.

I wondered if Dr. Chin felt the same.

WHILE WE FINISHED UP in Kathmandu and prepared to head to Dhaulagiri's base camp, I fumed. I was angry at the way Dr. Chin had been treated.

Our delay in arriving on the mountain meant we'd missed our best window for climbing; a nasty weather system had now blown in with devastating results. Heavy snow had buried our fixed lines, and by the sounds of it we weren't going to find them. Meanwhile, our tents on the mountain's higher camps had been pummeled by powerful winds, and some were in ribbons. When I arrived at base camp by helicopter, joined by Gesman, Mingma, and Geljen, the morale of the team was in equally bad shape. Our supplies had run out, too. We were screwed.

I understood the importance of climbing Dhaulagiri quickly, but the growing unity within the Project Possible team was also important. I'd learned that organizing an expedition party was the same as organizing a group of soldiers in war: They needed purpose and incentive, but food and downtime were vital, too. Without periods of rest and recovery, individuals or the whole team had increased likelihood of failure in the heat of a battle.

So I announced to the guys that we were withdrawing from the mountain to regroup together. A little drinking and dancing were in order, and we rode in 4x4s into Pokhara for a week of partying. We even hired some motorbikes and cut about the fields at high speed for an afternoon.

The group's spirit was lifted and our brief period of rest and recuperation paid off. On May 12, we summited Dhaulagiri at 5:30 p.m., battling 45-mile-an-hour winds and heavy clouds for 20 hours nonstop, digging our way across deep hills of snow to ascend a few yards at a time.

Much of the climb was done alpine style, where we operated for the most part without fixed lines, making exceptions for a particularly technical ridge, or rock face. It was an exhausting effort, and it certainly wasn't safe. But even in the extreme weather, ours was proving to be a brave and highly skilled team. When the wind abated momentarily, the team exploded forward, climbing as quickly as possible before the next squall arrived, at which point we'd lean into the storm, bracing ourselves until it was time to move up again.

There was no room for complaints. Wallowing in misery or inviting fear into our thinking wouldn't help us. Whenever the team rested, I only allowed them to sit for five minutes; when time was up, I made sure to be the first one to stand, and then to break trail. I figured it was best to lead by example. But though I was eager to move quickly, I wasn't about to risk the lives of my teammates. When Ramesh started to feel unwell with altitude sickness, I told him to get down to safety.

But Kasang was struggling, too. Although he'd gained some experience climbing the 8,000ers, he wasn't as physically agile as his older brother, Mingma. Also, an intense toothache was bothering him, and he seemed to deteriorate as we edged into the death zone. At times, Mingma had to prop him up as we struggled to the top. I was worried.

Kasang is not as strong as his brother. Is he going to make it?

Then, an awful realization struck me: If the two siblings were taken by an avalanche or fell into a crevasse together, the family's bread earners would have been wiped from the earth in one cruel stroke. Kasang seemed to be having similar thoughts. When we finally made it to the summit, he patted me on the back.

"Maybe it's wrong to have both brothers on the mountain at the same time," he said. "If something goes wrong, who will look after the family?"

I pulled Kasang close. "I promise we'll make it home together, brother."

At times, the conditions threatened to overwhelm us during our descent; the mountain's mood turned increasingly hostile, and the winds were so powerful that, at times, it was impossible to see. Though I wore protective goggles, my eyes burned and as we worked our way to base camp.

Still, I sensed that a shift had taken place. Gesman had shown me on Annapurna that we were an elite unit. But the Project Possible team had now discovered a unique bond, too. Intense loyalties had developed between us because the stakes we were facing were so huge.

I knew Mingma and Geljen could be trusted during the pressure of a search and rescue operation; Lakpa Dendi had already proven himself to be tough during his work on the G200E. The group had my back, and I had theirs. As in the SBS, we shared an unrelenting pursuit of excellence.

We'd need every connection in that bond to hold firm if we were to survive Kanchenjunga.

12

INTO
THE DARK

A t 8,586 meters above sea level, Kanchenjunga is the third tallest mountain in the world—but it may have been the toughest expedition within Phase One. That's saying a lot, considering the daunting kill rate of Anna-purna. Still, Kanchenjunga was renowned for being brutally tough to climb; few people had the resilience, luck, or strength to reach its peak, because the ascent to the summit from Camp 4—itself pitched 7,750 meters above sea level—was a soul-breaking grind. Despite only having around a thousand meters in altitude to scale, the distance to travel was long, and deep snows often impeded the ascent to the shoulder that ran toward Kanchenjunga's summit.

If they can make it to the final ridge, mountaineers are then exposed to awful winds and biting cold. The oxygen levels drop to 33 percent and the terrain is perilous chaos—a bewildering minefield of loose rock, ice-covered boulders, and blinding spin-drift. Psychologically, the route feels never-ending, the summit forever out of reach, and many people turn back long before making the top. On average, only around 25 climbers reach Kanchenjunga's apex each year.

I knew we had it in us to charge up Kanchenjunga—after all, we had climbed the first two mountains in double-quick time under difficult circumstances—but everyone on the team was feeling frazzled. We were battle-bruised from five days on Dhaulagiri, fixing lines, and digging up rope buried by heavy snowfall while carrying 65 pounds of gear on our backs. When we arrived at Kanchenjunga's base camp on May 14, the team fell into a short period of relative luxury, stuffing our faces with fried chicken bought in a nearby village while we prepared for the next 24 hours.

We were to move fast, pushing immediately to the top in one hit, rather than resting for a day at Camps 1, 2, 3 and 4, as with normal expeditions. Our intense work rate was born of necessity: We were already acclimatized to high altitude, and because of our fading energy levels, to stop and rest could mean lost time. I'd have fallen asleep on the spot; Gesman and Mingma, joining me for the push, were tiring as well.

We set out in high spirits, climbing quickly through the valley to Camp 1, spiking our heart rates and shocking our bodies into action. Beneath us, the snow-covered terrain was booby-trapped with hidden crevasses. Above, the lower slopes were notorious for dropping heavy avalanche payloads and rockfall onto unsuspecting climbers. The weather had created still more dangers.

A number of boulders around us were frozen together, and under the day's high sun any thawing ice had the potential to trigger small avalanches. Taking turns as sentries, one of us scanned the ridges above for potential bombardments, while the other two hurried to the nearest point of shelter. If we heard the cry, "Rock!" the group dove for cover. At first, our rapid tactics worked well; our energy levels were high.

"We'll climb this mountain as fast as we can, brothers!" I shouted, excitedly. "When you're panting, you can't sleep!"

By 5 p.m., we were zipping up our summit suits at Camp 1. The expedition parties already on the mountain were into the thick of their respective summit pushes; at 7 p.m., a lot of them were already leaving Camp 4. (On Everest, which has the longest climb in terms of altitude from Camp 4 to peak, mountaineers generally leave at around 9 p.m.) In the fading light, I noticed their head-lamps flickering high above us, which worried me a little. The distance between the high camp and the peak looked challenging.

I knew we'd have to move fast if we were to make the summit in good time. But my optimism began to fade when I noticed Gesman lagging; he'd struggled to keep up with the momentum Mingma and I set as we pulled ourselves along the fixed lines. And though I was feeling strong as we moved toward the peak, the thought of waiting for Gesman to catch up with us was unsettling.

First of all, there was always a risk in carrying a passenger. Our chances of making it away from a mountain as deadly as Kanchenjunga in one piece were low if we were held back from making the summit window—the time in which it's safe to ascend the peak and still turn around safely. Second, it's possible we'd be stranded on the descent, unable to move up or down in the dark if weather conditions deteriorated and we were stuck between camps. We hadn't planned for an overnight stay.

By planning to climb and descend the mountain in one hit, we only carried essential equipment such as oxygen, emergency rope, food, and a few personal items. The plan was to charge onward, fighting to stay awake whenever we paused for a breather.

"Guys, whenever we're partying in Kathmandu, we're happy to dance until six o'clock in the morning," I said. "That's for fun, and we manage it, no problem. But climbing Kanchenjunga is for something rare; we'll all get rewarded, and this might change our lives if we succeed. We don't need to rest."

The trick was to present a psychological reframing of what was sure to be a painful experience. The emotional switch helped us eat up the meters—but physically, we were suffering.

At times, during my then relatively modest portfolio of high-altitude expeditions, it was possible to sense a disaster unfolding on the mountain in much the same way I could often sniff approaching trouble in war. On military tours, the work was mostly familiar; a soldier could remain fairly alert and functional without being fully focused, just as somebody could drive a car while at the same time engaging in conversation. If trouble loomed on the road ahead, it was still possible to maintain enough alertness to react and slow down, or even swerve.

By the same token, a soldier was able to understand that life was about to get ugly simply by observing the behavior of the human traffic bustling around. In some desert outposts, if locals suddenly disappear into nearby doorways and alleys, it was time to switch on: A battle was coming.

As we moved up to Camp 3 and beyond on Kanchenjunga, I experienced that familiar rush of anxiety and excitement. Trouble was brewing. I first sensed it after spotting a climber directly above us as we worked along a steep, icy slope. It took every ounce of strength to maneuver up the line, but we were moving steadily, though Gesman had long faded away in the distance.

The bloke ahead, a Chilean, was struggling. He was moving slowly, and we'd have to overtake him quickly if we wanted to reach the summit in good enough time to turn around and descend safely. I also saw that he was in no shape to finish the climb; even from a distance, he looked exhausted. The smart move was for him to turn around, but he was pressing ahead regardless.

I felt sympathy. Everyone has a meaningful goal when climbing an 8,000er. Some people are experienced alpinists who enjoy bettering themselves. Others have more personal ambitions: Maybe they're raising money for charity. Many people use an expedition to overcome mental health issues like post-traumatic stress disorder, or to celebrate their recovery from a nasty condition such as cancer; others are determined to set a personal record or some grander benchmark.

I'd learned in base camp that the Chilean climber—a man named Rodrigo Vivanco—fell very much into the latter category. Apparently, nobody from his country had ever made it to the top of Kanchenjunga, and yet two Chilean mountaineers were attempting the feat that very day. Rodrigo was working without oxygen; his fellow countryman had gas, and was now a speck above him in the clouds. The realization he would be the second climber from his country must have been psychologically draining, even if he was doing it in a more challenging style.

When we finally met on the line, I noticed Rodrigo's labored movements and tired breathing. He was exhausted.

"Brother, look, it's very late now," I said. "The summit is quite far away, so you need to be very, very cautious about this."

He nodded but seemed determined to push on. "No, I climb. I climb!"

"It's your decision," I said. "But what I'm saying is your pace is very slow, and the summit is still miles away."

It wasn't my place to force Rodrigo. Had he been a member of my expedition party or a paying client, I'd have ordered him down with a guide to safety at base camp. But I could only advise him, and Rodrigo had already brushed off my help. I sensed a moment of looming disaster; my focus sharpened. For a moment, I assessed the smaller details around us.

Physically, Rodrigo was in a bad way. *At what point would he collapse: on the way up, or the way down?*

Were we strong enough to rescue Rodrigo if that happened? *Probably. Gesman's flagging, but between the three of us we can manage it.*

Could we make it to the top of Kanchenjunga first and grab Rodrigo on the way back if necessary? *I'm feeling strong, the summit is in reach, so . . . yeah.*

I was fast learning that the biggest challenge for any climber was self-awareness; it's impossible for anyone to run or hide from themselves, *their truth*, on the mountain. My primary instinct at that point was to turn Rodrigo around. But once he'd announced his decision to press ahead, I switched to my secondary instinct: to concentrate on the mission.

I have to climb 14 mountains in seven months. This is the next one on the list.

My next step was to figure out how.

Fortunately, I understood myself as a person and a mountain climber, *my* truths. I knew it wasn't in me to wait around for Rodrigo, hoping he might revive himself and hurry up. Walking behind somebody as I worked toward my objective, in the hope they might move aside, had never been my *modus operandi*—and the chances that Rodrigo would briefly detach from his rope to let us pass were slim. He was burnt out. Instead, both Mingma and I unclipped from the line. We advanced past the Chilean as quickly as possible, continuing our rapid ascent in the first light of the morning. But climbing around Rodrigo was only the first in what became a series of high-altitude maneuvers.

The mountain was logjammed with people moving up and down the rope. Those heading toward the peak seemed to vibrate with urgency, but the mountaineers descending to the lower camps carried a different energy. Many were exhausted; others looked stressed. Some climbers even seemed to be teetering on the balance point between death and survival, having exhausted themselves on the way to the summit. The worst of them was an Indian climber who had slumped beside a rock with his Sherpa, seemingly unable to move either up or down while facing a terrifying reality. Kanchenjunga had exposed their truths.

WE SUMMITED AT NOON on May 15. Hugging Mingma, I shouted into the clouds and reached into my rucksack—we had photos to take and flags to unpack. The first one carried the Project Possible logo; another had the Special Boat Service badge printed across it.

"This is it," I shouted, repeating the regiment's motto. "By strength and guile, the only one, SBS!"

From our position, the peaks of Everest, Makalu, and Lhotse were in full view: the final three destinations of Phase One. This was the banner day I'd long dreamed of, bright blue skies arching overhead.

Still, time was fading fast. Gesman—finally, thank goodness—joined us 45 minutes later. But when I looked at my watch, I saw that we only had a few hours of daylight left. And who knew what trouble awaited us on the lines below? It was time to begin the long walk home. I was already switched on and ready for trouble, half expecting to carry a broken Rodrigo to safety.

Drama arrived almost immediately. The Indian mountaineer and his guide we'd seen earlier were still stranded 50 meters below us, unable to move and locked in the familiar death spiral of high altitudes: A stronger teammate desperately coaxes an incapacitated climber until, having hung around for too long, both find themselves in an equally perilous state. With no energy to escape, they both die. Here it was again—and now, both climber and guide were stuck to Kanchenjunga.

"What's the problem?" I asked, trying to rouse them. Some horrible attack of altitude sickness appeared to be overwhelming the mountaineer.

The Sherpa shook his head. "It's his oxygen—it's run out. My air has too. Now he can't move down and I can't leave him here, so I'm trying to convince him to come with me. But he thinks the next step will be his last."

A slow-moving car crash was unfolding in front of my eyes.

"We met you here before we got to the summit and you haven't made any progress?"

"No, brother. This man cannot make one step."

I looked down at the climber. "What's your name, buddy?"

"He's called Biplab," mumbled the guide. "He's stopped talking."

I checked him over. Biplab was conscious, thank goodness, but it was hard to tell whether he was suffering from HAPE or HACE. His Sherpa seemed in a bad way too, though he could at least stand and place one foot in front of the other, albeit slowly.

I wasn't going to leave either of them in such a precarious state. They were unable to save themselves, so it was up to Mingma, Gesman, and me to get them both down. Operating quickly was imperative. Some oxygen might be enough to get Biplab on the move, though all of us knew that if he couldn't descend at least to Camp 4, he was probably going to die. Our biggest hurdle looked to be psychological, rather than physical. Biplab was paralyzed by fear.

"We're going to get you home," I shouted, helping him to his feet.

We immediately moved into a CASEVAC setting. Mingma volunteered his oxygen cylinder to Biplab. Because the air was dangerously thin, the shock to his system would prove debilitating over a number of hours. But for now, Mingma could support the slightly more stable Sherpa, who was getting to his feet.

"Let's use our speed," I suggested. "The only way these people get better is if they get down. Oxygen is the biggest medicine for all of us."

I radioed down to base camp for assistance. "We've got two stranded climbers up here and we've given them our gas. We're going to conduct a rescue, but we need some more air. Can somebody from Camp 4 help us?"

My comms crackled. "Yes, we'll help," shouted a voice. "Three Sherpas are coming to you with oxygen."

I moved closer to check on Biplab, asking if he'd like to speak to anyone on the satellite phone. Although time was against us, I knew a shot of positivity could boost him during what was bound to be a long, tough descent.

"My wife," he said.

Soon, the distanced couple were connected. By the sounds of things, his entire family had gathered around one mobile, and Biplab was laughing. He'd located the inspiration crucial to making it off the mountain in one piece. There was a feeling of relief and hope. For a brief moment, I believed we were going to be OK.

But I was wrong.

Mingma and I grabbed Biplab's arms, Gesman held his feet, and we attached him to our safety rope. Together, we started the heavy, painful slog toward Camp 4. But because this was an unexpected rescue operation and we were without our usual kit, we had to improvise. On a rescue of this kind, the casualty would normally have been moved on a stretcher with one person at the front, while the people lifting the back of the stretcher worked as brakes. Any other available bodies chipped in by balancing the casualty and guiding the carriers.

This CASEVAC was very different, though. The terrain was a challenging mix of rock, snow, and ice, and the work was slow; we had to traverse, which required us to be methodical, especially when applying different technical rope skills to our descent. We pulled and lifted, the pair of us struggling under the weight of our semiconscious casualty.

Shortly after starting our rescue, I realized another climber was coming toward us on the line—but he was heading up, rather than down. Was it help? Whoever it was seemed to be working alone, and looked seriously ill equipped for the effort; every movement was labored and simply clinging on to the line appeared to be an incredible strain.

Then I recognized the summit suit. *It was Rodrigo!* He was still moving toward the top, and I experienced a sensation of dread. It was mid-afternoon, and there was no way he'd make it to the peak and descend to safety alone in the darkness.

As he moved closer, I grabbed at him again. "Look, brother, you need to go down now. It's nearly two o'clock."

But Rodrigo was still unwilling to listen. His body might have been failing, but his determination seemed unbreakable.

"No, the summit is very important for me," he shouted.

"Yeah, brother, but if you leave, you can come and summit next year. You are very, very slow, and you'll be dead soon if you don't turn around."

Rodrigo tried to push past me on the line. I recognized the telltale signs of "summit fever," a disorientating condition where someone becomes so obsessed with making it to the top of whichever 8,000er they're climbing that they forget the importance of executing the second part of the mission: getting home. I reckoned Rodrigo was addled by altitude. Without oxygen, his brain was probably unable to process information as readily as a climber working at lower elevations.

In some instances, when the end of a project is in sight, an unflinching desire to finish the job is essential. During the London Marathon, runners commonly collapse 650 feet short of the finish line. Some of them give up, but the majority find a way to get their medal: they stagger, crawl, or lean on another runner for assistance. At sea level an exhausted individual can make that final push; they won't die.

177

But above 8,000 meters, pressing for the finish line is incredibly dangerous, because in marathon terms, reaching the summit is like running 13.1 miles. *There's still another 13.1 to go.* The peak is only the halfway point, and it's very difficult to seek help if trouble arrives.

Rodrigo had made that choice, either through altitude sickness, or with a clear mind; only he would have known. Kanchenjunga's summit was his death-or-glory moment.

I shouted out to him as he moved ahead. "Look, brother, I cannot force you to get down from here now. Please be very, very careful—it's your life."

Then I grabbed the radio and called down to Camp 4, where I knew Rodrigo's expedition operators and camp support were waiting. This was their responsibility, not mine. I'd twice tried my best to talk him out of what was sure to be a suicide mission. Now, it was their turn.

13

IN TIMES
OF CHAOS

We had no time to wait. With Biplab so close to death, we descended from the summit ridge as quickly as we could. Every now and then, our casualty groaned faintly. This was the good news: At least Biplab was still alive. The bad: We'd been forced into hefting him through the peak's rocky field, where the work was roughest; he was taking a number of bruising hits. But we had no other way to transport him effectively.

During my military career, I'd performed a series of CASEVAC drills where I'd learned that speed was of the utmost importance. When transporting a seriously injured soldier to lifesaving medical treatment, a few extra cuts and bruises in transit were considered collateral damage; the alternative was to take extra time and care, during which an injured operator might bleed out. Biplab was in much the same situation, and we had no time for subtlety or tender bedside manners. The elements were also worrying; as the temperature dropped with the sun, the mountain would slowly take our souls.*

Strange things stick with a person during chaotic events. I remember the perfect visibility on Kanchenjunga that day, and the bright blue sky around us. Whenever I took a second to check my surroundings, or the line below, the views resembled a postcard or one of those aerial photos from *National Geographic* magazine. An hour had passed already; our route home was clearly laid out below, with Camp 4 visible in the distance. But taking into account our current speed, I estimated we were approximately six hours away, and I prayed Biplab could hold on for that long. Still, he was only one component in a rapidly deteriorating situation.

How was Gesman holding up? At what point would Mingma feel the effects of altitude sickness? Where was the help?

At around 8,400 meters, as I planned our descent, looking out hopefully for our reinforcements and those promised oxygen cylinders, I noticed another climber slumped in the snow ahead of us. From a distance he seemed OK, his eyes fixed on the moun-

---

* Here's the science. When it comes to CASEVACs in war, medics have what's called a "golden hour"—the time frame in which to get an injured soldier away from the battlefield and to a hospital. Extracting a person in that time gives the wounded a greater chance of survival, though, of course, those odds change according to the severity of the wounds. When it comes to altitude, time is important, but altitude is vital: As soon as you start bringing down a casualty, more air hits their body, and blood flow, breath, and heart rate begin to normalize, helping the vital organs. Not only oxygen is helpful for survival; increasing the barometric pressure—the atmosphere's weight—is imperative too, and like air it decreases at altitude. This is why some climbers have died at high camps, even when they're given oxygen.

tains ahead. Maybe he was taking in the scene? But as I got closer, I recognized the same awful expression of fixed terror I'd seen in Biplab an hour or so earlier.

I shook the man's shoulder. "Hey, are you OK?"

"Yeah, I'm OK," he said, introducing himself as Kuntal, as if it were simply another afternoon on the mountain. But the man's eyes wouldn't meet mine; he seemed hypnotized by the landscape. Then I registered the awful reality: *I think he's snow-blind.*

"Why are you staying here?" I said, checking over his situation. When I looked at Kuntal's oxygen cylinder, it was empty.

"I can't get down. My guide has left me. My team left me, too." He seemed resigned to the end. His voice was eerily calm. "I think I'm gonna die."

I looked at Mingma and Gesman sadly. Was this really happening again? Whatever expedition team was responsible for Kuntal had seemingly decided his climbing days were over and that he couldn't be saved—and now we were forced into making a heavy, morally loaded decision.

Do we leave Kuntal to die, too? Or do we risk the lives of our casualties further by adding another person to the risky rescue operation?

As far as I was concerned, there was little room for debate: On previous missions, I'd been taught to leave no operator behind. The rules may have been different during high-altitude expeditions, but my attitude was hardwired. And it was the reason I used oxygen in the first place.

"Let's get this dude down as well," I said.

I unclipped my mask and placed it around Kuntal's face. Though I'd been working with bottled air throughout our ascent's final stages, my vital organs weren't jolted by the sudden lack of oxygen. It didn't whoosh from my lungs; my heart rate hardly rose. I knew my deterioration at high altitude would be slow, but I trusted my body to weather the storm for a few hours, by which point the rescue team from below might arrive.

I steadied myself further by remembering I'd previously survived on Everest for several hours with HAPE. The fact that I'd recovered quickly gave me hope, but my ever decreasing chances of survival on Kanchenjunga felt unsettling. When I'd saved Seema on Everest, it had only taken me around an hour to get from her original position to Camp 4. But that was because I'd had oxygen.

Six people were attempting to escape Kanchenjunga; three were incapacitated, and the others, while physically mobile, had given away their oxygen. Our descent to Camp 4 was now going to take us a lot longer. I figured that if help didn't arrive soon, one of us might die.

And where were the climbers that were supposed to be helping?

I called down for assistance again. A voice told me not to worry, reassuring me that help was on its way. *Was it the same person?* Through the scratchy radio interference, I couldn't be sure. But when I looked down at Camp 4 in the fading light, I still saw no sign of activity. Perhaps our rescue team was gathering together in a tent to plan their mission. If so, they'd have to move fast, because our resources were dwindling at an alarming rate and we were taking hit after hit.

An hour on from resuming our snail's pace evacuation, Gesman's strength faded. He'd already suffered frostbite on his toes during the rescue of Dr. Chin on Annapurna three weeks earlier, and his feet were prickling and tingling again: a sure sign the cold was taking another gnaw at his flesh. For a moment, I became worried by his behavior, too. When I turned around to check on the group, I noticed that Gesman had yanked away Kuntal's goggles and was jabbing a finger toward his eyes.

Had Kuntal died? Or did Gesman have HACE?

"Brother! What are you doing?"

"He's lying," shouted Gesman, furiously. "The guy can see. Look!"

He pulled back a hand, as if preparing to smack the casualty across the face. Kuntal flinched. Then he flinched again. Apparently Gesman had noticed Kuntal reacting to one or two moments of danger—but how could a blind man hesitate before making a risky step he couldn't see? When I leaned over Kuntal and repeated the same test, he cowered with every poke and prod.

Gesman was right!

I groaned. Had we known that Kuntal was not in fact snow-blind, we could have moved at a faster pace and covered more ground. Now he was helpless, he wasn't thinking straight, and my temper broke. I grabbed Kuntal by the hood of his summit suit and pulled him close.

"What the fuck, man?" I shouted. "We three are risking our lives for you, carrying you like a dead body. And you're pretending to be snow-blind. Why?"

But Kuntal was too weak to answer. Despondently, Gesman grabbed his shoulders, lifted him up, and we continued walking into the shadows falling across the mountain. I didn't have the energy to waste on rage—not with the lives of so many people on the line—and my anger passed quickly.

IT WAS AS IF we'd been abandoned. Nobody seemed to be coming.

I must have radioed down to Camp 4 or base camp more than one hundred times, and with each communication I became increasingly disheartened. But despite my rising frustration, I worked to maintain a sense of calm, convincing myself that assistance *was* on the way. Oxygen *was* coming.

At least 50 people were sleeping in the tents below. Nearly all of them had summited Kanchenjunga that same day, and a rescue party would only take around two hours to reach our position. Among them were experienced alpinists and solo climbers.

Surely out of all those climbers, a small group will feel inclined to help?

With every radio call, the unease increased. Hours passed, our situation became increasingly desperate, and yet the same response was delivered over the radio every time.

"Someone is on their way to help, Nims."

"They're coming."

"Not long now . . ."

But from what I could tell, that someone hadn't even left Camp 4, unless they were stupid enough to climb without a headlamp. No telltale lights were approaching from below.

It was around 8 p.m. Judging by my watch, we'd been working through the rescue mission for several hours. The weather was fairly calm, thank God, but it was bitterly cold. Gesman, Mingma, and I had the skills to survive. But the oxygen we'd given the casualties was worryingly low and morale was fading, due to the lack of support from below.

Kuntal, withering under the stress of altitude sickness, seemed unable to communicate. Biplab was deteriorating, too. Then, as we resumed our trudge, I noticed something different about his body as we lowered him, foot by foot, over rock and ice. His pained groans had stopped; the instinctive, muscular spasms that braced against our every movement were gone.

Biplab was dead.

Desperately I checked his vitals. "Please don't let all this work have been for nothing," I sighed.

But he had no pulse; Biplab wasn't breathing. I even poked him in the eyes, the one action that usually triggers a response in a seriously injured person. But there was no reaction. When I glanced down at his oxygen cylinder, I realized the awful truth. Biplab's air had finally run out, and his body had failed immediately. Because of the rapid physical decline, my guess was that he hadn't been acclimatized properly as he'd moved up and down Kanchenjunga's lower camps in the weeks leading up to his summit push.

"I'm sorry, brother, we did everything we could," I said sadly, pulling his hood down around his eyes.

I looked angrily at the lights of Camp 4. The suggestion that help was on the way had been bullshit, and every request for assistance had been ignored—but why? I felt betrayed.

People are nasty, man, I thought.

The mountain showed me the truth about who, and what, I really was—on both the climb up and on the way down, as I'd worked to keep our small unit alive. I could hold my head high. But the painful reality of people I once respected within the community was also revealed: mountaineers sleeping in their tents as a

185

man died on the line above them. The people who had claimed, over and over, that help was on its way.

Their truth would be impossible to escape.

GESMAN LOOKED at me fearfully. His frostbite had become increasingly painful, and now it seemed as if he could barely walk. He had to go down now, as quickly as possible, without being hampered by our rescue mission. At first he protested, arguing that he wanted to fight with the rest of us. But unless he descended to the lower camps, Mingma and I would likely have another casualty to work with. We couldn't take the risk. Gesman walked off into the darkness as we said our farewells and apologies to Biplab, leaving him to the mountain. Carrying him longer would only slow our escape.

Assessing our situation, I reckoned our position was ordinarily around half an hour from safety—but only if we all were in condition to walk fairly quickly. With two incapacitated individuals to care for, the journey was likely to take a couple painful hours, maybe more. But we had no choice other than to put in the effort. Having descended away from the death zone, nearly a thousand meters in altitude, Biplab's Sherpa was now able to move more freely. Together, Mingma and I pulled and dragged Kuntal, while I cajoled the guide during breaks from our heavy lifting. But Mingma was beginning to struggle, too. He was showing the first signs of altitude sickness, and when we next stopped to catch our breath, I could tell something was wrong.

"Brother, I can't feel my legs, my face, my jaw," he said. "I think I need to go down now. It's probably HACE. You'll have another body to worry about if I stay here with you for too much longer."

Mingma was the strongest Sherpa guide I'd ever known. He wasn't the type to make excuses, or to look for an easy way out. But he was also experienced enough to know when his limits were met, and that to push past them up there would mean certain death. Though I'd be alone on the mountain with a seriously injured climber and a Sherpa, I couldn't stand the thought of losing a team member to the mission.

To make matters worse, word then came on the radio that another climber had been reported missing on the mountain. "If you see him, make sure to bring him down," crackled the voice from base. I stared angrily at the lights flickering in the distance at Camp 4. Still, nobody was moving toward us. Hugging Mingma, I sent him on his way.

"And tell the others down there what's happening," I shouted after him.

What was I doing? Was I really in the best position to conduct this rescue? I was out of oxygen. I'd been on the mountain for more than 24 hours and was physically destroyed, especially after those five grueling days on Dhaulagiri with barely any rest; I estimated I'd had a total of nine hours of sleep in that time. Every muscle begged me to stop. But nevertheless, I dragged at Kuntal's weight for another two hours, the Sherpa helping from time to time, until I arrived at a physical crossroads.

Option one was for me to stay with the rescue party, while hoping that help and oxygen might arrive soon. However, seeing as nobody had stirred from the tents below, the likeliest outcome was our death from cold and lack of air. The second option was to leave Kuntal where he was, moving quickly in a journey that would take me 15 minutes down to Camp 4, where I could beg for a rescue party to save him. I knew enough people would be well rested by the time I made it down; several climbers were certainly powerful enough to execute the mission, despite having summited Kanchenjunga that morning. If I could rouse them, we had a good chance of saving Kuntal and the guide. I was taking option two.

"Listen, this oxygen is about to run low," I said to Biplab's Sherpa. "If Kuntal's anything like Biplab, we'll lose him soon after. But there are people in Camp 4 that I think will listen to me—they'll come to his rescue. Either you can stay here with him, or you can come with me. It's your call."

As I made my descent, the Sherpa tailed me, both of us confident in saving Kuntal's life, when a strange sight appeared. Not 50 yards ahead was an old man wandering aimlessly in the snow. He looked ragged, manic; his beard was matted with ice and he was dressed in a reflective summit suit that pinged away light from our torches like laser beams.

At first, I wondered if the altitude had finally warped my mind. Was HACE kicking in? No. I quickly realized that I was seeing the other missing climber, who I later learned was called Ramesh Ray. And behind him was a reassuring sight: headlamps flickering below us in the distance. A rescue party was on the way. We rushed down to the lost mountaineer, holding him up until the glowing blobs became people, and the people turned into shouting voices.

"This guy needs to go down," I said as we gathered. "You're in a better place to take him than me. And the other guy, Kuntal, is over there."

I pointed to where we'd left our casualty with a small oxygen supply. "He's not far away. Take some air and rescue him."

My mission was done. Biplab may have been lost to the mountain, but at least his guide and Kuntal would soon be safe. I hoped Ramesh Ray was OK as well. Descending into camp around one a.m., I found Mingma and Gesman's tent and crawled inside, pulling a sleeping bag around me for warmth. But resting felt impossible. I was angry at how our calls for help had been ignored. Why were we lied to, over and over, on the radio comms?

The thought of hanging around for too long with those people felt demoralizing, and I knew I'd find it impossible to look any of them in the eye when they woke. I brewed a tea and sat silently until it was time to leave the mountain.

I RUMMAGED THROUGH MY BAG for a pair of fresh socks and packed my kit. I was going to wake Gesman and Mingma, and then I was going to descend to base camp, ignoring waves from passing climbers, avoiding the gaze of anyone who approached me. But first I was going to call Suchi.

Biplab's death had broken me.

I patched a call through to our home in England. Straightaway, she knew something was wrong, because I rarely called her from the mountains. "Nims, what's up?" she asked. I could hear the fear in her voice.

"I've failed," I said, fighting back tears. "I've failed."

I retold the story, my sadness twisting into anger. "The climbers up here were thinking only of themselves. They say they're bad-asses, they boast about how they can climb this mountain and that

189

mountain . . . but where are they now? If one of them had just brought up some air, we would have been fine. He would have lived."

Suchi tried to soothe my distress, but I was too upset to listen. My mood darkened even more after I woke Mingma and Gesman. Rodrigo was dead, too.

During the rescue, stuck between the summit and Camp 4, I couldn't see Kanchenjunga's peak. But word had reached Mingma that, from lower down, the Chilean's headlamp was visible. It had flickered at the top all night, unmoving, until eventually the battery burned out. His body was now another frozen reminder of a bleak 24 hours on the mountain.

At least Kuntal had been rescued and was on his way to a hospital in Kathmandu—or so I believed. While we descended through Kanchenjunga's camps, a helicopter passed overhead. It was flying toward a pickup point higher on the mountain, and I figured Kuntal would be retrieved.

I was relieved, happy our work hadn't been for nothing; I'd been so determined to keep everybody alive. But when I arrived at the bottom of the mountain, I was told that the chopper had only collected Ramesh Ray. From what we could tell from the people around us, Kuntal had been left where we'd positioned him, even though the rescue party had been so close they could have reached him easily.

I felt sick, realizing the poor guy was probably still on the mountain and there was no way he'd survived—not without oxygen. I raged at Mingma and Gesman.

"These people! They take the glory on social media, but they wouldn't do the job on the ground. They disgust me. When the shit hit the fan, where were they? I'll tell you: hiding in their tents!"

War had taught me two things about handling mortality. I understood that soldier die in battles because they are fighting for a cause (much as mountaineers die at high altitude, testing their endurance in an unforgiving environment). But sometimes, death happens in preventable incidents, and men and women working in a war zone are killed by friendly fire.

In the mountains, distressed climbers die because they, or the people around them, are ill equipped to work effectively in deteriorating circumstances. Those situations, to a degree, are painful but understandable; they are usually caused by human error or accidents. But the deaths of Biplab and Kuntal felt totally unacceptable, because their endings had been settled by choice. Somebody could have made an effort to help. *They could have been saved*.

And I still have no idea why the rescue never came.

As far as I was concerned, there were no excuses. In the cases of both Indian climbers, some of the guys sleeping below us could have moved into action if they'd wanted to; they'd been resting for hours. They'd also moved slowly up the mountain, camp by camp, over a few days, whereas I'd barely slept for five straight nights and had then climbed Kanchenjunga in one push. Yet I'd been the one doing the rescuing.

I also knew from my experience in running guided expeditions that putting the lives of paying clients first was imperative, no matter how determined they were to reach the summit. In those situations, my job was to bring them back to reality, or haul them to safety. But it wasn't like that for everyone: The high-altitude mountaineering world, as I was learning the hard way, could be heartless and cruel.

As we flew to Everest Base Camp for the last three peaks in Phase One—Everest, Lhotse, and Makalu—I tried to refocus on the job at hand. Three men were dead, but my primary mission still lay before me.

I had to leave the ghosts of Kanchenjunga behind.

SUMMIT FEVER

The jokes and sarcastic comments about my ambitions were beginning to quiet down a little.

But while my expeditions were gathering more attention on social media, and an increasing number of potential investors were coming forward, I couldn't afford to let down my guard. Though Everest, Lhotse, and Makalu felt like home turf because of my climb a year previously, none of them were to be taken lightly. Every 8,000er was a challenge, and it bothered me that people were becoming dismissive of the world's tallest mountain.

No, Everest wasn't as dangerous as Annapurna, Kanchenjunga, or K2. And yes, a number of not-so-skilled climbers had made it to the top, thanks to the work of the excellent Sherpas assisting them on the way. But it was no easy ride. If the weather was clear and calm, it was possible to reach the peak without too much stress. But if conditions deteriorated at the higher camps and the shit hit the fan? Well, then the chances of survival were slashed dramatically. People died.

In the Everest death trap, expedition parties at base camp had been ripped apart while resting in their tents. Avalanches sometimes roared down the mountain, devastating everything before them, as the tragedies of 2014 and 2015 had shown. Once the climbing started, the treacherous Khumbu Icefall, which divided base camp from Camp 1, was notorious for its fracturing seracs that twitched and moved as the glacier shifted three or four feet a day.

It was beautiful in the Khumbu Icefall, like an alien planet from a science fiction film. But its shimmering terrain was deceptive. A number of climbers had been killed or seriously injured by ice chunks as they sheared from the mountain. And though I loved the drama of climbing through it, the icefall was a sketchy place to be; it was impossible not to feel exposed. And that's before a mountaineer even negotiates the challenges of the peak, like the Hillary Step, and the exhausting climb back down to safety. Everest is no joke.

Yet, despite these risks, the mountain was developing a cushy reputation. By the time I attempted it again during Project Possible, people were complaining that it had become little more than a playground for superrich climbers with little experience on high mountains. The old guard of mountaineers—those who'd scaled Everest 30 or 40 years ago—argued that many climbers relied entirely on their guides and Sherpas and were undeserving of making it to the top.

Other critics pointed to the Nepali government and the fees associated with climbing Everest. Mountain permits were too cheap, they said, and anyone could buy their way in, regardless of skill (although the cost of gaining access was still beyond the reach of most people). A permit to climb the mountain ran about U.S. $10,000 in 2019, and that didn't include gear and provisions, flights and accommodation, or hired guides.

Regardless of expense, there was no debate that Everest was overcrowded. The ledge leading up to the Hillary Step could resemble a city crossing as dozens and dozens of people clogged the fixed lines, either waiting for their moment of glory on the highest point on Earth or attempting to move down the mountain as they tried to descend.

It was a frustrating experience for everyone. By waiting for other climbers to finish ahead of them, some mountaineers were being denied their shot at reaching the summit. Or worse, they were being delayed for so long that their descent felt increasingly precarious as daylight faded. With all the to-ing and fro-ing, a volatile mood at the peak was not uncommon.

My attitude toward the mountaineering politics swirling around Everest was to tune out any negativity as best I could. As far as I was concerned, it was still the highest point on the planet and needed to be respected, though some of the grumblings were legitimate. Overcrowding was definitely a problem, but there were ways around it. If the line toward the summit was congested, a serious climber could always pick another plan—and there were plenty of old routes to be explored or reopened.

I'd noticed that when people failed, if they were unable to top the summit or were forced back by fatigue or altitude sickness, they had a tendency to blame others: their guides, fellow mountaineers, or even the individuals responsible for managing Everest.

That drove me crazy. In life, I was always encouraged to admit to a mistake. If ever I made a misstep on a military operation, I would mention it to my teammates. By shining a light on my failings, I was able to improve, and I would never use the excuse that a mountain was impossible to climb because of traffic. I'd plan and find another route to the top.

A bigger issue, as far as I was concerned, was the Himalaya's deteriorating environmental health. In 2015, the head of Nepal's mountaineering association, Ang Tshering, announced that the human waste left behind by expeditions had the potential to become a major health hazard; given that the mountain had become so popular, the spread of disease was a serious concern. Just as worrying were the impacts of climate change, which had become increasingly obvious and unsettling. Though Nepal was a developing country, it still lacked the resources wealthier countries enjoyed.

The Himalaya were its greatest asset; they brought in huge amounts of money in tourist revenue. The spirit of the Nepali people, humble and kind, added to the country's appeal as well. But as a community, the region was suffering from the effects of global warming; it didn't take a meteorologist to discern the considerably lower levels of snowfall. The mountains now thaw much earlier in the season too, and the increased melt causes floods and mudslides throughout the region.

When I summited Ama Dablam in 2014, scooping up snow from Camp 1 to melt for drinking and cooking was possible. But when I returned in 2018, the snow was nowhere to be seen and we were forced to carry gallons and gallons to the higher camps, adding multiple pounds of weight on our backs. I also noticed similar changes when climbing Dhaulagiri in 2019; when I looked to the peak, the glacier had almost faded away. The sight was heartbreaking.

A year later, as I readied myself for the final three mountains of Phase One, I realized Project Possible now presented me with the platform to speak out on climate change, a position I'd hoped to reach when I first announced my idea. People were now watching my progress. I needed to alert them to the damage being inflicted around the world by posting one or two comments on social media, each one outlining my fears.

At that point, though, I felt like I was screaming into the dark. Although my social media numbers were growing and I'd gathered followers in the tens of thousands, they weren't yet astronomical numbers—nowhere near the hundreds of thousands that would arrive during the mission's latter stages. Despite these figures, however, I was still proving that with a little imagination and some serious effort, people were capable of taking on tasks the larger world couldn't imagine.

I'd climbed my first mountain in 2012, and not seven years later, I was on my way to working through all 14 8,000ers in seven months. I'd proven to everybody that it is never too late to make a massive change in life. And if I could pull off such a project and show the world that a positive mind-set could fuel such far-reaching results, what would that say about the potential for environmental efforts around the planet? As people responded to my comments on climate change, I felt humbled—and emboldened.

Among the voices I was interacting with online were kids, teenagers, and young adults on the verge of making their first big life decisions, such as who to vote for or what career choices to make.

Some of them—the type of people emotionally invested in the future of the Himalaya and the environment—were considering their first mountain climb. I wanted to show them exactly what was happening to the world at high altitude: both the good and the bad.

I'd already decided that my efforts should begin close to home. I insisted our missions be as environmentally friendly as possible; I was the expedition leader, so I had it in my power to instigate change. Everything we took to the mountain we brought back down with us, including oxygen cylinders, which seemed to litter peaks across the Himalaya. When it came to briefing clients before climbs, I always made my position very clear.

"You come here for the love of nature, but if you don't respect it, you've got no place in my expedition," I told them. "If you don't follow the rules, you can take your money and leave." Overall, most people on my climbs turned up with a passion for the environment. Getting them to follow my protocols wasn't too tricky.

The impact of climate change, as I often told people, was universal. For too long, many of us have been guilty of regarding our houses as the only home we have, but that's simply not true. We weren't built for hiding indoors; we're outdoor animals, and the wider environment around our towns and cities is where we should be investing our money and attention—because when the force of nature hits, nothing can stop it. I've seen Nepali villages ripped apart by mudslides and flooding; from a distance, the carnage looked like the aftermath of a bombing raid.

Throughout 2018, California was ravaged by a series of wildfires that scorched nearly two million acres of land; the same environmental catastrophe struck Australia a year later. What was it going to take for people to pay attention? The biggest problem facing humanity at this moment in history is our inability to think long-term. Ours is a crowded planet, and we worry about the days, weeks, and months ahead. But when it comes to contemplating the health of our environment in 20 or 30 years' time, we tend to switch off. Maybe it's too scary to contemplate; it's certainly sobering.

I soon realized the best way to draw attention to our planetary health through Project Possible was to shout about it from the mountaintops. And then, an opportunity to highlight some of the conflicts between nature and man arrived much sooner than expected.

I WAS KEEN TO BREAK my speed world record for climbing Everest, Lhotse, and Makalu. In 2017, I'd gone from the peak of Everest to Lhotse in 10 hours and 15 minutes; by the end of my trip with the G200E team, I'd climbed all three mountains in five days. But on my way to Everest Base Camp for the Project Possible expedition, I decided to try to cut that time by 50 percent. I believed in my mental and physical strength, and although those mountains were giants, I was familiar with their dangers.

Accompanied by Lakpa Dendi—one of the guides who'd helped the Gurkhas during the G200E in 2017—I set off a little later on Everest than some of the other expeditions, climbing on May 22. As we moved over the Hillary Step, dawn cracking the sky above, I noticed the flash of cameras and the flicker of headlamps ahead. A few groups there were moving slowly, tired from climbing so far. We soon stepped past them to reach the summit; the view, after three hours of climbing from Camp 4, was mind-bending.

The morning sun crested the Himalaya, and as other climbers joined us, everyone seemed energized again; the guys who looked spent moments earlier were suddenly full of life. It was as if the new sun had delivered us all a fresh burst of purpose and optimism, even in the freezing cold. *If only I could soak up the light all day.* Then I felt a tugging at my summit suit. It was Lakpa.

"Brother, we should go," he said. "If you want to break that record, we need to turn around now."

I nodded, grabbing a few photographs, and stepped off the peak. But a few yards on, I came to a chaotic scene. A long line was snaking around the thin crest leading away from the Hillary Step. At first I thought a few dozen people edging toward us until I realized the crowd was bigger—much bigger. Around 150 climbers were squeezed onto the fixed line, with the group moving slowly in both directions. We tried to edge down the rope carefully, checking in with each person we passed. But I sensed a growing mood of panic.

Some people were angry. They'd invested a lot of money, time, and effort to scale Everest, and their progress had been stopped dead, like traffic behind a motorway pileup. I feared some climbers were taking serious risks with their lives, plus the safety of those around them, by not making the call to descend before their oxygen became perilously low.

Others worried about what was fast becoming a dangerous situation. One climber complained that his toes and fingers were becoming frostbitten, and the ledge leading from the Hillary Step was an intimidating place for any expedition party to cling to, especially if exposed to the high winds that often whip the mountain above the high camps. Anyone moving along the ridge faced dangers on either side: To the left a 2,400-meter drop; to right, 3,000 meters. A climber falling from that height wasn't coming back.

The people I worried for most were the climbers lost amid the chaos, fearful and emotionally spiraling. I'd often thought that anxiety at high altitude was like a drowning event; in the middle of the ocean, people who think they're about to go under will grab at anything or anyone for buoyancy, even their loved ones. They thrash and panic, often yanking the nearest person down with them in a desperate attempt to survive. Mental breakdowns above 8,000 meters were similar: people flapping and making reckless decisions, often impacting the safety of the climbers around them.

With summit fever and anxiety building among the different groups, I sensed the mood on Mount Everest approaching boiling point. People argued around me; somebody was about to freak out or act recklessly. Several lives had been lost on Everest already that year, and something drastic needed to happen if the body count was to stop growing.

I climbed a small rock ledge overlooking the line of climbers. The scene below was ugly, and when I attempted to guide people as they moved up and down the line, few in the scrum listened. Both lanes of traffic had claimed right-of-way, and neither side wanted to give ground. Collisions were taking place every couple of minutes; a succession of frantic overtaking maneuvers threatened to wobble someone from the safety rope at any moment. At times, quicker climbers descending shouted aggressively at slower ones ahead.

"It takes you half an hour to cover five meters," one climber yelled to another ahead of him who was clearly struggling at the top of the line. "If you let us pass, everything will be clear."

I noticed a Sherpa, conscious of the anarchy, begging his clients to turn around, fearful for their health. Some agreed reluctantly. Others ignored him. It was madness.

I had to exert authority.

I started organizing the congestion, though the problem with adopting such a bold position was the mountain-climbing community: It was packed with alpha males and females, exactly the type of people I'd encountered in the special forces. I'd learned during service that the best way to work with these personalities was to pretend to be bigger and better than all of them. I also knew that in life-or-death situations, where the management of interconnected groups and individuals was the key to success, people involved tended to listen if control was exerted. Nobody wanted to die.

At first, I ushered through climbers who'd been waiting the longest. I was like a traffic policeman, but instead of cars I waved through mountaineers. Some of them were so fatigued they seemed to have forgotten the basic skills required for high-altitude climbing. I checked in with Sherpas guiding clients who were visibly struggling, to see if they could continue. If they couldn't, I suggested the guides send them down.

In the end, I remained below the Hillary Step for close to two hours. With every assessment, I knew any chance of breaking my own world record was diminishing. But once the logjam cleared, about 90 percent of the crowd had either summited with enough time to turn around, or were already winding their way along the ridge and down to Camp 4. It was time for me to make the same move, and heading across to Lhotse was now my primary objective.

If I wanted to break my record for climbing Everest and Lhotse, I figured I was at least three hours behind schedule. Yet I wasn't overly concerned; if I could fight off fatigue and shave an hour or so off my previous time, I'd still fulfill my promise. Lhotse is a steep mountain, though, and as I pulled myself along the fixed line, putting one foot in front of the other, my quads and calves burned. To prevent my muscles from failing, I switched techniques, sidestepping up the mountain like a crab, focusing the strain on the iliotibial bands in my legs.

Lhotse, brutal and beautiful, rose before me. Its couloir, a narrow gully that led to the peak, was lined with black rocks that sparkled in the sunlight. Beyond lurked the massive presence of Everest, standing tall, dressed in cloud, a line of climbers visible as they descended toward Camp 4.

There were also a number of unpleasant reminders of the harsh and unforgiving nature of life at high altitude. I passed at least three corpses along the way, the most unsettling being a man in a bright yellow summit suit, his jaw set askew in a rictus grin. Apparently, he'd been stuck there for years.

When I topped out and turned around in a time of 10 hours and 15 minutes, matching my time from 2017, I kept thinking of the man in the bright yellow suit. *That could be you if you don't take care, brother.* I still had plenty of hard work to do.

After Everest and Lhotse, I climbed Makalu quickly, helicoptering to base camp and resting up for a few hours before moving to the peak with Geljen. The lines had been fixed, the snow was shallow, and we moved fast and light, in 18 hours, reaching the summit on May 24.

Phase One of the mission had been executed. And I'd broken one of the two promised world records: I'd climbed from the summit of Everest to the summits of Lhotse and then Makalu in 48 hours and 30 minutes, smashing my time from 2017.

Annoyingly, my holdup on Everest stopped me from improving on the time taken from the summit of Everest to the summit of Lhotse. But the bigger objective was still in play. Phase One of Project Possible had been smashed in 31 days, and I buzzed at the effort.

Could anybody doubt me now?

15

THE POLITICS OF A MOUNTAIN

T he scene under the Hillary Step was still weighing on me. It had been crazy up there, close to catastrophic. Did people understand what it really took to climb Everest these days? Twenty-four hours earlier, I'd scrolled back to the photo of those waiting climbers. Then I logged on to Facebook and Instagram and uploaded the images, not for one second picturing the political headache to come.

Before long, my shot of 150 climbers, clustered along the thin ridge below the Hillary Step, was pinging around the world. On social media it received click after click, like after like. And although a lot of the attention was focused on the chaos of that morning, the image's quality helped too.

As any high-altitude mountaineer will testify, it's tough to take a half-decent picture above 8,000 meters. Because of altitude's effect on the body and brain, the simple act of taking off gloves, rummaging around in a pocket for a camera, and then pointing and shooting, can be exhausting. If someone wants a portrait, lifting the camera to take a selfie can be challenging in itself, and not a lot of Sherpas are qualified photographers. Unless a climber is fortunate, a lot of shots that come back from death zone expeditions are blurry or out of focus. But I'd gotten lucky.

While waiting to leave Makalu's base camp, with Phase One of Project Possible complete, I scrolled through my laptop, emailing potential investors and sponsors, reminding them that I was on track to complete my mission. Then, a professional photographer friend messaged me with an idea: What if I sold the Everest picture? So many people were commenting on it; plenty of others were sharing it with their mates, and one or two climbers had even asked for a copy. Could this be a clever way to drum up extra funding?

I advertised the print online, offering to sign a limited number of copies, and slapped on a price tag of about U.S. $425. I wasn't entirely sure how much money I could expect to make, but I was keen to make up the shortfall in financing for Phase Two. I needed all the help I could get.

One of the things I'd learned living in Nepal was that Everest makes money—a lot of money. Where there's money, there's politics. And whenever politics is involved, trouble is sure to follow. Apparently, a number of people had registered complaints with the Nepali government about my image from the Hillary Step on social media, and were accusing me of working to give the country a bad name. The truth was that well over one hundred people had approached the mountain at once, all of them hoping to top out during a short weather window of three days.

(Interestingly, some complaints came from people directly or indirectly connected to guiding companies that were rivals to my own. Some of them even asked the government to ban me from climbing in the Himalaya, which would have prevented me from finishing Project Possible.)

When the authorities learned I was hoping to make a little cash from the same photograph, they called me in for a meeting, but the cat was very much out of the bag by then. After I left base camp, the picture gathered 4,000 comments on Instagram and was splashed across newspapers and websites around the world. But an incorrect narrative of what had taken place underneath the Hillary Step was circulating and, in many people's minds, my photo was being mis-construed as a daily event. Suddenly, the public was calling for a cap on the number of climbers allowed onto the mountain.

The backlash was fierce. Certain social media voices seemed skeptical about its authenticity; they claimed I'd created the image to draw attention to the politics surrounding the mountain, the environment, or to hype up my mission. But they hadn't heard my side of the story. Figures in the mountaineering community were reacting angrily, too.

In the *Nepali Times*, a climber and good friend of mine, Karma Tenzing—who summited Everest a week prior to my summit push—explained how the mountain had been quiet during his ascent. He'd also posted a photo of the empty ridgeline, argu-ing, rightly, that my experience had been a once-in-a-season occurrence (though once in a season is too much when the risks were so high).

It "has been portrayed around the world as an everyday event at the summit," he complained, in an article entitled "Most Days, It's Not So Crowded on Mt Everest."

But Karma's anger wasn't aimed at me; he was frustrated by the knee-jerk response of people calling for the number of people climbing Everest to be capped. He later argued on Twitter against restricting access:

Weird seeing non-mountaineers voice opinions about the rush to summit of #Everest. No, don't cap the number of climbers! These are "real" climbers who've paid their dues & are qualified & remain. With only 3–4 clear window days to summit, this will happen every darn year. I feel you should voice yourself only if you've been in the mountains and climbed the deadly Khumbu Icefall trying to avoid any killer falling ice, climbed to Camp 3 with brute jumar strength pulling yourself up for hours and hours and then to Camp 4 where the air has hardly any oxygen. Finally making it to the summit, dead tired after 12 hours of intense climbing (with 3 days of no sleep & non-stop walking) only chocolate bars for nutrition. After that, making it down to Base Camp walking for 2 days calculating every step in case you slip & fall. Only then, I'll hear your opinion.

PS: Even with very little climbers on the 15th and 16th, folks perished in Camp 4 and above. In the end, the climb to the summit ain't a catwalk or easy as in photos. #Stupidity.

I couldn't argue with his position. When I eventually returned to Kathmandu, I was invited to meet with several concerned politicians, including representatives from the Tourism Department. They wanted to know what I'd experienced and why I'd decided to sell my photograph. This annoyed me. The day before, I scanned online for similar pictures, either from that summit push or any other year. There were dozens and dozens. By the time of my appointment, I was feeling slighted. *Why are they picking on me?* I arrived with a PowerPoint presentation on my laptop and a gallery of old images detailing the lines on Everest.

"Is it because I'm trying to do something different?" I asked, when we settled down to talk. "So far, I've been nailing these mountains in the way I said I would. I'm putting the focus back on the Sherpas. Why are you treating me as the enemy? I'm not the first to take this kind of picture. It just so happened mine captured a lot of attention."

I registered one or two nods of understanding around the table. Someone pointed out that complaints had been raised about me selling the photo online. It was their job, they said, to get to the bottom of what was happening on Everest.

"Yes, fine," I said, "but let's get to the point: The line is there. If you're saying it's a bad situation, why don't we do something about it? Are you just going to hide it? Or, now that everybody knows about it, are you going to fix it? This situation can cost people's lives. It's been like this for years, but it doesn't have to be so crazy. Maybe the time to make a change is now."

I worried that their first suggestion when looking to correct the issue of congestion on Everest might involve a financial adjustment. A number of people online had proposed that the overcrowding problem was solvable simply by increasing permit costs. If the price point became much higher, they argued, fewer people would feel inclined to visit Everest. Meanwhile, the government could still make the same yearly profits from those adventurers with the cash to climb. But it still bothered me that certain people in Nepal, and beyond, wanted to reduce Everest to a luxury available only to the very rich.

"Whatever you decide, can you please not increase the cost of climbing Everest?" I said. "A price shouldn't be placed on nature. The mountains are there to be enjoyed by all."

I then explained that although there was an argument for introducing certain restrictions on who could climb and when, they had to be fair. For example, the problem was easily fixed by creating a qualification system. As with Gurkha Selection, the process would be designed to weed out those who could from those who couldn't.

For example, only mountaineers who could prove they'd successfully topped an 8,000er, such as Manaslu or Cho Oyu, could apply for a permit to climb Everest. (Or perhaps they could climb a series of 6,000- and 7,000-meter peaks in Nepal, which would generate more money for the local community.) Adjusting the Everest climbing calendar might help in the future, too.

The problems in 2019 were because the lines on Everest were fixed very late in the mountaineering season, which had created a backlog of climbers waiting to make their summit push. Once the ropes were set, everybody made their ascent from base camp at the same time, creating the traffic jam. Resolving that logistical issue would help to ease congestion.

"How about we fix the lines on Everest a month earlier, in April, when the season starts? So, when people arrive, they can have a full month to pick and choose when they'd like to summit."

The people at the table nodded and told me my suggestions would be taken under consideration. The pressure on them was rising; 11 mountaineers had died on Everest that year already, and a number of new rules would be implemented by the end of 2019. The Tourism Department ultimately asked climbers to prove they'd already scaled at least one 6,500-meter peak in Nepal—which wasn't quite as challenging as my idea, but was at least a start.

Elsewhere, Sherpas working on the mountain needed to prove their experience if they were to guide on Everest, and every climber had to validate good health. Of course, all these proposals had some downsides. Almost every Sherpa would qualify under the new criteria, and health certificates were easily forgeable. But again, they were a step in the right direction.

After all the tragedy I'd experienced in the Himalaya during Phase One, these efforts, although not perfect, were better than nothing.

MUM WASN'T GETTING BETTER. Her heart condition was worsening.

As she rested in the hospital, she received regular updates on Project Possible from Binesh, a friend of the family. He'd come into our orbit when I joined the Gurkhas in 2003, after all the kids had left home and Mum and Dad were on their own. I hadn't known they were struggling with the stresses of day-to-day life in Chitwan until I visited them on leave.

One afternoon I took the local bus with Mum. But when it rumbled into view, I noticed that the carriage was jam-packed: a commuter trip from hell. During busy times, the drivers accepted passengers only if they were traveling for longer distances; it was a way of charging more money. Because our destination that afternoon was only around four miles away, our chances of getting on were slim, and we'd probably have to wait a while for the next bus.

Sure enough, the driver tried to wave us off. "I can't take you," he said.

Undeterred, Mum stepped up to get on, but then a bus conductor shoved her away and slammed the door shut. I couldn't believe it; I lost my temper as the bastards drove off. I ran home in a fury to get my motorbike, bombing through the streets until I caught up with the bus. Pulling in front, I got on board and berated the conductor.

"Never, ever do that to anyone!" I shouted as he cowered in a seat. "Especially not to elderly women." The guy looked terrified.

"I'm not having you do this anymore, Mum," I said, when I finally got home. "I'm going to get a car for you; that way you won't ever have to use the bus again."

This plan had two downsides: The first was that Nepal sometimes charged as much as 288 percent tax on purchased vehicles, which meant I'd have to get a loan from a Kathmandu bank. The second was that neither Mum nor Dad could drive. And so, having bought a car, I employed Binesh to take them grocery shopping whenever they needed food; he also drove them to their friends' houses for get-togethers and dinners. Before long, Binesh was very much a part of our family life, and by 2019, 11 years later, he was charged with caring for my parents while the kids were away working.

As I'd moved through the Himalaya in May, Binesh sat by my mother's hospital bed in Kathmandu and read her newspaper stories of my expeditions and world records. He showed her video clips from Facebook and explained how I'd rescued Dr. Chin. Binesh even told Mum about the tragedy on Kanchenjunga.

Once my meeting with the Tourism Department was done, I visited her in the hospital as much as I could, holding her hand while I retold my stories. After a while, she looked at me and smiled. "It sounds like my son is unstoppable," she said.

Mum knew how important Project Possible was to me, and she'd come to accept my passion, even though some of the risks I took worried her. She also knew that I would do everything in my power to get her and Dad into an apartment together, once my work was done. But seeing her in a hospital bed, attached to wires and blipping machines, was upsetting. Tears streaked her cheeks as we spoke. Mum was everything to me; she'd made me the man I was, and I hated the thought of leaving her behind. For a moment I felt a stab of doubt.

With Mum's poor health, was Project Possible still justifiable?

If I couldn't finish this, what would happen to Suchi and me?

And what would become of my reputation if I didn't deliver on my ambitions?

Mum seemed to sense I was worried. "Nims, you've started this mission now," she said. "So complete it. Our blessings are with you."

I squeezed her hand and promised to return home safely again as soon as I could. And then I remembered.

Quitting was not in the blood.

I MOVED INTO PHASE TWO of Project Possible at the end of June 2019, which would take me to Nanga Parbat, Gasherbrum I and II, K2, and Broad Peak. By then, the conversation surrounding my goals had shifted within the mountaineering community, but only slightly. Yes, a number of people were making encouraging noises about the speed at which I'd climbed all six mountains in the first chunk of the mission. But plenty of others were casting doubt on me, too.

The most common complaint was that Nepal was my home turf; people argued I'd probably understood the local culture and terrain better than climbers from another country, and it had given me an advantage. That was fair enough, I suppose, though it conveniently overlooked the fact that I'd been climbing for only seven years. Others even claimed that Project Possible was only successful because I'd traveled between some base camps by helicopter, whereas in Pakistan the infrastructure for that type of mobility wasn't available.

Yeah, stand by, guys, I thought, feeling a little annoyed. You don't even know . . .

On the other hand, I understood that Pakistan presented a different challenge entirely. It was certainly a more unpredictable region in which to climb. The weather was known for being vicious on K2; across Gasherbrum I and II, huge storms could blow in out of nowhere, bringing whiteout conditions to an otherwise sunny day. The logistical support at base camps across the Karakoram mountain range, such as communications and accommodations, was also less sophisticated than in Nepal. I would have to trek between base camps, rather than taking a helicopter.

Overall, though, my biggest stress when climbing in Pakistan was the threat of my team being wiped out in a terrorist hit on Nanga Parbat. My experience with the people of Pakistan had always been fantastic; they were lovely. But an attack from Taliban forces was a very real concern during the months building up to Project Possible.

The backstory to this issue began on June 22, 2013. That day 16 Taliban fighters, dressed in paramilitary uniform and wielding AK-47s and knives, moved into base camp, dragging 12 climbers from their tents and tying them up with rope. Everyone's passports were confiscated; photos were taken of each captured climber, and their smartphones and laptops were smashed with rocks. Eventually, the group was led to a field outside the camp and executed. Only one man escaped, Chinese mountaineer Zhang Jingchuan, who managed to free himself from his binds as the shooting began.

With rounds ricocheting around him as he fled, Zhang escaped into the dark barefoot. The poor bloke was dressed in only his thermal underwear, but he hid behind a rock, turning hypothermic, until he felt safe enough to crawl back to his tent, rummaging around for a satellite phone and some warm clothes. Around him, 11 people, friends and colleagues, had been massacred. Knowing the terrorists might still be nearby, he moved fast, calling the authorities for help. Later that morning, a military helicopter hovered above base camp and Zhang was rescued.

I'd heard the story while in the special forces, and the atrocity made our fight seem all the more relevant. But when Project Possible rolled around several years later, the very real threat of a Taliban attack during the mission felt unnerving, especially as I'd be operating on their turf in Pakistan. Any fighters could arrive quickly, because it took only a day to trek to the Diamer District of the Gilgit-Baltistan region (where Nanga Parbat could be found) from the nearest towns. By contrast, the Karakoram range, where K2 and Gasherbrum I and II were located, was 10 days away, and getting there required passing through a number of military check-points. I would also be unarmed and unable to defend myself if life got noisy as we waited in base camp.

This wasn't just about me; several others were on the team, and none of them possessed military experience. The other concern was the profile I'd generated while organizing Project Possible. I'd talked openly about my ambitions in my quest for funding, and my social media presence had grown; this had made me a high-level target for any terrorists looking to make a name for themselves. My background in the military was hardly a secret; anyone with an ax to grind about my involvement in the war on terror would find me exposed and vulnerable on Nanga Parbat. I'd have to work carefully.

There was some good news on the funding drive, at least. While planning my climbs in Pakistan, I was painfully aware of what was still needed to complete the mission on schedule. Everything I'd earned so far had gone into Phase One, and I needed a huge cash injection. But luckily, we had a lifeline.

A number of my mates in the special forces had worked alongside Bremont, a British watch company. Following an introduction through a friend, they'd initially offered to give me 14 watch faces as I prepared to leave London for the Himalaya and Phase One. The idea was to take each of them to the summits during Project Possible; ultimately, they would be turned into a unique watch. All the watches would then be auctioned off, with most of the money feeding back into the expedition costs. But by the time I'd completed Phase One, Bremont wanted to increase their involvement.

"We want to sponsor and promote Project Possible and advance you $280,000, interest-free," the company announced.

I was thrilled. I had no other funding on offer at that time, and without financial support, the completion of the project looked unlikely. But with the backing of Bremont, which would also provide publicity for the mission—now to be called Bremont Project Possible—a large chunk of my expeditions in Pakistan could be paid for. With a few more guiding expeditions and another injection of cash from my GoFundMe page, raising the necessary funds for the second phase was within reach. But there was a major catch.

"We'd love to be named as your sponsors before you climb Nanga Parbat," my contact at Bremont said.

I paused. The company's input was invaluable, and announcing its involvement was something I was delighted to do—but only after I'd safely climbed Nanga Parbat. I needed to stay off radar from the Taliban until then.

"Look, because of my military background, I can't take a single risk," I explained. "It only takes one bad dude to say, 'OK, this guy's going; here's $200 to brass him up.' Someone will take that offer up in a heartbeat."

Fortunately, Bremont understood. The last thing anybody wanted was for Project Possible to end in a bloodbath. As it was, Nanga Parbat had its own plans for finishing me off.

16

QUITTING'S NOT IN THE BLOOD

worked hard to bombproof the Nanga Parbat mission.

To confuse any potential terrorist attackers, I booked three different flights into Pakistan throughout July, hoping to cover my tracks. It added a couple grand to the tab, but that was better than being on the wrong end of an ambush or kidnap. I also wasn't publicizing any of my movements on social media until I'd made it away in one piece from the Diamer District.

As a final precaution, I separated myself from our private client, an accomplished mountaineer who paid to top Nanga Parbat alongside the team. I decided she would be safer if she rendezvoused with us at base camp. If something kicked off, I didn't want anybody else to suffer in the blowback.

Even my teammates were forced into a procedural change or two, which included an adjustment to our relaxed attitude in the mountains. During treks, we liked to smash back the booze and play loud music, and we often brought a raucous atmosphere to most base camps where there was very little to do, other than to sleep, eat, and chat. With a small Bluetooth speaker, the Project Possible team was able to transform any dining tent into a club after dark, banging out Nepali pop hits and loud rock music into the early hours of the morning as we passed around bottles of beer and whisky.

The drinking and dancing had first started in Annapurna, and continued after the vicious Dhaulagiri climb; together we kicked back, having survived a life-or-death expedition. As far as team-building exercises went, it was an immediate hit: I noticed that some of the quieter lads opened up about the mission after a few beers. Others found the confidence to talk about their fears at high altitude, or their ambitions once the 14 mountains had been climbed. By partying together, everybody felt more included in the project; we were able to communicate and connect, which created a sense of cohesion. We also had an understanding among the crew that, yeah, we were there to work hard—but we had room to mess around, too. Getting sloppy wasn't an option, though. Whenever we partied through the night, I made sure to wake up earlier than everyone else. I meant business, I demanded excellence, and it was important everybody around me knew it.

At first, that rowdy spirit extended into our arrival in Pakistan. When a van arrived to take us from Islamabad toward Nanga Parbat, the driver's radio was playing. We turned up the volume even louder, singing and shouting as we started our journey into the mountains. But almost immediately, I received a sobering reminder of what we were taking on when the renowned Pakistani mountaineer Muhammad Ali Sadpara called.

Ali had climbed Nanga Parbat a number of times already. He was more than familiar with the region, and I'd asked him to operate as our base camp manager. But hearing the music and singing in the background as we spoke, Ali delivered a stern reminder of our need to be unseen and unheard during the coming week.

"Nims, I've been told about your reputation," he said. "I know you like to party through the night. You drink; you play loud music. But in Pakistan, that won't happen. This is not Nepal. No messing around!"

His warning spooked me a little bit, though he was right: Because of my situation, it was wise to keep a low profile whenever possible. Staying alert was key, too, and as we later started our trek to Nanga Parbat, the team trudged silently through villages at night and past trekking lodges, ever focused. Once at base camp, I drew upon the defensive skills gathered from my military training as the sun went down, remaining switched on, checking in with the tents and the guys who were chatting quietly.

The vibe was eerie. Every now and then I'd watch the horizon for approaching lights, or some sign of any unusual activity. But my sentry patrol was only half the job. Having realized that my position could be compromised by a tweet or Instagram post from one of the other expedition parties waiting at Nanga Parbat, I called together the different team leaders, briefing them about the importance of discretion, especially when tagging people on social media. I couldn't take the risk that a terrorist group in Pakistan might pick up on the info and strike at us.

"The reason I'm working covertly is because of the security issue," I said. "What happened here in 2013 was brutal, and it's not 100 percent safe, even now."

Someone argued that I was overreacting, but I wasn't having it.

"A terrorist cell hoping to reach base camp could probably get here in 24 hours. And if they come, they won't end it with me. So, don't let people know I'm here—*please*."

I was erring on the side of caution because it seemed best not to take the risk, especially when there were plenty of other dangers to stress about. I'd rather die in an avalanche than in an execution.

A **FEW EXPEDITION PARTIES** had taken up residence on Nanga Parbat before our arrival, including climbers from Jordan, Russia, France, and Italy. One or two of them had been busy, and the Jordanians in base camp were claiming to have fixed the lines leading from Camp 2 to Camp 3. Elsewhere, an international team had apparently fixed the lines from Camp 1 to Camp 2, and their climbers had later gone on Twitter, boasting how the ropes had been fully secured. Among the expedition parties, this was widely accepted, and we planned accordingly. (Because we wouldn't have to fix any lines early on, we could perform a load carry of equipment on our way up, with rucksacks weighing around 65 pounds.)

Everybody was accustomed to trusting other climbers on the mountain, and as soon as we settled, I led an acclimatization rotation from base camp toward Camp 1, with a plan to scale the Kinshofer Wall—an intimidating, sheer face of ice and rock negotiated with ice axes—to Camp 2. But after we started our ascent, a heavy weather system closed in around us. The mountain was blanketed by a snowstorm and our luck worsened once we passed Camp 1. The lines set by the international team were nowhere to be found.

The fear that the line had not been fully secured nagged at me. But hoping the ropes were cloaked in the whiteout, we dug furiously through the growing drifts. The fast digging made for heavy work. Meanwhile, the terrain around us was so steep that gathering snow had the potential to avalanche, unloading from above and rushing through the rocks like a lava flow.

It wasn't long before I recognized an all-too-familiar whooshing sound: A huge rush of powder poured in from overhead and smashed everyone sideways. My eyes were on Mingma as he reached around for a sign of buried rope. The white swallowed him up in an instant.

I panicked. *Was I about to lose him?*

Gathering my senses, I crawled through the billowing fog and powder around us, hoping for some indication that he'd survived until, thank goodness, his frame came into view. Mingma had saved himself from a fatal drop off a nearby ledge by forcing his arms into the drifts around him. But his position was precarious. In the chaos, his legs had twisted and his grip on the snow was barely strong enough to hold his weight in place. One wrong move might collapse the powder around him, releasing him for at least a few hundred yards.

Given the slope, it was unlikely Mingma would die in the fall, but he'd definitely suffer a serious injury if he collided with one of the nearby rocks on his way down. Slowly we worked our way toward him. By fixing a couple of ice axes into the snow as makeshift handholds, we were able to give Mingma a firm grip, and he untangled his limbs before climbing his way to safety. Bloody hell, he was lucky to be unhurt.

I'd had enough, and the lines weren't there. So, grabbing our gear, we abandoned our plans to move up the Kinshofer Wall. As the team descended to base camp, I became determined to confront the international crew for having misled me on Twitter. I was furious—sick and tired of people lying to others on the mountain, especially after Kanchenjunga—and this time, the bullshit had thrust my team firmly into the line of fire. I was also annoyed with myself—I'd been too trusting. When I found some of the international climbers, my anger at their phantom lines and Mingma's near-death event intensified. I stormed into their tent.

"Why did you fucking lie?" I shouted. "Why did you say you'd fixed the lines when you hadn't? I nearly lost my most capable guy because of you."

To my surprise, they made no attempt to bluff their way out of it.

"Nims, we're sorry," said one of the group. "The lines are *partly* fixed. We put the word up on Twitter, but maybe it wasn't detailed enough. We didn't expect you guys to be looking at it too."

"Yeah, but it caused me to plan differently. I'd have gone light rather than carrying a superheavy load."

I shook my head. From the sounds of it, they'd made the post to impress their sponsors and followers on social media, and this was a worrying realization. At that point, I realized the only trustworthy people on Nanga Parbat were the guys from Project Possible. But I also understood our summit push wasn't going to be made any easier if I started brawling with everyone else in base camp.

I checked myself; it was the right moment to simmer down. I knew there was no point looking for a scrap when the option of diplomacy remained on the table.

"Listen, brothers, we have to be on the level here," I said, lowering my voice. "From now on we'll only deal with accurate information. To climb this mountain, we need to have a bombproof plan."

Somebody pulled out a bottle of vodka and some canned tuna. A truce was called. As a compromise, I suggested the line-fixing workload be shared between the different teams during our summit push, which was scheduled for the following week on July 3, when the weather conditions were forecast to improve.

Seeing that some ropes had been partly set between Camps 1 and 2, I suggested that the Project Possible team conduct the trail-blazing effort through the freshly laid snow, fixing lines where necessary before resting overnight at Camp 2. Later, if the Jordanians' old rope was still in place from the previous year, the different teams could share the workload as we climbed to Camp 3. From then on, I was happy for the Project Possible team to set the rope to Camp 4 for everybody to use, and then break trail to the top.

The international team nodded in agreement. *We had a plan.* Word was spread to the rest of the teams resting in base camp. The misbehavior had been nipped in the bud—for now.

The following morning, when the climbing began for real, the Project Possible team broke trail across the mountain toward Camp 2, digging out any submerged rope before resting in our tents for the night. We were thankful for the sleep, limited though it was. Handily, the Jordanians proved to be a powerful unit, unafraid of sharing the heavy workload as they led the way to Camp 3 the following day. Some sections of their lines from the previous year were easy to find, but some had been buried under a layer of snow. To climb, we needed to pull the line free—but the powder wasn't too deep, so it made for fairly easy work.

But with our work under way, a couple of the expedition parties seemed unable to stop themselves from bickering. Some people moaned that certain climbers weren't putting in the required effort, or were just following slowly on the line. At least two teams were planning to ski off Nanga Parbat once they'd summited, and they sounded keen to outdo one another. (A French climber had already summited ahead of us, alpine style, and performed the same feat.)

The breaking point, as far as I was concerned, arrived when one experienced mountaineer refused to help with the rope-fixing effort. His excuse? That it was more important to concentrate on flying the drone he'd brought along for a film he was making. I felt pissed off again. Everybody wanted to fly drones and capture exciting film footage; I knew I did. But on expeditions where a series of climbing parties had opted to work together, shirking responsibility was considered bad form. Teamwork and the overall mission took priority over personal agendas.

Though we weren't directly involved, the squabbling was distracting. Throughout my career, I'd enjoyed working in a team, just as everyone around me did; this meant that all of us in the squadron were able to trust one another implicitly. In the military, I understood my priorities: The mission and the group came first. Nobody was going to step over me or take unnecessary risks that might jeopardize the life of my teammates—least of all for personal success.

Nanga Parbat was reemphasizing some of the harder lessons I'd learned on Kanchenjunga. Some people were only out for themselves.

My frustrations with the other teams turned up a notch the following morning after we'd stayed overnight at Camp 3 and broke trail across a steep incline to Camp 4, where the snow was deep and the line-fixing effort proved physically intense. To prepare for our summit push, the expedition parties decided to rest at Camp 4 for a few hours, though there was little chance to sleep. Six people were crammed into one tent, because we'd decided to travel across the mountain with as little equipment as possible.

When the departure time arrived, I heard chattering outside the tent. The other teams had gathered together and were waiting for us to lead yet again, when they could have easily taken the initiative themselves. They were relying on us; they wanted the Project Possible team to break trail for them. For a little while, we stayed inside, wondering if any of them might take on the job, but nobody moved an inch. Once more, it was down to us to lead the way. I was annoyed, but my frustrations increased even further when the intel I'd been given about our final summit push turned out to be a little off the mark.

Some sections of Nanga Parbat, between the lower camps, comprised stretches of hard ice that required climbers to bite into the terrain with crampons while working cautiously along the line—if one had been fixed, that is. Without one, mountaineers might slip and fall, skidding across the mountain like pucks on an ice-hockey rink. If they were lucky, a self-arrest might stop them from picking up too much speed. But on compacted snow and ice, gravity could launch an individual to his or her death.

So tackling ice of that kind without a fixed line was less than ideal. And yet, here we were, approaching the peak of Nanga Parbat, stepping gently across a slippery spur coated in the stuff without a rope, because informants claimed a line wasn't needed from Camp 4 to the summit. That might have been true for previous expeditions, but not for ours.

A few days earlier, I'd been burned by claims regarding the international team's fixed lines. Now I was being burned again, and the slope we were traversing was pitched at a steep angle of around 50 degrees. I should have triple-checked my intelligence. And then triple-checked once more.

When I looked down, the exposure was intense and base camp was visible through the clouds. My heart pounded. My hands felt sweaty. As a group, we decided to sidestep across the icy incline; one misstep might hurtle me past the other teams climbing below, exploding my body on the rock. I looked at the others, who seemed to be moving fairly steadily. Then I called out to Geljen. He had taken on most of the trailblazing between Camps 3 and 4, and when we'd awoken for the summit push that morning, he looked like a dead man—the effort had been that intense. Geljen's face had been pale; he seemed broken.

Surely he was now feeling the fear too?

"Hey bro, is this not a bit sketchy?" I shouted.

Geljen laughed. "Fuck, yeah! It's crazy, Nimsdai. Let's be super-careful."

Knowing it wasn't just me, I exhaled a sigh of relief. But that one tingle of fear caused me to reevaluate our situation. I switched on, kicking my crampons into the mountain, the metal teeth shredding chunks of ice away until a deep foothold appeared. I then gouged out another with my ice ax. And another.

"Guys, kick out a path for the others!" I shouted. "Otherwise someone might take a lethal fall up here."

We carved our way to the very top. Having dug out a visible trail, the team eventually topped out around 10 a.m. on July 3. Some way below us, arguments and angry confrontations were still playing out. But teamwork and shared focus had pushed Project Possible to the top of our first Pakistan 8,000er.

I SWITCHED OFF. Only for a second or two, but it was nearly enough to kill me.

I'd been keen to get to the base camp quickly, resting overnight at Camp 4 before descending early in the morning. Having moved away from the Kinshofer Wall and into the soft powder that had nearly sucked Mingma away a few days earlier, I stepped down carefully, holding on to the line on a super-steep slope of around 60 or 70 degrees—a gradient that should have caused me to take greater care.

Why I became distracted, I don't know. But when a climber from below shouted that I should get off the line, I unclipped my carabiner and stepped back, and then down, without thinking. I guess the guy hadn't wanted any extra tension on the rope, which was unreasonable. But I was happy to give way, seeing as he was caught up in what seemed like a minor meltdown. It was nearly a fatal move.

My previous military analogy for focus involved being able to remain fairly alert and functional without being 100 percent switched on, in the same way that someone is able to drive and talk at the same time. But when unclipping from the line and stepping back, I relaxed momentarily, and my concentration levels dropped. It was a sloppy move—the equivalent of texting from behind the wheel at 90 miles an hour. I skidded backward, landing on my back and banging my head before spinning and sliding down the mountain at a rapidly increasing speed. Yard after yard passed by in a blur as I started falling more and more quickly.

I'd been in sketchy falls before, but I hadn't panicked. During a parachute-training jump with the military, I once pulled at my release cord, only to watch as the chute sailed away. Rather than panicking as I hurtled through the sky, I followed my training and released my reserve. The second canopy billowed open around me, thank goodness.

This was a similar experience, and every second counted. I yanked at the leash holding my ice ax in place, burying the pick into the snow, hoping to slow my speed in a self-arrest. Once I'd come to a stop, it would be possible to walk back to the rope. But the ax wouldn't hold. I'd had a malfunction. It was time to reach for the reserve. I stabbed with the ax again, but the surface was too fluffy and I couldn't pump the brakes.

Now was the time to panic. I was in free fall, and only once I'd spotted a brief glimpse of the rope alongside me did I realize I had a fighting chance of survival. Reaching out, I grabbed hard, pulling myself to a stop. Somehow, miraculously, I hadn't been killed. The fall was bound to launch me off Nanga Parbat, which would have made for a messy end—and all because I'd taken my eyes off the ball for the briefest of moments.

As I clipped myself back onto the line, my legs wobbling a little, and I made a promise to myself—*I'll always concentrate; I'll always get down safely.* As far as mottoes to live by, it was as good as any. I crept down the mountain slowly, repeating the words over and over.

There was no time for celebration. We moved away from Nanga Parbat without much fanfare.

I was lucky to be alive.

17

THROUGH
THE STORM

P roject Possible was teaching me lesson after lesson, both on and off the mountain. At sea level, I was developing my skills as a fund-raiser, one-man PR machine, environmental campaigner, and political mover. Above 8,000 meters, I'd learned more about my true capabilities under pressure: where I could lead and stay calm while managing potential disasters like severe altitude sickness, avalanches, and rescue operations.

I never moaned when the going got tough. Instead, I followed the principles of war and led by example, maintaining team morale through hard effort and positive thinking. That style of work didn't always translate into civilian life, where elemental dangers rarely came into play. But on a mountain, where ever changing weather systems could flip the balance from survival to death, those leadership qualities could make all the difference.

There were occasions when the advance team was setting up our tents at base camp as a nasty weather system blew in. A panicked call would come over the radio: "Nimsdai, it's snowing heavily on the mountain. It's going to be a rough climb!" Rather than wallowing in negativity, I'd make a smart-ass comment to lift the mood. "Come on, bro, what do you think we're getting on a mountain—a bloody heat wave?" I reveled in the challenge of leading my team into battle, across challenging terrain where the weather conditions were often grim. The hard work felt both rewarding and inspirational.

During moments where the burden of leadership seemed too much to handle and I grew tired, I reminded myself of my reputation as a Gurkha, a special forces operator, and a record-breaking climber. That was usually enough to shake away any negativity. Reminding myself of the motivations that had kick-started the project helped me to power through any episodes of extreme tiredness.

But most of all, I had belief. When operating at sea level, I often felt as if I didn't belong, that it wasn't my place. But in the big mountains, I seemed unbreakable. I remembered the stories I'd heard about Muhammad Ali and how, even in his senior years as a fighter, he never considered defeat. Likewise, Usain Bolt during his gold-winning Olympic races.

At the base camp of every mountain, I tried to think the same way, never once imagining that the summit above me might be out of reach. Instead, I told myself it was there to be achieved. *You're going to make this happen,* I would say. *You're the man here.*

To some people, that might sound egotistical, or overly ambitious, or perhaps even dangerous. But it was never about ego; the

234

mission was bigger than that. I wasn't being nonchalant or dismissive of the mountain's power. Rather, I strived to possess a supreme level of belief in my ability and what I was about to do—and that was the most powerful rocket fuel of all.

Now, Gasherbrum I and Gasherbrum II (GI and GII)—the 11th and 13th highest mountains in the world—were next on the Phase Two schedule. We had no time to ease up.

Despite the funding problems plaguing the mission, my goal was to stay focused. Mum and her health concerns in Kathmandu were stresses I had to manage as best I could, as was the extreme fatigue I was experiencing.

But some issues were beyond my control. The journey from Nanga Parbat to Skardu, and then to the shared base camp of GI and GII, was slated to take eight days; the route wound through areas Taliban fighters were known to patrol. It was important that everybody remained on high alert until we reached the Karakoram range. (To cover our tracks further, we camped away from the trekking lodges on the road.)

We had no time to rest. We drove nonstop for 24 hours for the first part of the trip, the entire team and all our gear jammed into a minivan. When a landslide on the road threatened to halt our progress, we unloaded our backpacks and equipment and packed them into another vehicle on the other side. I knew that to rest unnecessarily when a hostile force was in pursuit could be a suicidal move.

Before we'd started walking, we'd hired mules and porters to carry most of our equipment the rest of the way. Time was against us; the mountain season was coming to a close. And following Nanga Parbat, I'd decided I didn't merely want to break the record for climbing the region's five 8,000ers, which was two years. I wanted to destroy it. Now, I'd proclaimed my goal to climb the five tallest mountains in the world in 80 days.

"We can't go at the normal speed," I told the porter. "Let's double up the mules and porters. If we can get to GI in three days, I'll still pay you for the full eight."

He wasn't convinced. "Nims, it doesn't matter if the mules carry 65 or 90 pounds. They always travel at the same speed."

"Give it a go," I said. "You get one chance. I don't want it to affect the mission."

But my request fell on deaf ears. The following morning, as we were about to depart from Askole—the starting point for most treks in the Karakoram region—the porter arrived with the same number of mules, adamant that reinforcements were pointless. On the first night, we waited for four or five hours for our porters to catch up with us as we camped. The same thing happened the following evening. And on the third, I became wound up.

"Fuck this," I snapped. "You know what? You guys are too happy to work in your comfort zones. We need to move faster."

I checked in with Mingma, Geljen, Gesman, and the others. "If we can carry our climbing kit by ourselves, we'll be so much quicker. Are you willing?"

The team nodded; everyone was in agreement. We left camp at 4 a.m. and arrived at the bottom of GI around 5 p.m., covering 34 miles in 13 hours, while carrying a lot more than 75 pounds a person. All of us were exhausted, but unbroken.

Despite the enormous effort it had taken to get there, I felt ready for the Karakoram stretch of the mission, confident we could tackle the tests ahead, but respectful of what I was about to take on. Gasherbrum I, although not carrying the ominous, headline status of K2 or Annapurna, was still a worrying adversary; more than 30 climbers had died there since 1977. It wasn't a mountain to take lightly, especially after I'd come so close to disaster on Nanga Parbat.

I had a funny relationship with fear. The common perception was that Gurkha soldiers never experienced terror or anxiety, but the reality was different. Being afraid was human nature; we had only figured out how to manage its debilitating effects. Rather than allowing negative emotions to paralyze us, we transformed fear into an inspirational energy, a motivator. On other occasions, I used it as a reminder of the primary mission's overall importance and the value of staying calm. "I'm scared because this means something," I'd tell myself.

In war, for example, one role of the special forces was deliberate detention: arresting a wanted and dangerous individual. During those situations, my life was secondary to the operation; capturing the target was our goal. Meanwhile, the pride I felt for the institutions I represented was way bigger than concerns I might have held for my own health or mortality. That attitude silenced any negative thoughts regarding what might happen if someone opened fire on me, or whether I'd lose a limb or two in an IED detonation. The same rang true on the mountain.

I often acknowledged that the odds I might die were high during an expedition, and there was a chance I could seriously hurt myself. But that's as far as I went. I never contemplated how it might happen, or the pain I might experience during my final moments. Instead, I focused on my reputation as a hard-core mountaineer; I recalled the importance of being brave and acting with integrity. Strength and guile could take me anywhere, and with the courage of 10 men I would prevail. If the weather turned bad or the mountain looked primed to avalanche, I used my nerves to focus, mainly by treating the environmental dangers around me in the same way a military unit would work to outwit an enemy. I looked over my resources and assessed the hostiles ahead, then figured out the best tactics to neutralize them.

Having settled in at Gasherbrum I and Gasherbrum II's shared base camp, I focused on how to overcome any traps the mountains might have laid for me. Then, I put aside any bad thoughts from my tumble on Nanga Parbat—and in doing so, another dialogue with the mountains began.

So, come on then—this is you versus me.

Settled in at base camp, I noticed that a storm seemed to be brewing. But it was little worry; my team had the assets to overcome any looming dangers. After all, extreme altitude climbing was a mind game as much as a physical endeavor.

This is yours, Nims. This is where you come alive.

I wasn't being disrespectful. After Kanchenjunga, I'd deliberately adopted a neutral attitude toward the peaks I was about climb. Of course, overconfidence was a dangerous position to take; it can lead to corner cutting and laziness, and I'd received a lesson on trust and intelligence gathering on Nanga Parbat. Trepidation is also dangerous; it causes you to overthink when you need to be in a flow state. So my default setting before any climb was pitched somewhere in the middle: neither fearful nor overly relaxed. But my aim was always to be aggressive: *Whenever I attack a mountain, I attack 100 percent.*

I knew, more than anyone, that nature didn't care about reputation, age, gender, or background. It was equally indifferent to personality: The mountain couldn't give a shit if the people exploring it were nasty or nice. All I could do was to place myself into the right frame of mind; then I'd be able to tackle the challenges above.

Deep powder? *I will break trail like one hundred men.*

Avalanches? *I can mitigate.*

Crazy whiteouts? *Bring it on.*

I needed to make myself a solid force on every mountain, capable of smashing through any obstacle. Then it was go time.

THE AMERICAN WRITER Mark Twain once wrote that if a person's job was to eat a frog, then it was best to take care of business first thing in the morning. But if the work involved eating two frogs, it was best to eat the bigger one first. In other words: *Get the hardest job out of the way.*

As we waited in base camp, a battle plan was set. GII was very much the smaller frog, and we intended to take it at a relatively leisurely pace, resting in some of the lower camps as we climbed. But GI was the bigger, uglier test, so I wanted to take it first with Mingma and Geljen—hopefully, in one hit.

The work was grueling. Nobody had dropped off any air for us in advance, so the team needed to load up with oxygen cylinders, a full mountain kit, equipment, and supplies. But after we set off following two days of rest, it didn't take long to figure out we were still exhausted by our trek from Nanga Parbat. We wandered through a crevasse-scarred gully on the mountain's lower slopes—a longer but less impressive version of the Khumbu Icefall—and our energy levels depleted quickly. Thank goodness, fixed lines would take us all the way up, and I was fairly hopeful of finishing GI in pretty good time.

I'd previously topped Makalu, the world's fifth highest mountain, in 18 hours after climbing Everest and Lhotse and barely sleeping for four or five days. Following a rough expedition on Dhaulagiri, we had scaled Kanchenjunga, the world's third highest, in similar circumstances. I reckoned we had it in us to do the northwest face of Gasherbrum I, at 8,080 meters, in one push. By my estimation, we'd reach the summit around midday.

One of the challenges was the Japanese Couloir, which bordered a steep, 70-degree ridge that divided Camp 2 from the higher camps. Once we'd climbed above it, our job was to pull ourselves to the top, the final stages of which involved a traverse across another sharp incline. The work was damn tough; it took us much longer than expected. By the time we'd negotiated the Japanese Couloir and reached Camp 3, the sun had fallen. We had no way to press on. We needed a new plan.

To forge ahead in the dark was potentially suicidal; we weren't entirely sure of where the summit was, there wasn't a route marker in sight, and we could easily become disorientated figuring the precise route up, even with our GPS technology. Tragedy wasn't hard to envision: One of us could become confused and fall into a crevasse or off a cliff edge.

The more pressing issue was our lack of equipment. Because the plan had been to push toward the summit in one go and we'd failed, we now felt exposed. To complete the expedition in time, we'd need to stay at Camp 3, where we had at least an old, broken tent to crawl into. Once in shelter, we could rest up for a few hours until the time came for our summit push in the morning. But because the team had traveled light, apart from our oxygen cylinders, we had no food between us. And for warmth, we had only our summit suits, plus one sleeping bag.

Our only respite from the biting cold was to huddle together, our body heat saving us from the plummeting temperatures. At 3 a.m., too cold to sleep, we roused ourselves for the summit push. It took 90 minutes for everyone to get the kit together. We were exhausted.

The climb to the top was a desperate slog. We moved up the slope without ropes, perpetually confused as to which way to turn in the dim, early morning light. *Was the peak to the left or the right?* I couldn't tell, but I needed to know for certain we were heading in the right direction. There were too many horror stories of climbers scaling one summit, only to be told after making it back to base camp that they'd reached a false peak. Exhaustion was threatening to overwhelm me with every step, and I didn't want to suffer as a result of a navigational error. So I called to base camp and was patched through to a climber who'd made it to the top a couple of weeks previously.

Following his directions, we found our way to the summit, taking in the sight of GII and Broad Peak in the distance. The three of us trudging, exhausted, to a razor-thin edge of rock that marked our turnaround point, the reality of GI dawning on us. This was a challenging mountain, and despite my promise to be neutral when considering the tests ahead, I'd underestimated it a little.

My first summit pushes at high altitude, such as Dhaulagiri and Everest, were strange experiences where the importance of timing had been cruelly revealed. Occasionally, I'd pushed myself too hard as I climbed, then suffered exhaustion and altitude sickness in the fallout, as had happened on Everest in 2016. I had watched with horror as climbers from other expeditions made their summit pushes too slowly, or too late, and then were unable to descend, due to fatigue and poor judgment. Sometimes those miscalculations were fatal; on other occasions, the climbers were rescued.

Keen not to repeat those same mistakes on my early climbs, I rushed down from the summits of Dhaulagiri and Everest, hoping to stay out of trouble above the high camps, rather than soaking in the views and enjoying the moment. In a way, I didn't understand my true strengths back then. Climbers need to have confidence in their ability—it's everything on the mountains, and mine was not then fully formed.

That changed with experience. While climbing Everest with the Gurkhas in 2017, I stayed at the top for two hours. During Project Possible, I'd spent an hour or so on the summits of Annapurna and Makalu, reveling in my latest achievements and celebrating with the rest of the team. I took pictures and videos, hung flags, and credited the people at home who were helping me along the way. I made time for myself because I knew it was in me to travel all the way down to base camp quickly—maybe in a few hours or so if the conditions allowed. For a lot of people, that same trip might take a stressful eight to 10 hours.

Not that it was easy for us, though. We often climbed down in extreme weather conditions, where the wind threatened to tear us from the mountain and whiteouts dizzied us on precarious inclines; the team rarely crawled home. But experience had changed my attitude: I came to understand the importance of resolution on every mountain. Most of all, though, I made sure to take in the view.

Those top-of-the-world perspectives, where nature could be both beautiful and violent, had power. I remember standing on the summit of Everest for my first time with Pasang. I'd just overcome a dangerous brush with HAPE; my fingers and toes seemed close to snapping in the metallic cold. But the first glimmer of sunlight through the peaks changed everything. Everest's energy shifted from dark to light, death to life, and I knew I'd make it home.

Seeing the Himalaya stretching out before me, the top of GI had a similar effect. Our struggles felt distant, from another lifetime—especially now, with the mountaintops glowing, clouds around them burning away. A new day was kicking off; everything was going to be all right.

Then gravity pulled me out of my comfort zone.

The fear struck me as soon as we began our descent. When I looked down, the ground seemed to rush up at me as the memory of my tumble on Nanga Parbat flashed in my mind. Without a safety line, I suddenly felt vulnerable and exposed. I watched nervously as Geljen and Mingma turned around and began digging their ice axes into the slope, stepping down backward, as if just another routine descent. *But was it?* I wasn't so sure. My legs were wobbling, the adrenaline was racing, and for the first time in the mission I feared for my mortality. Self-doubt hit me like shrapnel.

It would be quite easy to slip here. *Would I die?*

We weren't tethered together. *Why didn't I bring rope?*

If I lost my balance, I'd go into free fall. *Would a self-arrest fail me again?*

These emotions shocked me, but I was vulnerable because I'd forgotten one of my most important rules: I'd underestimated the mountain. The realization was like a slap across the mouth. Another unfamiliar reality was even scarier: My self-confidence was unexpectedly in ribbons. I turned around and drove my crampons into the ice, moving down slowly, cautiously, step by step, my heart racing. Once we'd made it to flatter ground, I felt more at ease and walked confidently to Camp 3, praying the loss of self-belief had only been temporary.

Then I remembered the sporting greats I loved: The mark of a true champion was the way they reacted to a fall or defeat. Muhammad Ali was knocked down in fights before fighting to victory. Usain Bolt had false-started or been beaten in smaller championships before taking gold at the Olympics. My tumble a week earlier could be seen as an equally minor setback; it was unsettling, but with time and work I could put it behind me, especially if I summoned the Gurkha mentality. First, though, I needed to dust myself off and get back in the game.

THERE WAS ALWAYS room for more drama.

As we moved down to Camp 2, checking in with base camp, a message from another expedition pinged my satellite phone.

"Nimsdai! There's a climber called Mathias stuck at Camp 2. Can you call out to him and bring him down?"

I sighed. The time was around 3 p.m. and seeing as we were within touching distance, there was no reason not to help. After locating Mathias, the three of us waited patiently as he gathered his things. Five minutes passed. Then 10. Mathias announced he would be ready in "just a few," and so Geljen pressed down to the next camp, assuming we'd catch up fairly quickly. After a quarter of an hour had passed, we were on the move again. I was freezing cold and exhausted, and the delay had cost us dearly.

From nowhere, a heavy weather system swept in, and within minutes we were swaddled in cloud that dumped a blanket of snow on us. Our visibility was reduced to nothing, and in the confusion I heard a cry. It was Mingma! He'd been sucked into an unseen crevasse. I crawled across to find him, fearing the worst, careful not to plunge into another hidden maw. But when I peered into the hole, Mingma was there, peering back at me. By sheer luck, his bag had snagged on the edge, fixing his body in place. With some careful wriggling, Mingma was able to free his arms, grabbing on to the ice as we lifted him away from trouble. That was now two near-death scrapes he'd survived in as many mountains.

Between my fall on Nanga Parbat and now Mingma's accident on Gasherbrum I, it was as if the mountain gods were trying to swallow us whole. And if Mingma could slip into an unseen crevasse, would Geljen be OK? Without a clear view through the clouds to Camp 1, he might step away from the line and disappear into the mountain. I grabbed my radio and tried to call him, but there was no answer. Then I heard a faint beep and a crackle of static in my rucksack. *Geljen had left his comms behind!*

I took a moment to assess our situation: There was no way up; the route was shrouded in mist. Climbing down wasn't much better, as the snow was too heavy to see through.

At first, the three of us tried digging a hole into the snow with our ice axes. If we could create a break from the growing wind and whiteout conditions, we might stay warm enough by cuddling up close. But as we hacked and chipped away, there wasn't enough room to protect us all. I knew if we hung around much longer, we might die. The time had come to take an even riskier step.

"We're going to have to get back up to Camp 2," I said.

I looked at Mathias. "Is there enough room for us to get into your tent up there?"

He nodded. We had a shot at survival at least, but it was a risky one; Mingma's experience had showed how easy it could be to fall into a crevasse. Cautiously, we climbed back up to Camp 2. Every now and then, I'd radio down to the expeditions below, hopeful that Geljen might have made it down to Camp 1. But nobody had laid eyes on him.

Was Geljen still alive?

I feared the worst. Only after we'd made it above the cloud, beyond the freezing squalls, and squeezed into a tiny two-man tent, did I feel safe. Then my radio beeped and coughed with static.

"Nimsdai! I'm home!"

It was Geljen. He was in one piece and had borrowed a radio from another climber. For a moment, we had room to breathe.

18

THE SAVAGE MOUNTAIN

We endured the night, shivering in the cold for hours. As we climbed down the following morning, my confidence gradually returned. I felt stronger and more comfortable with the extreme exposure. By the time we reached base camp, the worst of the wobbles I'd experienced at the top of GI were behind me, although I guessed I wasn't yet back to 100 percent. My plan was to work hard on bombproofing my emotions through Gasherbrum II, because I'd need every ounce of emotional resilience to survive the more challenging terrain of K2. For now, I had to focus on the primary mission by embracing an age-old military adage: Prepare for the worst, hope for the best.

When I looked up from Camp 1 to GII—a peak considered relatively benign—I steeled myself for a challenge, though I looked forward to climbing at a more traditional pace this time. We weren't planning on climbing it all in one hit. Instead, the team would rest at Camps 2 and 3, like normal people.

As we worked our way up the mountain, GII's moods were calm. We summited on July 18, and from the summit we could see K2, the world's second highest mountain, in the distance. Its sharp peak, curved toward the sky like a shark's tooth, glowed pink in the sunrise.

I'm going to be on top of that. And I'm going to show the world how it's done.

Not everyone shared my optimism, however. As I made my way down GII, I learned that K2 had been in an unforgiving mood. A number of veteran climbers were stalled at base camp, and several expeditions were holding out for a suitable weather window; some had been waiting for months. The Pakistani authorities issued around two hundred climbing permits (including to Sherpas) that year, but almost all of those climbers had packed up and gone home.

I passed several teams trekking away from the mountain as I arrived, many of them stopping to tell us their K2 horror stories. At least two summit attempts had taken place, but on both occasions horrendous conditions beat back the line-fixing teams. They'd only made it past Camp 4 and onto a section called the Bottleneck, a thin couloir positioned below the peak at 8,200 meters above sea level. Meanwhile, a number of ridges along the way were apparently primed to explode with avalanches. Even the Sherpas were in fear of what might happen up there.

When I joined up with the others at base camp, I was pulled aside by Mingma Sherpa, who had serious expertise on the big mountains. He had twice set the lines on K2 in recent years and was regarded as a fearsome climber within the guiding community. This time, though, Mingma had been spooked by the mountain.

"Nimsdai, it's so, *so* dangerous to climb," he said, pulling out his phone to play several minutes of video footage captured from his attempt at the summit a few days earlier. "Take a look . . ."

The clip made for sobering viewing. The snow was chest-deep in some sections, which wasn't going to be a physical issue for me or my team. But every step was loaded with risk. At one point, according to Mingma, the lead climber in the fixing team had been swept away by an avalanche. Luckily, he'd survived, but the video certainly had me worried.

I gathered my team around me. "Tonight, we drink," I said, patting Mingma on the back and sparking a cigarette. "We party hard. And tomorrow we plan."

It was time to prepare for the worst.

THE MISSION was in jeopardy.

As I met with the various expedition parties at base camp and figured out how best to tackle K2, an update arrived regarding my permit request for Shishapangma, the world's 14th highest mountain and the final peak on the project schedule. So far, the problem reaching it was geopolitical. Located in Tibet, it was up to the Chinese government to rule who could climb it and who couldn't. And for the entire mountaineering season of 2019, China had granted no one access to the peak.

I'd hoped they might make some exception, given the scale of my mission, but the news wasn't great. The Chinese Mountaineering

Association (CMA) had turned me down flat, citing a number of safety concerns. Shishapangma was to remain closed, no exceptions. The chances of my climbing the final mountain of Phase Three seemed increasingly unlikely.

It was hard not to feel disheartened. So far, I'd scaled every peak on the schedule in the time and style I'd promised from the outset. The team had proven self-sufficient and effective, and we'd worked with speed. Now, bureaucracy could crush my ambitions.

But I wasn't going to let it derail me. There would be some way of finishing off the job. *There had to be.* For now, though, it was important to absorb the latest intelligence on Tibet and the Chinese permit issues, before boxing it away emotionally. With K2 to deal with, shutting the door on any negative thought became important. The politics and paperwork could wait.

In hindsight, this was the right move. Climbing K2 was a test of both psychological and physical resilience, and there was little room for distractions. Yes, it was a tough mountain to summit and the conditions were often unforgiving. But I believed my team had the psychological minerals to manage the workload, though I feared the news about Shishapangma might knock them off course. Maintaining a positive mood was vital, and despite the increasing levels of fatigue, everyone in the expedition party seemed fired up.

So far, my tactics for the big peaks had been to lead experienced Nepali climbers to the top of mountains they had yet to scale; then they'd have the in-demand credentials to work there in the future. (When climbers tackle an 8,000er for the first time, they always prefer guides who've climbed it before, because they know the route and its dangers.) This was my way of setting them up for the future, while preserving their immediate energy for the good of the overall mission. Once the project was finished, they would be held in high esteem.

I also had to consider how best to tackle K2. Before showing up at base camp, I'd toyed with the idea of first taking on Broad Peak (12th highest mountain in the world); a small expedition party had climbed it a few days previously, and all the trailblazing and line fixing had been completed.

But when I spoke to other climbers at K2, I realized some of them had been waiting for my team to arrive. They wanted to see if we could finish the rope fixing before deciding whether to pack up and go home. That increased the pressure on us. But I liked the idea of helping climbers realize their dream of scaling one of the most dangerous peaks on Earth.

I certainly needed all the experience and manpower I could get. On K2, the weather was set to be horrendous, with high winds and painful cold predicted for the next few days. I understood that failure on K2 would mean I'd have to make a second attempt at it, or more, before climbing Broad Peak—and by that point the Pakistan climbing season would be over.

Time was tight, and I mission-planned accordingly: We had to fix the last lines on the mountain above Camp 4. Meanwhile, I hoped to climb K2 with Gesman and Lakpa Dendi Sherpa, but the mountain's unforgiving nature and dangerous conditions around the peak required a strategy featuring near military precision.

"Guys, this is a risky climb," I said. "The work is going to be rough. My plan is to assess the situation from Camp 4. Gesman and Lakpa Dendi, you're coming with me. If it's too dangerous up there, we'll come down and I'll swap you out. Mingma and Geljen, you'll then fall in behind and we'll go again. I'm going to rotate two guys every time so you can rest, but I'm going to lead this thing from the front. And I'm only giving up when we've made at least six, seven attempts at the top."

There was another pressing issue to deal with. Many of the climbers waiting nervously at base camp were rattled by fear, and some of them appeared beaten already. They'd learned that dangerous weather had held back the South African–born Swiss explorer Mike Horn—known for climbing Gasherbrum I and II, as well as Broad Peak and Makalu, all without oxygen.

Knowing that big-time mountaineers were unable to scale K2 was unsettling the expedition parties still there. Some even wanted to go home, and it didn't help that several people were noticeably freaked out after seeing an avalanche sweep away a line fixer ahead of them. The incident had left scars.

One afternoon, Clara—a woman from the Czech Republic, whom I'd known to be a very strong climber—came to my tent. She was scared.

"Look, Nims, I don't think I can do this. It's too much."

The morale at base camp was clearly broken, and it was up to me to fix it. When I gathered the expedition parties together for a group briefing, I outlined my plan, detailing how I intended to use my guides to help forge a path to the top and that everyone could follow in behind me. Then I tried to lift the group's self-belief. I preferred not to prepare or operate when surrounded by bad energy and pessimism. On K2, I sensed the battle was being lost in the mind—but the climb was within everybody's grasp if they showed enough heart. Positivity was crucial.

Some may wonder why I cared so much about the confidence of other climbers. It would have been easy for me to be selfish; I could have moved over to Broad Peak, climbed there first and returned to K2 later, once the other parties had left. Instead, I wanted to show them the impossible was within reach.

"You've already been up to Camp 4," I said. "You only turned back because there were no fixed lines beyond that, and the conditions were bad. Since then, you've had time to rest. You're strong."

"But it's so tough up there," said one climber.

"Look, brother, don't talk yourself out of it. I've just climbed back-to-back mountains without sleep. In Nepal I made rescue attempts, and then climbed again the next day. You guys haven't had to do that. You're in a much stronger position than I was on Everest, or Dhaulagiri, or Kanchenjunga. We'll lead the way and a day later, you'll summit."

I told them about the U.K. Special Forces Selection process—how around two hundred people put themselves through it every year, knowing that sometimes only five or six people would qualify. "There's always a high risk of failure," I said, "but those two hundred people all started out from a point of positivity. They didn't quit before the first day."

I reminded them that approaching K2 with a negative mind was the fastest route to failure, or death.

"You can rest in the jungle when you're tired and still survive. You can give up in a desert without food or water for a few days and still be rescued; you won't die instantly. But death happens fast on the mountain, and to give up or be halfhearted will only cause you to stop. And to stop is to freeze and die."

I knew the climb would prove hard going, regardless of my enthusiasm for adventure. Beyond the hair-trigger avalanches and screaming gales on the famous Abruzzi Spur route of the mountain—the most popular line to the top—K2 had another booby trap in its armory: the Bottleneck.

At that point on the route I'd have to rely on my oxygen supply, though there were still immediate dangers to negotiate. The Bottleneck bristled with seracs and was pitched at around 55 degrees, requiring a cautious traverse while keeping a watchful eye on precarious seracs overhead.

It was an unnerving approach, but we had no alternative. The Bottleneck was the fastest route to the top, although according to some stats, a worrying percentage of K2's fatalities happened there; in 2008, 11 climbers were killed over two days, most of them in ice avalanches during that particular stretch of the climb.

Timing was also an issue. With the conditions, it was important to hit the Bottleneck at around 1 a.m. during a summit push. In the middle of the night, the terrain is colder and the snow tends to harden, so it is possible to break trail through it without slipping and sliding around. Any later, and most climbers in the Bottleneck find the surfaces softer and trickier to negotiate.

Climbing at that time also offered me a psychological advantage. In the dark, I wouldn't be able to look up at the intimidating seracs above.

We took our time climbing, fixing any damaged anchors, while still determining our route to the top, which was marked by a series of physical and emotional tests. Our backs were weighed down by rope, anchors, and oxygen; between Camps 1 and 2, we had to negotiate the House Chimney, a 100-foot-tall wall of rock, so called because of a "chimney" crack that ran through the middle of it (and because an American mountaineer, Bill House, was the first to climb it in 1938). Luckily, we scaled it fairly easily, making the most of some fixed ropes that dangled from the top.

Later, beyond Camp 2, was the infamous Black Pyramid section of the mountain: an imposing, triangular rock buttress that stretched up for 1,200 feet and required us to scramble over a perilous stretch of rock and ice. We worked slowly, taking our time to avoid a disastrous slip. But my body was feeling weird. I'd started out strong, but as we approached the Shoulder, a glacial hump manageable without the use of fixed ropes, I had a worrying gurgle in my guts. Then another. My bowels were cramping and knotting, and I recognized the warning signs of explosive diarrhea. I prayed the sensation was temporary.

By the time we arrived at Camp 4 at 3 p.m., my stomach had settled a bit. But I knew the situation would be doubly tricky, as we were fixing lines in tough conditions. Above us rose the Bottleneck and the sky-scratching summit of K2; on a good day, we might expect to take six hours to reach the top. The Bottleneck was followed by a short but challenging ice ridge that eventually led to the peak. I'd heard stories of climbers being fatally blasted by high winds near the summit; unable to hold their footing, they were blown off the side of K2 and plunged to their deaths.

I decided it was best to worry about those things when they arrived. For now, my most pressing concern was how to manage the lurching in my stomach. On troublesome expeditions there were always events that couldn't be planned for, no matter the moods of the mountain.

I decided to adjust my thinking, pulling out my camera and grabbing several reconnaissance photos, zooming in to the image to pick out the best route around the Bottleneck. I wanted to find an alternative line, should the well-traveled route prove trickier than expected. My team had gathered around me. We were fully geared up with ice axes, crampons, snow bars, ropes, and ice screws. We were ready. The time had arrived to deliver my war briefing.

"Guys, we are the best climbers from Nepal," I said. "It is time to show the world what we are capable of. Let's get this done."

We pulled on our heavy packs and oxygen masks. Then we started our climb to the top, moving with the energy of a hundred men.

19

A MOUNTAIN MIND

We made our summit push at 9 p.m., eventually reaching the Bottleneck at one in the morning. The adrenaline pulsed through me; I knew the seracs were hanging over us like a toothy jawline. It required only one to crack and crash for all of us to die, or for a chunk of falling ice to shred through our rope, pulling the team down the mountain with a violent yank. Moving slowly across treacherous terrain, I focused my thoughts, ignoring occasional stomach cramps as we advanced up the summit ridge to reach the peak.

At the summit of K2, my heart was full as I braced against the wind. But the buzz of success was strangely fleeting. Having reached the top of one of the world's deadliest mountains on the morning of July 24—a climb that was steeper and riskier than the world's highest—I was reluctant to take in the clear blue skies for too long, or to enjoy the now.

I wanted to get down as soon as possible, because (1) my stomach had been feeling weird for a few days, and I guessed that climbing down might prove as uncomfortable as climbing up; (2) I wanted to hit Broad Peak as quickly as possible on the next expedition; and (3) the sooner I completed the Pakistan phase, the sooner I could deal with the pressing issue of gaining the permits for Shishapangma. There was no room for reflection or emotion this time.

On occasion, my attitude toward climbing a mountain was similar to the psychological position I'd adopted for military operations. In both, I was never sure I'd come back alive, and once a mission was finished, it was often best to leave safely and efficiently. Of course, I was always supported by information: Before military jobs, we worked from the gathered intelligence regarding the enemy, their location, and their capabilities. On climbing expeditions, we relied heavily on our knowledge of the mountain, weather reports, and our equipment. But some factors were forever beyond our control in both scenarios.

In war, unexpected hostiles might be lurking nearby; during climbs, a rockfall might explode from nowhere. Once a team steps into action, the unpredictable becomes a dangerous opponent. The best approach to neutralizing it is to work steadily and methodically, without emotion.

I wasn't a robot, though. I had moments when the Project Possible mission felt overwhelming. Sometimes I even prayed for death, in moments when the very thought of putting one foot in front of the other felt too draining to contemplate.

These events, though rare, usually happened during trailblazing or line-fixing efforts, where I'd become so exhausted after climbing for 20 hours or more that to close my eyes, even for a second or two, caused me to slip into sleep. As my body began dropping to the ground, my brain would jolt, shocking me awake like one of those falling dreams when a person drifts off too quickly, their muscles relaxing all at once, triggering a hypnagogic jerk where the brain imagines the body tumbling from bed or tripping over a step. On some peaks, fighting off the urge to snooze became a never-ending battle.

Sometimes the elements seemed capable of overwhelming me. Climbing through extreme weather conditions with sudden drops in temperature caused my bones and extremities to burn. Hurricane winds whipped up spindrifts that ricocheted off my summit suit. Weirdly, banner-day conditions were sometimes equally demoralizing; on Kanchenjunga, under clear, still skies, every muscle in my body trembled with pain as I struggled to bring those casualties to safety.

Each step felt torturous as I heaved their weight toward Camp 4, and every now and then I briefly imagined the sweet release of an avalanche collapsing above me. Picturing my fall in the whiteout, I felt the eruption sucking me down deeper, a rock or chunk of ice knocking me unconscious. Out cold, I'd suffocate quickly, blissfully free of pain; the suffering would come to an end. Thank goodness, those thoughts were always fleeting.

I've never been someone who grumbles about pain in front of others, or opens up about any emotional hurt I might be experiencing (not too much, anyway). I feel weirdly exposed even writing down these ideas; it's a vulnerable process. But a lot of that strength came from being a soldier, where an alpha-male culture encouraged silent suffering.

The guys I served with rarely grumbled about discomfort or discussed any psychological hurdles they might be overcoming. I followed suit, managing my issues alone during selection. Sometimes Suchi would ask me what it had been like and I'd mumble a vague description. I suppose admitting pain and accepting its reality was part of my job, but doing so would increase my chances of becoming crushed by it. What the U.K. Special Forces required were people who could grin and bear it. So I sucked up the agony and laughed as much as I could.

My combat mentality later helped me to overcome the turbulence of the death zone. For one, I was able to use discomfort in positive ways by turning it into motivational fuel. During rare moments of weakness, where I'd briefly envision turning around, I'd think: *Yeah, but what happens if I give up now?* Sure, quitting would have brought some much needed respite. But the relief would prove temporary, and the longer-lasting pain of giving up would be bloody miserable.

My biggest concern throughout the mission was not finishing, either through weakness or dying. So I used the potential consequences of failure as a way of *not quitting*. I pictured the disappointed people who had once looked to my project for inspiration, or the joking doubters who would inevitably make comments in interviews and call me out online. Imagining their faces fired me up. Most of all, it felt important that I complete the 14 expeditions in one piece. I needed my story to be told truthfully and in full, because my success was not a coincidence.

Then I remembered the financial risks I'd taken. I visualized my parents living together in the not-too-distant future, once my mission was completed, and the love I had for them was enough to inspire positive action. My heart and intentions were pure, and I didn't want failure to sully them. So at my lowest ebbs—such as in the middle of a daylong trailblaze—I forgot about the aching muscles in my legs by simply imagining the burn of humiliation. I was soon able to make another step through the heavy snow, or along the rope, until one step became two, two steps became 10, 10 steps became 100.

No way was I allowing myself to quit, so I also recalled my undefeated record. *I have reached all my objectives, from the Gurkhas to the Special Forces and then at high altitude. Now is not the time to break down.*

In many ways, this was the echo of an old mind trick I'd used in war. When trying to negotiate pain, I often worked to create a bigger, more controllable hurt, one that would shut out the first: replacing an agony that was beyond my control. If my pack felt too heavy, I'd run harder. Any backache I'd been experiencing was soon overshadowed by the jabbing pain in my knees.

On K2, I moved faster to forget the cramps in my bowels. But I also once climbed with a grinding, pounding toothache, the result of a condition called barodontalgia, where the barometric pressure trapped inside a cavity or filling changes with the high altitude. (Some people have complained of fillings popping out during a mountain expedition.)

On that occasion I had no option to turn around—I had a group of clients to lead—so instead, I worked toward locating a second, more uncomfortable pain: one I could turn off if necessary. That day, I climbed nonstop, working for a full 24 hours at a speed that left me fighting for breath. My lungs were tight, and my whole body was in turmoil. But by the time I reached the summit, the throbbing in my gums had been forgotten.

Suffering sometimes creates a weird sense of satisfaction for me. The psychological power of always giving 100 percent, where simply *knowing* I am delivering my all, is enough to drive me on a little bit farther: It creates a sense of pride when seeing a job through to the end.

I remember times throughout Phases One and Two of the mission when the thought of leaving my warm sleeping bag filled me with dread. I knew the temperatures outside would be painfully cold, and the climbing would be hard. But to stay cocooned in relative comfort would have slowed down the mission; I wouldn't be giving 100 percent. The best option was to move quickly and purposefully. Simply unzipping the door and pulling on my crampons helped to motivate me for the next push.

Though a physically small step, this was a huge psychological gesture during an expedition, because it showed desire. In much the same way that making the bed first thing in the morning is a mental cue that a new day is beginning, so the arduous effort required to pull on my boots and crampons was a trigger for the work to come. Self-discipline was my biggest strength during the mission. I was always the first to get up, even when it felt horrendous to do so; at times, I wished someone could encourage *me*. Instead, I had to motivate myself at all times to step away from the relative comfort of my shelter.

Once I was outside, it was far easier to plan for the conditions; to hang back and rely solely on computers or radio communications for an indication of what was going on with the weather felt like a shortcut, and taking shortcuts during expeditions would have suggested to everyone around me that I wasn't fully committed. In turn, one halfhearted effort might have led to countless other halfhearted efforts on the climb.

The knowledge that I was giving 100 percent also served as a motivational factor during the fund-raising drive for the mission. I contacted a number of people who, on paper, were never going to help in a million years. One example was the successful entrepreneur and billionaire Sir Richard Branson: I sent him a handwritten note before the mission started that explained who I was, what I was doing, and why I was doing it. The letter was posted with the assumption that Sir Richard probably receives hundreds of similar requests every week, and that mine was another one to lob in the trash. I even sealed the envelope with wax and stamped an "N" into it with an embosser I'd picked up from a stationery shop. I didn't receive a donation in the end—but knowing that I'd explored all possibilities allowed me to sleep comfortably at night. I was leaving everything on the table; it was important to have zero regrets.

I needed to have balance, though, and I made it my job to practice patience at all times. Because of my desire to achieve so much in so little time, restlessness was an easy trap to fall into— for all of us. The group had been climbing for three months. It was highly unlikely we'd make it into the final phase before autumn, and that was only if Shishapangma was open for us to climb. In the meantime, we had to remain calm. There was no point in rushing at high altitude, or making rash decisions, seeing as we were waiting on events that were out of our control, like those permit applications. Every moment on the mountain was a next-level test, where restlessness might prove fatal.

New challenges were thrown at us every day. I had been going from mountain to mountain in quick succession, so it was important to assess my team, my expedition, and myself constantly. Were we ready? When is the best time for our summit push? Are our bodies too exhausted to climb?

I didn't waste a second. If I was pinned to a position by the weather, I rarely sat back and relaxed. While stuck at a base camp, for example, I worked on figuring out the best ways to tackle the incoming conditions, or I worked on funding the mission. I also used those moments to train or to calm my mind by taking in the environment and scenery. As a result, I often felt at peace while working at high altitude.

Most of all, I learned how to function effectively in unpleasant conditions. Throughout my military life I was trained to survive and succeed in almost any environment—and so I found it easy to work in the mountains. That same mind-set is available to every climber. It is possible for a novice to become accustomed to the harsh realities of life in base camps very quickly; after a few days or a few weeks, surviving even higher up the mountain becomes a habit for a lot of people, especially if they have positivity.

It helped that war had given me a low baseline in terms of personal comfort. As I told Suchi when financing the early stages of the project: I could live in nothing more than a tent for months and still find a way to earn money for the family. I'd previously lived in jungle, mountain, and desert environments for work; anything else felt like a luxury. I was primed to function effectively at high altitude.

As we moved down K2 and readied ourselves for Broad Peak, my mind felt strong. Ten peaks had been ticked off the list. Discomfort was fuel.

THE SECOND PHASE came to a close, and the fantasy of dying pulled on me once more. After resting at K2's base camp for three hours, and meeting with Mingma and Halung, we pressed on to Broad Peak, the 12th highest mountain in the world at 8,051 meters above sea level.

The pressure upon me was building. I'd hoped to top out on Phase Two's final mountain in one day, but more and more challenges were stacking up. We were wrung out, both physically and emotionally, and I was still feeling sick. Worse, my kit had been soaked through on K2. As we prepared at base, I made sure to air out the equipment as best I could. But I had no way of drying my heavy summit suit in such a short period of time.

When we started out for Camp 1, my trousers and coat felt like a sodden, squelchy bear hug. At a much higher altitude, that unpleasant sensation could become potentially dangerous, particularly if the moisture inside my suit turned to ice; I would freeze quickly. So at Camp 1, I took advantage of the high sun and dried out my kit as best I could. The importance of nailing Broad Peak as speedily as possible was becoming increasingly evident to everyone. But the mountain gods had made other plans.

Broad Peak was smothered; a heavy snowfall had landed shortly before our arrival, burying the fixed lines. And though a couple of climbers who'd made it to Camp 4 a couple days earlier had marked a light path, a lot of their footfalls had been filled in; we had to trailblaze a path to the very top.

The burden of heavy work was upon Mingma, Halung Dorchi Sherpa, and me, and as we charged through the powder, my body seemed unable to cope with the workload. Not only was the rope to the summit buried, requiring us to yank it up through a few feet of snow, but we were also having to lift our knees high, over and over, for any forward momentum.

My breathing was labored. The energy levels I'd once carried in reserve were depleted, and my guts still rumbled like a blocked drain. Every now and then, I'd steady myself against the stomach cramps until I couldn't ignore them anymore. Nature was finally taking over.

Oh no, I thought, looking around desperately for somewhere to unload. But my current position was too dangerous, and taking a dump at high altitude was no joke. Perching on a steep slope, with or without rope, while fumbling around with the zippers and Velcro of a summit suit in subzero temperatures, was an awkward situation; I'd be exposed and likely to fall in the most undesirable circumstances. So I pushed ahead in agony until I noticed the mountain leveling off above me, around 650 feet in the distance.

This is my chance, I thought as I charged ahead, my lungs burning.

The climb seemed to be never-ending, but the pain in my legs and chest overwhelmed the churning in my guts, until finally I was able to locate a spot where I could hold myself without too much effort. I unzipped my suit and dealt with a very unpleasant level of personal hygiene.

Physically, I felt near failure. Realizing that a record-breaking time for finishing the Pakistan 8,000ers was within reach, I leaned heavily into the mountain mind; I closed down the pain in my cramping stomach by striding forcefully to the top, stage by stage. By the time we'd made it to 7,850 meters, the effort was finally taking its toll, and my back and legs were buckling. Although the discomfort in my guts was fading, I was exhausted. Slumped in the snow, extreme pain flooded my muscles and bones. Whenever I coughed, the taste of blood clung to my tongue—a sign the high altitude was impacting my body.

Broad Peak had worn me down, but with our morale in a precarious state, it felt wise to outline a clear plan of action; not explaining the situation, as obvious as it might seem, could sometimes give a team a misjudged set of priorities or expectations. The bottom line was this: The route to the top of Broad Peak was difficult and required us to climb a steep couloir to the ridgeline. From there, we could work our way over to the true peak, hitting the very top at sunrise.

"Guys, we're all beat up," I said. "The conditions up here are tough, so we should rest a bit, regroup, and then work really hard to the top."

In my condition, this was set to be one of the more grueling events of the mission's second phase. But we were on the move again a few hours later, oxygen masks strapped across our faces. Having climbed to around 8,000 meters, my breathing felt increasingly labored, and when I checked in with Mingma and Halung, they confirmed that, yeah, the workload seemed even more challenging than usual. Halung had trailed behind us for some time, and had been unable to help with our efforts as we climbed.

At first, I attributed our combined slump to the physical fallout from K2. But the decline in energy was still alarming, and when I checked our oxygen cylinders, the awful truth about our slowing pace was revealed. *We were out of air!* Even worse, the fixed lines had finished, so we would need to traverse the last 50 meters or so to Broad Peak's summit as quickly as we could, alpine style. I'd been presented with one of those life-or-death decisions that were so common during combat, where evaluation and decision-making would prove key.

Option one: Retreat by returning to Camp 3, where we could gather some extra oxygen and push for the summit a day later, though a system of bad weather was due to rush in.

Option two: Get the job done, without a visible route to follow while relying on our GPS system to steer us onward and keep us clear from a nasty fall off the mountain.

Option two it was, then.

We walked across the mountain's ridgeline, carefully kicking in our steps, working toward what looked like Broad Peak's highest point. But once we arrived, another, higher promontory emerged through the clouds ahead. And another. Managing the emotional highs and lows under intense exhaustion was challenging enough. But now, in the gathering clouds, navigating with our GPS was becoming impossible.

Though the worst of the weather wasn't upon us yet, it was still bitterly cold and windy—we were shrouded in thick cloud, and barely able to see in front of our faces. Considering that none of us had climbed Broad Peak before, we weren't entirely sure which way to go. (And for exactly these reasons, mountain climbers like to work with experienced guides.) Only by communicating with our radio contacts in base camp, Kathmandu, and London—all of whom were linked up to another GPS to track our location—were we able to get a steer on our exact position. Voices in the clouds told us to move left, right, or forward.

The work rarely eased up; we were at our limits. Extreme fatigue gripped us all, and as we became increasingly disoriented, our lives were very much on the line. One of us could easily take a fatal misstep or make a stupid decision. Like those confused climbers I'd heard about prone to hallucinations or delirium in the death zone, we'd been exposed. At one point, I looked down and realized we'd been climbing alpine style for some time, having forgotten to connect ourselves to a rope*—a critical priority for high-altitude safety.

Disconnected from one another, I knew that if Mingma, Halung, or I slipped, we would have little chance of arresting a fall; a horrific slide from the mountain into a sheer drop below would follow. But if we were all linked, the combined weight and effort of the group might help to slam on the brakes. Our oversight was due to extreme tiredness. I pulled out a length of line and lashed everybody together.

Although I liked to carry the bare minimum equipment and supplies during a summit push, Mingma often traveled with one or two luxuries. During a short rest, I noticed him rummaging through his rucksack until he pulled out a packet of Korean coffee. Tearing it open, he tipped the ground beans into his mouth, gesturing that we all do the same. The powder was bitter and sticky; we coughed on the acrid taste. But a caffeine kick was soon working through our system.

Before long, Broad Peak's summit flag appeared in the distance. We hung around for as little time as we could, laughing bleakly at how the mountain had nearly killed us, and taking only a couple of pictures before descending again. We felt little joy. I couldn't wait to get down, and the team had been angered. It felt as if Broad

---

* When climbing this way, if one of the team slips and falls, the others on the line hit the ground and dig their ice axes into the snow and ice, preventing anyone from sliding off the mountain.

Peak had defeated us, even though we'd reached the top in tricky circumstances.

Mingma and Halung opted to sleep at Camp 3 for a few hours. But fogged with exhaustion and eager to get home, I continued down, wandering into a layer of thick cloud. *Big mistake.* I was soon confused, unable to locate the fixed line that led to the bottom of Broad Peak. At one point, I found myself perilously close to the edge of a sheer drop. I cursed my luck and poor judgment. Why do you do these things? I thought. My damp summit suit was freezing; I was cold and unable to focus on the terrain ahead. And what I really wanted to do was sleep. Suddenly, surrendering seemed like a viable option.

If I died here, then all of this pain would end.

It had happened again. I was being overwhelmed by the effort, but I wasn't beaten. Before any military operation, I found that a sure sign of approaching failure was to enter it believing defeat was in the cards. The only way to succeed was through positive thought.

I needed to kick-start my revival.

Turning my thinking around, I found fuel: I saw myself a year down the line, fuming at my inability to pull through at the end. I thought of the people who had put their faith in me, the friends I had made along the way. And most of all, I considered Suchi and the family. *They needed me to get back.* Finally, I envisioned the finish line, my ascent on Shishapangma and the reception in Kathmandu as the world learned of my successes. The fog of despair was lifting.

Make it happen. You can't give up here.

With the sun rising higher, it didn't take long to figure out that somehow I'd moved away from our earlier route. Our ascent had taken place mainly in cloud and at night, and we'd followed the fixed lines up to Camp 4 for much of it; we'd only found ourselves in trouble after hitting the ridgeline. When the satellite technology proved too problematic, our radio comms had then guided us to the top.

Thinking that I'd be able make it down by sight alone, especially in such thick cloud, while exhausted, was an error. I needed to reconnect with the ridgeline somehow; by doing so, I hoped to locate the fixed line, and from there I'd be able to switch into auto-pilot. I had only to look out for some visual cue. I scanned the horizon for footfalls in the snow. And there, a hundred or so meters above me, was a barely visible path, gouged into the powder by our earlier trailblaze, the prints shadowing a length of rope.

I turned around, using all my strength to go up, then to go down again, all the way visualizing the spoils of success and the fury of failure.

20

THE PEOPLE'S PROJECT

A s I worked my way back from Broad Peak to home in Nepal, the obstacles in my path seemed to grow in size and stature. I decided to knock them down one by one. The big issue was Shishapangma. The Chinese and Tibetan authorities were still denying the paperwork required to climb it, which left the mission schedule in chaos. Finding a solution required me to hustle, but despite my reluctance to admit defeat, I also needed a Plan B—a fallback option that might replicate the effort required to climb a 14th peak.

I thought about climbing one of the other 8,000ers again—maybe Everest, Annapurna, or K2. In the end, I decided that if worst came to worst, I should repeat Dhaulagiri. The climb was gnarly, and it had also been my first 8,000-meter expedition. I also penciled in Everest as a bonus mission. Fifteen death zone peaks in seven months wasn't quite the original objective, but it might help silence any trolls throwing shade on my achievements in the weeks and months to come.

In the meantime, more world records had been broken: I'd finished the Pakistan 8,000ers in 23 days; I'd climbed the world's five tallest mountains (Everest, K2, Kanchenjunga, Lhotse, Makalu) in 70 days (when I initially planned to do it in 80). But I understood that failure to complete the ultimate mission would result in some level of pushback.

My other plan for climbing Shishapangma was to find an alternative route into Tibet. If sneaking across the border via some backdoor route were viable, we might be able to scale the mountain without alerting the authorities. I checked the map. Accessing Shishapangma by trekking from the Nepali side into Tibet was certainly an option, but also loaded with risk.

The authorities were sure to be tracking my activities on social media. My project had become a highly publicized endeavor, with followers acutely aware of the limited time frame available to me. Border patrol soldiers could be ready for my arrival; I wasn't so keen on being apprehended, nor did I want to cause a diplomatic incident. A captured, ex-special forces operator was likely to receive some interesting questions after trespassing into Chinese territory. Meanwhile, the risk to my teammates would be just as high, and I didn't want their safety jeopardized for my cause. Getting into Shishapangma was a job I needed to do alone.

In the end, I temporarily shelved the idea. My best hope was to find some way of convincing the Chinese and Tibetan authorities to reverse their decision. If I could apply a little political pressure, I might have a chance to score a permit (though I knew it was pointless to use the U.K.'s diplomatic channels, because the relationship between the two nations was, at best, frosty). I was better off approaching the authorities via a Nepali conduit; Nepal bordered China, and the two countries enjoyed a friendlier understanding.

Besides, my mission wasn't about representing one nation or any single entity. I wasn't climbing the 8,000ers to boost the achievements of Great Britain or Nepal. Nor was I trying to enhance the profile of the U.K. Special Forces or the Gurkha regiment (though it had an undeniably knock-on effect). My goals went beyond culture or caste, regiment or country. I was representing the efforts of the human race.

I called friends in Nepal and pulled every string I could; I contacted everyone I knew with influence to arrange meetings with anyone with the power to help. To my relief, appointments were made with a number of government ministers, including the home secretary, the Minister for Tourism, the Tourism Board, the Nepal Mountaineering Association, and the Ministry of Defence. Eventually, I was granted an audience with the former Nepali prime minister Madhav Kumar Nepal, a politician with considerable links to the Chinese government. This was my chance.

When I was ushered into his office, I didn't feel awed by his stature; my previous career taught me the protocols of meeting people in authority. I understood the finer details of respect, the importance of civility and cultural integration. I also appreciated the value of people's time. Mr. Kumar was a busy man, and I had a limited window to present my motivations for completing the project. I sensed he didn't have much room for small talk or niceties.

I briefly summarized my motives behind the 14 expeditions,

first telling Mr. Kumar about my work enhancing the reputation of the Nepali climbing community. Then, I explained my attempts to raise awareness of environmental issues affecting the 8,000-meter peaks.

"Isn't this an expedition the Nepali people can unite behind?"

Mr. Kumar nodded silently. Was this going well, or badly? I couldn't tell.

"I also want this to be an inspiring story for generations of people, no matter where they come from. This endeavor is for mankind. That's why I'm working so hard, every day, to push the story out. Mr. Kumar, I want to prove the power of imagination. People have laughed at me and made jokes. But I'm still going strong. If I can get that Chinese permit, nothing will stop me from finishing what I've started."

Mr. Kumar was smiling now. "Nims, let me make some phone calls," he said. "I can't promise the Chinese will issue you the paperwork, but I'll see what I can do."

We shook hands. I felt positive. I had a hunch that if someone with the profile of a former Nepali prime minister backed my cause, then the Tibetan and Chinese authorities might soften their attitude.

And I needed all the positive PR I could get. At that time, few people outside of the mountain-climbing community or my social media bubble were paying attention to what I'd achieved so far. In terms of newspapers and magazines, radio or TV shows, my efforts had passed with frustratingly little fanfare.

How would things have been different if I was from America, Great Britain, or France? I suspected every outlet in the world would have noticed my effort. But I was a realist; the media companies with the biggest global reach were mainly owned by Westerners. The story of a climber from Chitwan and his attempts to scale the world's tallest mountains in record-breaking time didn't have the same impact as a mountaineer from New York, Manchester, or Paris doing the same. Though I was technically a British citizen, my nationality kept me under the radar.

And yet the mission was gathering momentum. My social media followers grew every day, and more people were commenting on my photos and video clips—particularly once my dramatic picture of the Hillary Step went viral in May (though annoyingly, many media outlets that ignored my attempts to scale the 14 8,000ers had conveniently forgotten to credit my work when using the photograph).

Having left the military with nothing in the way of public relations experience, I'd somehow developed a knack for gathering hundreds of thousands of followers. Although this was mind-blowing on a personal level, it wasn't enough to translate into huge expedition funds. Still, the messages I received were inspirational: Kids mailed me to say they'd written a story on the successful expeditions so far and drew pictures of my team in action. Others commented on my photos or promised to organize an environmental awareness program at school. A few more donations trickled in, too.

My project was fast becoming the people's project.

TIME WAS ON MY SIDE, at least. I had all of August to fund the final phase and landed a branding deal with Osprey, a prominent backpack manufacturer, along with the IT company Silxo. The two covered nearly 75 percent of Phase Three's logistical costs, and a little extra money was raised during an awareness drive for my work at the Nepali Mela U.K. This was a big deal; a *mela* is a festival attended by the Nepali community living in the U.K.

Yet my heart sank when an appearance was proposed. Working at the mela required me to move from stall to stall, each celebrating a different aspect of Nepali culture, while being introduced to various people of influence. Then I'd have to ask for money. The embarrassment was huge: I'd never begged for anything in my life, and the idea dented my pride. I was an elite soldier, and going from person to person appealing for support and donations felt like a step too far.

This is not for me, I thought sadly.

But what other option did I have? The very idea of my expedition had been alien and unfamiliar from the outset; it made perfect sense that the funding process would seem alien and unfamiliar, too. I turned my attitude around.

Yeah, Nims, you're embarrassed. But that's your ego talking, which is nothing. Think of the endgame here. This isn't about how you feel. It's for the human race.

I moved through the stalls, shaking hands, making contacts and taking donations of 5, 10, and 15 British pounds until I was exhausted. Though my pride was dented, I also felt relief in knowing I'd given 100 percent, as I'd done with those letters to Richard Branson and a list of other business types, even though nobody had responded.

The strain was building, though. For much of the year I'd managed the project while dealing with booking agencies, mountain-climbing associations, and now the Chinese and Tibetan authorities. Planning the logistics for the three final climbs—Manaslu, Cho Oyu, and Shishapangma—was taking its toll on me. Though Suchi helped with some administrative details, I was essentially working alone; at times, the paperwork and planning felt as stressful as my summit push on Broad Peak, or a night spent rescuing climbers on Kanchenjunga. I was emotionally drained.

Then Mum fell sick again.

Her condition was worsening. Throughout the mission, her spirit had inspired me; it urged me onward in turbulent moments, and I was determined to see out the 14 mountains with her in my heart.

But I was in a difficult position. After climbing the 14 8,000ers, I'd be free to work on other moneymaking projects and bring my parents together in Kathmandu. Now, time was against me—that was becoming more obvious by the week. Mum was hospitalized yet again, and according to the doctor, her chances of making it through another heart operation were slim.

"Ninety-nine percent of people who have had this procedure at her age have died," said the surgeon.

She was placed on a ventilator and, fearing the worst, I called my family to Nepal. My brothers were living in England, and my sister, Anita, flew from Australia. There was a very real chance we might have to say goodbye to Mum.

Although we hadn't always seen eye to eye about my personal ambitions, my family was everything to me. Before starting the first mission phase, I'd had a tattoo of all 14 8,000ers etched into my back. Beginning at the top of my spine, the promontories of each mountain were spread across my shoulder blades in an epic tapestry. The tattoo was a statement of everything I hoped to achieve, and during its painful creation, the DNA of my parents and siblings, and Suchi, was mixed in with the inks. I wanted to carry everybody along with me for the journey, to places they would ordinarily never be able to experience for themselves.

My parents were both in their 70s and immobile; there was no chance either of them were going to see the Himalaya range spreading out beneath them from the top of Mount Everest. Nor were they going to experience the Dutch Rib on Annapurna, or K2's Bottleneck. Neither Suchi nor my siblings had shown any desire to climb with me either. But I wanted to take them to some of the world's most beautiful and inhospitable places—spiritually, at least. They were joining me on a journey of the soul.

I had another reason for having their DNA imprinted with my own: It acted as a sobering reminder, a voice of reason. The margins between making the right and wrong call in the mountains are fractional. I might take a risk and injure myself or a member of my team. At times, summit fever could cause me to push myself too hard, breaking the thin line between bravery and stupidity. By having my family on my back, I was constantly reminded of the people I was fighting for.

If I ever felt like taking a chance, I remembered Mum and Dad: They needed me to care for them when my work was done. I recalled how my brothers had sent me to boarding school with their Gurkha wages. I owed my family everything; all that I'd achieved so far was for them.

Mum understood that she was my inspiration. She seemed to be hanging on to life, knowing her death could shatter the dream of completing the 14 mountains.

In Hinduism, when a parent dies, the family embarks on 13 days of grieving, during which they mourn alone. Emotions are expressed freely, so that those left behind can get on with their lives and heal the huge sense of loss; the energy of mourning is turned into something productive.

If Mum passed, I'd have to lock myself away from everyone else to process, eating only once a day—and even then, I would only be allowed to eat a few vegetables. Although I wasn't a religious person, Mum was. I'd happily perform the ritual for her memory, even if it meant shutting down the last three expeditions.

But she was much stronger than we expected. Having undergone an invasive heart operation, she pulled through.

As I sat by Mum's bedside, holding her hand, I explained my plans for the coming month.

"I have only the three mountains to climb," I said. "Let me go do this."

She nodded and smiled. But she didn't have to say anything; I knew Mum was on my side. She always had been.

21

EPIC

Finally, progress.

After a full month of paperwork and politicking, my plan was to press ahead with Phase Three as best I could, first by climbing Manaslu and then by bouncing into Tibet shortly afterward for Cho Oyu. Meanwhile, the Chinese and Tibetan authorities were apparently warming to the idea of granting me an all-important Shishapangma permit.

Because nothing had been confirmed, I was hesitant to put too much faith in the news. So rather than taking my foot off the gas, I maintained a small campaign of public pressure, encouraging friends and social media followers to bombard both governments with emails and letters pleading with them to open the mountain.

Until that moment arrived, I focused my attention on Manaslu, where I would need to take extra care, given that I was leading a party of clients. A Nepali 8,000er with a high kill rate, it was ranked highly on the world's deadliest list.

Worrying about alarming statistics wasn't my job, but once the first rotation cycles for acclimatization up to Camp 2 started, I began to feel a little overwhelmed. I was so close to finishing the mission, but at the same time everything seemed off-kilter.

I was weighed down by the realities of Mum's health. The strain of completing the last mountains in the time I'd promised was a burden, too. And what about the financial implications of my career choices—no immediate pension, no security?

Not that I was going to let on to anyone about the true depth of my hurt. Whenever other climbers on Manaslu asked about the workload, or mentioned some of the adventures I'd experienced so far, I held back from discussing the mental obstacles. As ever, I chose not to acknowledge my pain.

That attitude, although undeniably pressurized, would stand me in good stead. After a week or so at Manaslu, a rumor spread through base camp: Cho Oyu was closing down for the season earlier than expected, and for some reason, the Chinese authorities had decided to evacuate the mountain by October 1. *Shit!* There were only two weeks left in September, and I had no choice but to interrupt my Manaslu expedition.

I did some calculations. It was conceivably possible to climb Cho Oyu and then rush back to Manaslu for the summit window with my clients. I didn't want to let them down; I'd given them my word I'd climb with them, and I wasn't going to break the promise. The effort would be massive, though—it ramped the pressure and left little margin for error.

Accompanied by Gesman, I packed up and traveled to Tibet via helicopter and road. After a series of border checks, I was allowed in for what had suddenly become a panicked expedition.

Once there, I worked tirelessly. My first job was to figure out how to climb Cho Oyu as quickly as possible, and I learned the line-fixing team had only reached Camp 2. After offering to help set ropes to the higher camps, we performed a load carry to Camp 1, dragging our oxygen cylinders, tent, and rope with us, before returning to base, where the real work could begin.

Because of the short window to climb Cho Oyu, a number of expeditions were gathering at the mountain. One of them was rumored to be Mingma Sherpa, who was planning to visit base camp with several high-ranking officials from the China Tibet Mountaineering Association (CTMA). He also planned to climb Cho Oyu around the same time we were.

I guessed Mingma might be able to grease the wheels for my permit application on Shishapangma, and between meetings on weather systems, trailblazing efforts, and workloads, I moved between tents, trying to find him—only to discover that the news of his arrival had been premature. But I left a message anyway, hoping to talk if he became available.

Elsewhere, I sensed a weird mood gathering among some of the mountaineers. Jealousy occasionally built between expedition guiding companies; the market was small, and competition for clients was fierce, especially on some of the tougher, more remote mountains. When a new presence joined the scene, their arrival sometimes created resentment among the existing organizations.

Thanks to Project Possible, my guiding company, Elite Himalayan Adventures—and with it, the likes of Mingma, Gesman, Geljen, Dawa, and the others—had begun to appear on the scene's radar. Our reputation was set to increase further if I managed to climb the final three 8,000ers on my list. We were on the verge of becoming a major player, but not everyone was happy about our achievements. As I prepared myself for the summit push one afternoon, a friend from another guiding company arrived at my tent with some troubling gossip.

"Nims, the Nepali climbing community is so proud of what you are achieving," he said. "Your name is out there and it's beautiful you're highlighting our capabilities . . ."

I knew him well, he was a nice guy, but he didn't have to flatter me. Something bad was coming. I could tell.

My friend continued, "But be careful, because some people are very envious of what is happening. They talk. And it takes only one push for you to disappear from the mountain for good."

That was it. The warning.

Somebody had made a comment—either as a joke, or as part of a more sinister plan to end me—and my friend was relaying the information. I wouldn't describe myself as a paranoid person, but I wasn't naive either. Even highly experienced mountaineers had fatal accidents at high altitude all the time. If a stranger or two from the line-fixing party, rival guides, wanted to push Gesman and me from the mountain while we weren't looking, what was to stop them from saying we'd slipped and fallen? The alibi was perfectly plausible. Very little evidence would support any suspicions that it had been deliberate.

The news didn't dent me emotionally. So a couple of jealous people were shooting their mouths off around camp. *Who cared?* But it was a hard reminder that not everyone could be trusted. In situations where faith between climbers is vital—such as a crew fixing lines in sketchy conditions—that was troubling. I asked my friend to act as an extra pair of eyes and ears for me during the expedition.

When our work began from Camp 2 later, I scooped up a long loop of rope and broke trail for 1,300 feet in one push. *Boom! Boom! Boom!* I strode forward. If people were feeling a little sore about the successes of Elite Himalayan Adventures, I would show them why our reputation was strengthening. With Gesman, I reached the summit of Cho Oyu on September 23. Our hard work and speed would do the talking for us.

I HAD NO TIME to celebrate. My weather window was closing, so I rushed back to Manaslu as quickly as possible. If the mission as a whole was a marathon, I'd found myself at the tricky 22-mile mark, where, with huge diplomatic hurdles ahead, the remaining distance seemed as daunting as anything before. I knew that once I climbed Manaslu, I'd have ticked off 13 of the 14 8,000ers. But Shishapangma still seemed out of reach, despite my lobbying efforts.

Could I finish what I'd started?

So many people were watching now, including those who'd initially dismissed my chances of making it this far. Some expert climbers had doubted I'd even last through Pakistan, so my efforts throughout 2019, even without Shishapangma, could still be seen as a kind of victory. Plus, the work of the Nepali climbers alongside me had garnered attention, which was another a success. Now I had to do only three more things.

The first was to finish Manaslu and the final mountain— hopefully Shishapangma, possibly Dhaulagiri and Everest.

Bringing Mum and Dad together under the same roof once more was the second. The third was to make the world pay attention to some of the damage we'd been inflicting upon the environment. And with the eyes of the climbing world upon me, I decided Manaslu wasn't simply a peak to be crossed off the list; it was a platform.

I climbed to the top and made my point.

"Today is the 27th of September," I said, as Gesman filmed me. "Here I am on the summit of Manaslu. We're not going to talk about Project Possible, but what I am going to talk about from the summit [is the environment]. For the last decade, it's pretty obvious there has been a huge, significant change in terms of global warming. There is a huge change in the melting of the ice. The Khumbu Icefall on Everest: Every day the glacier is melting; it's getting thinner, and smaller and smaller. Earth is our home. We should be more serious about it, more cautious, more focused about how we look after our planet. At the end of the day, if this one doesn't exist, we don't exist."

Nothing about my speech was really considered in advance. The words came from the heart, but they were the purest reflection of what I felt for the world. As far as I was concerned, the biggest challenge humankind would face in the coming decade or two had to be climate change, but fixing it required a course correction of massive proportions. All of us were insignificant specks on a huge planet, but the actions of an individual carried the potential to overcome the most insurmountable of problems.

If I could climb the death zone mountains in seven months—give or take the final peak—then what was to stop another individual from finding, and climbing, their personal Everest in the field of environmental science, alternative energy, or climate action?

My efforts were proving that everyone had the potential to go beyond what others thought was achievable. They were meant to stand as a glimmer of hope. Now I wanted others to use them for their own challenges and projects in a show of positive action. If my work creates a spark for change, however small, I'll be happy.

AND THEN Shishapangma was on.

The why and when of how it came to be was a dizzying blur of phone calls, emails, and meetings. But in the end it took just one effort to tip the balance in my favor: *Mingma Sherpa*. The man I'd nearly liaised with at Cho Oyu's base camp had learned of my efforts and was impressed by my keenness to explore every available avenue to the final peak. In Tibet and Nepal, humility went a long way.

Though I'd previously been rejected by the Chinese Mountaineering Association, I approached them again via Mingma, in a humble way. I was a firm believer in the equality of friendship: I believed everyone should be treated the same, unless they behaved in a manner that warranted otherwise. When people took the piss out of me, I put them back in their shoes; if somebody showed kindness, I returned the gesture. Everyone had the chance for redemption. Holding grudges against figures of authority because of a larger group decision didn't fit in with my ideals.

The news of my approved permit filtered back to me at Manaslu's base camp. A well-connected climber claimed to have heard that my application to climb Shishapangma was in the bag. "Nimsdai, it's happening," he said, excitedly. The other guys from the team began talking about a celebratory beer, but I struggled to share in their enthusiasm. I couldn't shake the fear that this was a false dawn.

I need to see the paperwork before I get too excited, I thought.

Fortunately, I didn't have to wait long. The CTMA got in touch; they wanted to chat. Having taken into account the scale of my project, they'd decided to open Shishapangma (a decision the government would ultimately approve) for a brief time so I could finish the mission. I let out a sigh of relief. After all the stress, a finish line was in sight.

There was one catch, however. Mingma explained that to access the mountain, the CTMA required he travel with me to base camp. At first, I felt unsure. Was it an attempt to muscle in on my hard work, or a way for the CTMA to grab a slice of the limelight for themselves? In the end, I parked my concerns and remembered the potentially positive impact of a successfully executed mission. If Mingma coming with us to base camp was the difference between completing the 14 mountains or coming up just short, then I was happy to have an extra body in camp.

In the end, I shouldn't have fretted. Mingma quickly proved himself an asset. He acted as a drinking buddy, an expedition resource, and a fixer for some of the more complicated aspects of the project. It turned out that Mingma was about the most con-nected individual in Tibet.

Despite his arrival, pressure still abounded from all angles. Sponsors called wanting to know why I hadn't posted more photos on social media or attached a certain hashtag. My wisdom tooth was pounding yet again. But the most pressing issue seemed to be the mountain's officious liaison manager. As we checked the weather and figured out the best date to climb, he stepped in with an ominous warning.

"The mountain is too dangerous," he said. "The weather is so bad."

He had a point; the snow was coming down hard. But I'd climbed in worse conditions. At first, I tried to make a joke. "No worries, brother," I said, clapping him on the shoulder. "I am the guru of risk assessment!"

The liaison manager shook his head. "Sorry, but no," he said. "If anything happens to you, it will be my responsibility. And there's an avalanche problem."

Wow, I thought. This dude is proving to be hard work.

In the end, I bent him with sheer force. I explained how I'd fixed the lines at K2 when nobody else had been willing to climb. I mentioned my efforts for the G200E in 2017, when the entire project hung in the balance. On top of that, I'd conducted 19 successful 8,000-meter expeditions in total—13 in 2019—and nobody had died on the mountain under my leadership, let alone lost any fingers or toes.

I explained my position, wanting to keep a lid on my frustrations. But I knew that to shout was to lose, and to lose control of my emotions at such a pivotal time could prove costly later. Eventually, the liaison officer agreed and granted me permission to take on the final hurdle. On the eve of the summit push, I sat at the foot of Shishapangma and gathered my thoughts.

Nims, take it easy, I said to myself. You are here now; you only have to stay alive. Don't take any unnecessary risks. Control everything. Stay calm, stay cool. The mission isn't done unless you come back home alive.

I looked to Shishapangma's peak. Clouds swept in, and an ominous rumble of thunder was echoing through the valley below. As I watched, it was impossible not to be awed by the size and scale of what lay ahead. No matter the weather raging around it, a mountain like Shishapangma always stayed solid. It never buckled or broke, and instead seemed impervious to the harsh elements swirling around its mass. I wanted to be like that.

I knew it was useless to judge Shishapangma's strengths and weaknesses at that point, because the giant peak ahead wasn't going to judge *me*. Instead, I felt a rush of inspiration. If I could channel the mountain's spirit, becoming bulletproof to pain, stress, and fear, then nothing could stop me. Before I rested for the night, I asked Shishapangma a final question, or two.

OK, will you let me do this?

Can I? Or can I not?

The answer blew in with the snow.

THE WEATHER on the way up was horrific, as if the mountain hoped to deny me the final climb—or at least discover if I was truly worthy of finishing the job. Winds of 55 miles an hour blasted Mingma David, Geljen, and me as we trudged up the mountain and through the lower camps, fixing the lines and anchors along the way. But nothing could hold me back, though an avalanche came damn close.

We'd been working our way to Camp 1 and for a few moments, as the team rested, I took the drone from my rucksack. Climbing Shishapangma was a big deal. As the culmination of the mission, it was sure to be emotional and I hoped to capture as much of it on film as possible. When the winds settled, I sent the drone into the air, filming the team as they stepped up the mountain in a short line.

Unexpectedly, the ground trembled. I was five or 10 minutes behind the others, and when I looked up, I saw a slab of snow had cracked below them and was slowly shearing away from the mountain. As it began its collapse down Shishapangma's slope, I became an accidental passenger. In effect, I was surfing the snow, and I could do nothing to fight its power.

I looked up and let the mountain gods decide my fate as I glided across the slope, the ground breaking up around me. In an instant, the powder had swallowed me whole and then puked me up. As I prepared to be pulled under and smothered for good, the world came to a standstill.

I looked down. The avalanche was billowing away below me, dissipating on the rocks and puffing up a white mushroom cloud. But the snow I'd been standing on had somehow come to a stop. The deities had spared my life.

I can't believe it, brother, I laughed. *You've come all this way and nearly died on the last expedition.*

The drone stayed in the bag from then on.

Ever since my fall in Pakistan, my confidence had returned in increments. After wobbling at the top of Gasherbrum I, surviving the night lower on the mountain in grisly conditions had helped. Fixing the last of the lines on K2, when other climbers had given up on the idea, was a psychological boost too. The pain of scaling Broad Peak in a state of exhaustion only underlined my fortitude when handling dangerous circumstances.

I'd suffered a mental blow on Nanga Parbat, but I'd managed to heal and grow from it. And as I worked my way back to the line where Mingma and Geljen were waiting, I felt surprised that the emotional aftershocks of yet another near-death experience were not impacting me. But by that point, having climbed nearly 14 8,000ers in such a short time, my crampons seemed fused to my body, my ice ax an extra limb. Now, I felt a little exposed whenever I was separated from those pieces of equipment, as I was when without my weapon in war.

For the push to Shishapangma's summit, we took a new line to the top, feeling confident enough to climb alpine style. The gradient was fairly mellow, and the weather calmed as we moved past Camp 2. When the clouds cleared around us, the winds died away and everything became peaceful.

I was calm, too. The last half of the climb on Shishapangma turned into a slow and steady trek, and though little in the way of technical climbing was required, the effort felt emotionally heavy as I stepped to the peak.

And now it was done.

As I stood there on the mountaintop in the sky, everything I'd achieved up to that moment dawned on me. I'd silenced the doubters by climbing the 14 highest mountains in the world in six months and six days. I'd shown what was achievable with imagination and a determined spirit, while shining a light on some of the challenges the planet and its people face.

I'd made the impossible possible.

In the distance I could see the white pyramid of Everest, the place it all began, and the feelings I'd bottled up for so long rushed at me at once: pride, happiness, and love. I thought of Suchi, and my friends and family. Most of all I thought of Mum and Dad. Tears ran down my cheeks.

In a way, the mission had been a process of discovery—not only on the mountains, but personally too. By climbing the 14 8,000ers, I was trying to figure out who the hell I was; I wanted to know how far out in the distance my physical and emotional limits were.

My drive was unusual. I'd learned that as the best runner in school, as a kid getting into the Gurkhas, and then as a pioneering member of the British Special Forces. Where did that desire come from? I'm not sure. But even as a small boy in Chitwan, I'd turn over rocks in the stream searching for crabs and prawns, and wouldn't quit until I'd peered under every single one, no matter the time or effort required to finish the job. Fast-forward 30 years, and nothing much had changed. My spirit was still the same; only the parameters had changed. But instead of exploring a local river, I was climbing across the world's highest mountains.

There on the summit of Shishapangma, after surveying the world and feeling the biting cold on my face, I called home and told Mum what I'd done.

"I've done it!" I shouted into the phone. "And I'm OK."

The line was crackling, but I could just make out her laughter. "Get home safe, son," she said. "I love you."

AFTERWORD

'm bigger than my ego.

I'm bigger than pain, bigger than glory, and bigger than my tears.

I'm bigger than my sacrifice.

I've overcome all these feelings, all these emotions, because I've lived for a bigger purpose, where me, myself, and I mean nothing.

I will keep going through hell. I will keep breaking boundaries. And I will keep moving forward.

These were just some of the realizations that landed with me in the aftermath of completing Project Possible. But really, the enormity of what I'd accomplished didn't hit me for days.

The following morning, hungover, I traveled back across the border into Nepal, where a hero's welcome was waiting for me and the team: the special forces of high-altitude mountaineering. Word had spread about my record-breaking achievements.

Not only had I managed to climb the world's 14 highest peaks, establishing a new record that many had deemed impossible, but I'd also posted the fastest time for climbing from the summit of

Everest to Lhotse and then Makalu. The Pakistan peaks had been nailed in 23 days, and I'd climbed the five highest mountains of Everest, K2, Kanchenjunga, Lhotse, and Makalu in 70 days, having announced my ambition to do it in 80. Additionally, I'd climbed the most 8,000-meter peaks in a single season (spring), by topping Annapurna, Dhaulagiri, Kanchenjunga, Everest, Lhotse, and Makalu in 31 days. In short, the mission was an overwhelming success.

I called Mum again. A party was being arranged in Kathmandu, and despite her condition, the doctors assured me she was well enough to travel. So I asked her to join me for a celebratory heli-copter ride. At first, she wasn't sure. I told her how important she was to me and how the mission had been the biggest achievement of my life.

"I want you to be a part of it," I said.

"Yes, I want to come," she said, eventually.

When we arrived at the Kathmandu Tribhuvan Airport, a marching band was playing. Dozens of photographers and jour-nalists where there, and a huge crowd circled the airport. I couldn't quite get my head around it. Up to that point, I think Mum consid-ered my climbing a crazy hobby, a risky project that filled me with joy. She didn't imagine the wider world was following my work—not on a big scale, at least. But seeing the crowds and fanfare, she finally understood.

As the rotary blades on the chopper slowed above us, a white Range Rover pulled around with the flags of Great Britain and Nepal fixed to the hood. The British ambassador to Nepal, Richard Morris, stepped out. Once we'd shaken hands, he thanked me for my efforts.

"We're so proud of you," he said. "What you've achieved is unbelievable."

When we were driven through the city to a reception, crowds followed us everywhere.

But there was more work to be done.

IN THE MONTHS after summiting the 14 mountains, I did everything I could to bring Mum and Dad together. I got a loan with a Nepali bank and borrowed money from my family while Elite Himalayan Adventures ran a number of successful expeditions. Following my success at 8,000 meters, my guiding services were in high demand, as were my motivational talks. With the financial returns, I found a nice house in Kathmandu that would work for both my parents.

At the start of 2020, we excitedly completed the paperwork and got ready to move Dad out of the old house in Chitwan and into the new family home. On February 25, Suchi and I flew to Nepal to bring them together. But when we landed, I received a devastating phone call. We were too late. Mum had died a couple of hours earlier. My heart split open. Everything I'd achieved was inspired by her spirit.

Through the hurt of the Hindu mourning ceremony, I reflected and grew. After emerging 13 days later, I looked to the positives, turning grief into a powerful energy. Because of the love and support of my family, I'd been able to push myself to the absolute limit, proving to the world that it was feasible to accomplish things no one had considered before. And I needed to do so much more.

One such hope was to encourage people to go beyond what they'd previously believed to be possible—either physically, mentally, or emotionally—with the idea that my mission could serve as an inspiration. For example, within the mountaineering scene, a number of climbers had figured that climbing all 14 mountains in such a short space of time was a suicidal move. But I knew I had it in me to succeed. And when I did, I was asked the same question over and over: Where had this self-belief come from?

The answer I sometimes gave pointed to an experience I'd had as a 13-year-old boy—one that taught me that overcoming any challenge was within everyone's reach, if they focused their thinking and their heart was full.

My village of Chitwan was located near one of the biggest rivers in the region. Despite not being a particularly strong swimmer, I'd decided to challenge myself one day by crossing it alone. Stripping down to my underwear, I waded in. The water pulled me this way and that, but eventually I made it to the other side. My heart raced and my limbs ached with the effort. I was exhausted.

Then the reality of my situation landed with a bang. *Fuck,* I thought, Now I have to swim all the way back. The work was intense, and as my muscles quivered, an awful terror welled up inside: I'd suddenly remembered the stories that had ricocheted around the village whenever a crocodile ate somebody in these waters, which had happened once or twice.

Better hurry up, Nims, I told myself. *That's if you don't want to be lunch.*

The effort soon became too much. As I reached the halfway point, I sensed my body could take no more. The river was pulling me under. But my head and shoulders were still above the surface!

And having stood up, I realized the water could only have been around four feet in depth and was only lapping around my chest. The currents were certainly fast moving, but I was able to wade toward the bank, alert for any predators that might be nearby.

Despite my fatigue, the adventure had taught me an important lesson: Fear was never going to hold me back from pressing ahead with my plans (though every now and then I had the tendency to get ahead of myself). And it established in me a mind-set with zero doubts and zero tolerance for excuses.

In fact, shortly after this experience I stopped celebrating my birthday. Every milestone date, I realized, fostered a psychology of negativity, where age was a determining factor in what a person could and couldn't do. *But you're too young! Oh, you're too old!*

Whenever people considered their years, it gave them a ready-made excuse to step back from a challenge they might have ordinarily accepted. Those words, my birthdays, meant nothing to me anymore.

That philosophy certainly applied to my mountaineering career. I'd started extreme altitude climbing at the age of 30; many people might have considered that too late a time to start, or worried about their lack of experience when attempting the peaks of Everest and Annapurna. But I wasn't falling into those traps.

Once Project Possible had been completed, I was unlikely to draw as much satisfaction from climbing an 8,000-meter peak as I had before. I demanded progress. So in the summer of 2020, I'd decided to take up paragliding, with the goal of topping an 8,000er and then speed-flying from one of its sheer walls and into the valley below.

Friends thought I was out of my mind, but for months I trained at Mont Blanc, learning how to barrel roll and spin with a wing that would fit into my rucksack. When I broke my tailbone in a hard landing, I didn't give up. I rested for 24 hours and fought through the pain before launching myself into the air again.

One day, I told myself, I'm going to fly from a mountain like K2.

But one thing Project Possible had taught me was that now I was no longer content to break boundaries in physical endeavor. I wanted to use my strengths to educate and inspire, too. And so through my social media platforms, I alerted the world to the Big Mountain Cleanup project—an initiative designed to undo some of the damage caused to mountains such as Everest, following the huge uptick in expeditions taking place there every year.

On an average expedition, climbers tend to create more than 18 pounds of waste; their footprint often includes abandoned tents, oxygen canisters, equipment, and fecal matter. Pollutants are washed into the nearby rivers and lakes, impacting the lives of people who live nearby, while increasing the risk of disease within local communities. By tidying up the rubbish left on the 8,000ers, we can help to protect and restore the environment on the mountains that need it the most—starting with Manaslu in 2021 and then Everest and Ama Dablam a year later.

The undertaking has a special place in my heart. I'd come to believe that it is up to everyone that explores the sacred ranges such as the Himalaya and Karakoram to take responsibility for the waste there—not only for the mountains themselves, but also for the communities that call them home. My hope is that the noise generated by missions like mine can help to shine a spotlight on similar conservation projects.

Elsewhere, the impact of my climbing those 14 mountains throughout 2019 was even more immediate. I learned that some elite mountaineers were now planning to tackle several 8,000ers in a year, rather than only one or two. The boundaries for what is considered achievable have shifted, and I am able to take a lot of pride in that. It is also great to know that the reputations of Nepali Sherpa guides have been amplified. The guys I've climbed with are being placed on pedestals, and rightly so: We worked as a relatively small expedition unit, in teams of three, four, or five, but we moved with the power of 10 bulls and the heart of a hundred men. They deserve all the spoils awaiting them, and as a tribute to the hard work throughout 2019, I gave our new line on Shishapangma a name: the Project Possible Route.

Most of all I realized that summiting the 14 peaks had been a launchpad. I needed more . . . but what?

The mountains, I now know, are there to be scaled; I have only to pick which ones to take on and the style in which I want to summit them. And although there are challenges to be conquered based on speed, style, and physical effort, there are no limits to the tests I could set for myself. The chances I might be killed while trying to attempt these missions may be higher than anything I've risked before, but that is the whole point: I have to push my limits to the max. Sitting tight, waiting it out, and living in the past have never been for me.

But I don't want to announce plans for the future—at least not just yet. I know that alerting the world to my ideas will only bring out the doubters once more. Instead, as I did in the military, I'll scheme from the shadows, because surprise can be one of the greatest tools in a soldier's armory.

And quitting is not in the blood.

LESSONS FROM THE DEATH ZONE

1. Leadership isn't always about what *you* want.

After making it to base camp at Dhaulagiri during Phase One of the mission, it was obvious that some of the guys on my team were struggling. Physically they were cooked, and their morale was broken. Though I'd just climbed Annapurna and conducted a stressful search and rescue mission, I felt fine. Still, I knew it wasn't smart to press ahead and push the others to their limits. Instead, I figured out what was best for the team.

It's easy to work at your own pace in a group setting, especially if you're the fastest or strongest in the pack. But the people around you will soon lose faith. They'll regard you as selfish, overly ambitious, and a bit of a dick. The general consensus will be that you don't care about anyone else, and the efforts of the team will fade away. When you need your colleagues to step up again, they won't bother.

Rather than pissing people off, put yourself in their shoes. Figure out how you can compromise: Is it possible to work in a way that benefits everybody? In this case, I took the team for a little rest and recovery. Yeah, we had to work through some terrible conditions a few days later as a consequence, but that one action told the team that the mission wasn't only about me.

As a result, they broke their backs to work for the cause over the following six months.

2. The little things count most on the big mountains.

Over the years, I've developed some techniques for lightening my workload when climbing 8,000ers. One of the most important involves my breathing. Whenever I'm at high altitude I wear a Buff, a thin sleeve of fabric typically worn on the head or neck, to protect my face from the sun and biting cold. But it's hard to wear without fogging my goggles or sunglasses with the condensation from my breath.

To solve that, I changed the way I inhale and exhale. Pursing my lips, I take air in through my nose and then blow down, away from the goggles. The cold air comes in through the Buff, warming it slightly, which protects my lungs from failing in subzero temperatures. It might sound like a minor detail—but that one technique saves my body from hypothermia, because the air I'm taking in is not as cold. It also protects my fingers from frostbite, because I don't have to take off my gloves to get to my goggle cleaning cloth (all of which is exhausting above 8,000 meters, by the way).

Taking care of the little things feeds into a bigger ambition. For you, that might mean knowing the finer details of a contract so you can succeed in a deal at work, or learning why buying the right running shoes for a 10K race can stop you from getting blisters. These small actions make a difference, much in the same way that a breathing technique, knowing exactly where my energy gels are, or keeping my ice ax within reach bombproofs me from stress on an 8,000er.

3. Never underestimate the challenge ahead.

I first learned about the dangers associated with underestimating a climb in 2015—but those lessons were learned the hard way. As an intermediate mountaineer still cutting my teeth, I climbed Aconcagua in the Argentinian Andes. It's one of the Seven Summits, and though not quite an 8,000er, it's still a challenging test of high altitude at 6,961 meters.

Mountaineers with ambitions of working in the death zone often use Aconcagua as an early test of their mettle; given it is a hike from bottom to top, and nothing is needed in the way of rope skills to summit, a lot of people figure it to be a fairly benign soul.

That was my attitude, anyway. Having flicked through a few climbing guides and magazines and stared at a ton of photographs featuring kids and old couples climbing to Aconcagua's peak, my attitude was a little dismissive. How hard can it be? Friends I'd made during my expeditions to Dhaulagiri and Lobuche East figured Aconcagua would be a breeze for me.

"You'll smash it," said one. "Trek to base camp in a day. Then take a day or two to summit and head back. No dramas."

I was so convinced of my ability, and Aconcagua's apparently gentle temperament, that I didn't bother packing a summit suit for my expedition. I was traveling during the summer months, at the start of the year when the weather is fairly warm in the Southern Hemisphere. As far as kit went, I think I packed some hiking trousers, a waterproof coat, and a pair of mountain boots. But once I entered the national park at Penitentes, snow started to fall.

Aconcagua is a remote mountain; it took a trek of 11 hours to reach base camp. Because I was traveling solo, without a guide, I had to use my map and compass to get there, as heavy drifts had smothered the paths normally marking the route up. When I eventually arrived at base camp and checked in with the other climbers on the mountain, the mood was gloomy. A number of people had made a push for the summit, but had been turned around by the elements.

"It's so dangerous up there," said a friend from the International Federation of Mountain Guides. "The avalanche risk is high, and the weather is seriously cold."

I figured I knew better. Having snapped up some boots from another climber—a pair far sturdier than the ones I'd brought along—and also borrowed a down jacket, I pushed to the top, the weather pressing in tightly around me. What should have been a straightforward hike became as grueling as my first ever climb on an 8,000er, and only 1,000 feet from the peak, I came close to giving up.

My vision blurred. Climbing without oxygen, and with altitude sickness kicking in, I felt close to passing out. All my hopes of becoming an elite climber seemed to hang in the balance. *Hell, Nims, if you can't make it to the top here, how can you expect to take on Everest?* I was shaken.

I took a sip from my flask and opened up a chocolate bar.

You have the speed to climb super quickly. Use it.

Pushing on to the summit, I couldn't wait to turn around, having learned another lesson at high altitude: *Never underestimate the mountain you're about to climb—no matter how easy other people think it might be.*

And another: *Be confident, but show respect.*

From then on, I did my due diligence on every expedition. I readied myself for the challenges ahead and told myself that any mountain had the potential to be my last if I didn't handle it with care. As a reminder of the pitfalls of what can happen when you let your guard down, I briefly underestimated Gasherbrum I during Phase Two of the mission, and it kicked me in the ass.

Whatever you're doing, treat your challenge with respect. You won't suffer any nasty surprises that way.

4. Hope is God.

You're not going to get to your dream just by fantasizing about it. But if you make it your ultimate goal, or god, and give yourself to it entirely, there's a good chance it will come your way.

As a kid, I got so angry at being beaten by a runner from another school in the district championships that I started getting up in the middle of the night in secret training sessions. I took that same attitude to the Gurkhas. If we were required to run 20 miles in training, I'd tack another 10 miles on at the end to push myself even harder, because I knew I wanted to make it into the special forces. The job had become my church, and I invested all my efforts in it.

So rather than thinking, praying, and waiting for your next project or challenge (and not doing it), commit to serious action instead.

5. A person's true nature shows up in life-or-death situations.

A lot of soldiers talk the talk. On the base they act like big heroes, happy to spout off about gunfights that they may, or may not, have been involved in. But the minute it kicks off for real, when bullets start flying and people are getting shot around them, they hide in the corner or panic.

The same attitude can be found on the mountain. At base camp, when the weather is sunny and warm, climbers take selfies and mess around, talking about how they're going to conquer the mountain. Once bad weather arrives and it becomes important to stay focused and disciplined, they lose their cool. Then their true personality emerges: They act selfishly, their work rate slacks off, and the safety of others is sometimes disregarded.

It's possible to learn a lot about someone when the chips are down.

6. Turn a nightmare situation into something positive.

During my first climbs of Everest, Lhotse, and Makalu, my oxygen was stolen on the mountain. I'd asked for cylinders to be left at a number of camps, but as I arrived at each one, it became apparent that the lot of them had been swiped. At first I was furious—an understandable reaction given the circumstances—but it was important to stay calm. Losing it would cause me to waste energy and maybe succumb to HACE in the process. As I've explained in Lesson 2, the little things count most on the big mountains. A negative response, like a tantrum, would only cost me dearly later in the expedition.

I calmed down and mentally turned the situation around. Rather than stewing in my own anger, I told myself that the air had gone to someone who needed it more than I did.

Maybe someone had severe altitude sickness and needed my cylinders to save themselves, I told myself, knowing it probably wasn't true. In which case, fair enough.

Yeah, this was a lie in some ways—though very different to the type discussed in Lesson 8. However, it was a vital self-defense mechanism. If I'd sulked and moaned about the circumstances surrounding my missing air, I would have wasted vital energy when I should have been concentrating on the mission ahead.

Thinking positively is the only way to survive at 8,000 meters. Nobody cheats death by wallowing in self-pity.

7. Give 100 percent to the now ...
... because it's all you've got.

There were moments in Gurkha Selection when a program of grueling work lay ahead of me: weeks of drills, marches, and exercises in unpleasant conditions, where I'd have to push myself to my breaking point. It would have been easy to feel overwhelmed by the workload, or stressed that day one's 30-mile run might burn me out for an even longer run on day two. Instead, I gave everything to the job at hand and dealt with tomorrow when tomorrow came around. It's the only way to handle an intimidating challenge.

The same attitude applied to my mission to climb the 14 death zone peaks. While working across a mountain, I tried my best not to think about the next expedition, because I knew I might not make it if I took my eye off the adversary ahead. To be focused on Broad Peak while scaling K2 would cause me to lose focus. And keeping energy in reserve was pointless. I had to give the day my all, because I knew the consequences if I didn't.

Tomorrow might not happen.

8. Never lie. Never make excuses.

I could have cut corners at times on the mountain. Following the

G200E in 2017, when Nishal offered me a helicopter ride from Namche Bazaar to Makalu's Camp 2, I turned him down. With his help, I'd have become the first person to climb Everest twice, Lhotse and Makalu in a single climbing season. But it wouldn't have been done properly. Sure, nobody on the planet would have known, apart from me and Nishal, but I'd have to live with the knowledge for the rest of my life.

It's easy to make excuses. You might be trying to give up smoking or alcohol. A sneaky beer, or a puff on a cigarette, is easy to shrug off. But by lying to yourself, you're consigning your goals to failure. Lying, or making excuses for sloppy actions, means you've broken a promise to yourself. Once you do that, you'll screw up, over and over again.

For example, it would have been easy for me to give up on K2, because so many people had tried and failed to climb it. Had I abandoned the project because of a lack of funding, nobody would have blamed me. But there was no way I was going to let myself off the hook with a convenient get-out clause.

If I say that I'm going to run for an hour, I'll run for a full hour. If I plan to do 300 push-ups in a training session, I won't quit until I've done them all—because brushing off the effort means letting myself down, and I don't want to have to live with that.

And neither should you.

APPENDIX TWO

FOURTEEN MOUNTAINS:
THE SCHEDULE

COUNTRY	SUMMITED	PHASE	PEAK	HEIGHT (METERS)
Nepal	4/23/2019	1	Annapurna I	8,091
Nepal	5/12/2019	1	Dhaulagiri I	8,167
Nepal	5/15/2019	1	Kanchenjunga	8,586
Nepal	5/22/2019	1	Everest	8,848
Nepal	5/22/2019	1	Lhotse	8,516
Nepal	5/24/2019	1	Makalu	8,485
Pakistan	7/3/2019	2	Nanga Parbat	8,125
Pakistan	7/15/2019	2	Gasherbrum I	8,080
Pakistan	7/18/2019	2	Gasherbrum II	8,034
Pakistan	7/24/2019	2	K2	8,611
Pakistan	7/26/2019	2	Broad Peak	8,051
Tibet	9/23/2019	3	Cho Oyu	8,201
Nepal	9/27/2019	3	Manaslu	8,163
Tibet	10/29/2019	3	Shishapangma	8,027

THE WORLD RECORDS

Fastest time to climb all 14 mountains above 8,000 meters:
six months, six days

Fastest time from summit of Everest to summit of Lhotse and summit of Makalu:
48 hours and 30 minutes

Fastest time to climb the top five highest mountains in the world—Kanchenjunga, Everest, Lhotse, Makalu, and K2:
70 days

Fastest time to climb all five 8,000ers of Pakistan—K2, Nanga Parbat, Broad Peak, GI, and GII:
23 days

Most 8,000-meter peaks during a single season (spring): Annapurna, Dhaulagiri, Kanchenjunga, Everest, Lhotse, and Makalu:
six in 31 days

ACKNOWLEDGMENTS

When writing a book of this kind, it's hard to remember all the people who helped me to make Project Possible a reality, but I'll do my best here. Hopefully, I won't miss anybody.

Without the support of my expedition sponsors, Project Possible would never have happened. At the top of the thank-you list stands Bremont, who made a series of Project Possible watches (available on its website) and helped me over the financial hurdles that threatened to stop my dream from becoming reality. A salute also goes out to Silxo, Osprey, Ant Middleton, Digi2al, Hama Steel, Summit Oxygen, Omnirisc, the Royal Hotel, Intergage, AD Construction Group, Branding Science, AMTC Group, Everence, ThruDark, Kenya Airways, KGH Group, Marriott Kathmandu, and Premier Insurance.

Logistical support for the mission was provided by Elite Himalayan Adventures, Seven Summit Treks, and Climbalaya. Although my team and I did the majority of filming above base camp, we had some assistance for the forthcoming movie of my story courtesy of Sagar Gurung, Alit Gurung, and Sandro Gromen-Hayes, who also joined me at K2 Base Camp and climbed with me on Manaslu. And I'd like to thank everyone working hard to put the hours of footage together at Noah Media Group, especially Torquil Jones and Barry, and thanks also to Mark Webber for the introduction. Help on the mission also arrived from the SBSA and Ambassador Durga Subedi, and from so many key figures from Nepal: the Nepali government, Nepal Mountaineering Association, Tourism Department, Tourism Secretary Kedar Bahadur Adhikari, former prime minister of Nepal Madhav Kumar Nepal, Deputy Defense Minister of Nepal Ishwar Pokhrel, Inspector General of Police Sailendra Khanal, and Sonam Sherpa of the Yeti Group. A big thanks has to go to Brigadier Dan Reeves for all his help.

In the U.K., an administration team helped me to figure out a way of managing PR, and all the other logistical issues that kick in while climbing to the top of an 8,000er. Most of all, this includes my supportive wife, Suchi, plus Project Possible's helpers: Wendy Faux, Steve and Tiffany Curran, Luke Hill, and Kishore Rana. Thanks also to all the clients that joined me on Annapurna (Hakon Asvang and Rupert Jones-Warner), Nanga Parbat (Stefi Troguet), and Manaslu (Steve Davis, Amy McCulloch, Glenn McCrory, Deeya Pun, and Stefi Troguet), plus everyone from all over the world who donated to the mission on GoFundMe and supported the project by picking up merchandise. Many organizations helped me along the way, and I'm extremely appreciative to all of them, but my gratitude especially goes out to the Nepali climbing community, my Sherpa brothers, and the Gurkha and Nepali communities: Myagdi organization UK, Madat Shamuha, Magar Association UK, Friendly Brothers Dana Serophero Community UK, Pun Magar Samaj UK, Pun Magar Soci-

Acknowledgments

ety HK, Pelkachour and Chhimeki Gaule Samaj UK, Tamu Pye Lhu Sangh UK, and the Maidstone Gurkha Nepalese Community.

My team from the 2017 record-breaking climbs of Everest, Lhotse, and Makalu also deserves a mention: Lakpa Sherpa, Jangbu Sherpa, Halung Dorchi Sherpa, and Mingma Dorchi Sherpa.

Without my family, none of this would have happened. Mum and Dad indulged my adventurous spirit as a child and allowed me to follow my heart to the mountains after I'd promised to bring them together under one roof. My brothers, Kamal, Jit, and Ganga, and my sister, Anita, encouraged me to follow the noble life into the Gurkhas, and there's a long list of friends to name-check in and out of the military: Staz, Louis, Paul Daubner, Gaz Banford, Lewis Phillips, C.P. Limbu, Chris Sylvan, Dawa Sherpa, Ramesh Silwal, Khadka Gurung, Subhash Rai, Govinda Rana, Thaneswar Guragai, Peter Cunningham, Shrinkhala Khatiwada, Dan, Bijay Limbu, Mira Acharya, Stuart Higgins, Phil Macey, Rupert Swallow, Al Mack, Greg Williams, Mingma Sherpa, Danny Rai, Dhan Chand, Shep, Tashi Sherpa, Sobhit Gauchan, Shiva Bahadur Sapkota, and Gulam.

This book wouldn't have happened without the hard work of everyone at Hodder and Stoughton, especially Rupert Lancaster, Cameron Myers, Caitriona Horne, and Rebecca Mundy. Thanks to my agents at The Blair Partnership, Neil Blair, and Rory Scarfe. Finally, I would like to thank my friend and brother, Matt Allen, for putting his heart and mind into capturing my story. Without his help (from his heart), the book wouldn't have been possible.